D0120076

The Story of Celtic
An Official History

The Story of Celtic
An Official History

Gerald McNee

Stanley Paul

Stanley Paul & Co Ltd
3 Fitzroy Square, London W1P 6JD

An imprint of the Hutchinson Publishing Group

London Melbourne Sydney Auckland
Wellington Johannesburg and agencies
throughout the world

First published 1978
© Gerald McNee 1978

Printed in Great Britain at The Anchor Press Ltd
and bound by Wm Brendon & Son Ltd
both of Tiptree, Essex

ISBN 0 09 132410 6

Contents

The Chairmen

Dr John Conway	1888–1890
John Glass	1890–1897
J. H. McLaughlin	1897–1909
James Kelly	1909–1914
Thomas White	1914–1947
Sir Robert Kelly	1947–1971
Desmond White	1971 until present day

The Managers

Willie Maley (Match Secretary, Hon. Secretary and Secretary-Manager)	1888–1940
Jimmy McStay	1940–1945
Jimmy McGrory	1945–1965
Jock Stein	1965 until present day

Note: Assistant manager Sean Fallon was in charge of the team for the whole of the season 1975–6 as Jock Stein recovered from serious injuries sustained in a car accident. The following year Sean Fallon was put in charge of scouting and Davie McParland, a former Partick Thistle player and manager and also Queen's Park manager, was appointed first-team coach and assistant to Jock Stein.

The Celtic Honours

The European Champions Cup 1967
The Coronation Cup 1953
The St Mungo Cup 1951
The Victory in Europe Cup 1945
The Empire Exhibition Trophy 1938
The Glasgow Exhibition Trophy 1901–02

Note: All of these are held on a permanent basis by the club except the European Cup, a replica of which was given to Celtic by UEFA.

Scottish League Championship Winners

1892–93	1906–07	1915–16	1937–38	1969–70
1893–94	1907–08	1916–17	1953–54	1970–71
1895–96	1908–09	1918–19	1965–66	1971–72
1897–98	1909–10	1921–22	1966–67	1972–73
1904–05	1913–14	1925–26	1967–68	1973–74
1905–06	1914–15	1935–36	1968–69	1976–77

Scottish Cup Winners

1891–92	1907–08	1924–25	1950–51	1970–71
1898–99	1910–11	1926–27	1953–54	1971–72
1899–00	1911–12	1930–31	1964–65	1973–74
1903–04	1913–14	1932–33	1966–67	1974–75
1906–07	1922–23	1936–37	1968–69	1976–77

Scottish League Cup Winners

1956–57	1967–68
1957–58	1968–69
1965–66	1969–70
1966–67	1974–75

Glasgow Cup Winners

1890–91	1906–07	1920–21	1938–39	1963–64
1891–92	1907–08	1926–27	1940–41	1964–65
1894–95	1909–10	1927–28	1948–49	1966–67
1895–96	1915–16	1928–29	1955–56	1967–68
1904–05	1916–17	1930–31	1961–62	1969–70
1905–06	1919–20			

Note: The 1974–75 Final between Celtic and Rangers ended in a 2–2 draw and the clubs were declared joint holders.

Glasgow Charity Cup Winners

1891–92	1902–03	1914–15	1920–21	1937–38
1892–93	1904–05	1915–16	1923–24	1942–43
1893–94	1907–08	1916–17	1925–26	1949–50
1894–95	1911–12	1917–18	1935–36	1952–53
1895–96	1912–13	1919–20	1936–37	1958–59
1898–99	1913–14			

Note: The 1960–61 competition was the last one played among the Glasgow clubs and the trophy was shared between Celtic and Clyde after a 1–1 draw. Over the next few seasons a Glasgow Select met English First Division teams but in the end the competition ceased.

Dedication

To my little Dara Marie whose first year of life has been dominated by the constant clicking of a typewriter – and to the Celtic Football Club.

Acknowledgements

The author wishes to thank Celtic chairman Mr Desmond White and directors James Farrell, Tom Devlin and Kevin Kelly for their much appreciated help in writing this book. Also the management and staff at Celtic Park and *Celtic View* Editor Mr Jack McGinn and his staff; Mr Tommy Welsh for some valuable documentation. Finally, the author wishes to express gratitude to his wife Rosaleen for her patience during the many months of compilation.

The photographs are reproduced by courtesy of: *Scottish Daily Express*, *Scottish Daily Record* and *Sunday Mail* Ltd, Mr Jimmy McGrory, Mr Hugh Brit and the Celtic Football Club.

Foreword

by Desmond White, Chairman

Because of the success of two previous Celtic books by Gerald McNee – *And You'll Never Walk Alone* and *A Lifetime in Paradise* – my fellow directors and I were pleased that he undertook the task of writing a full and up-to-date history of Celtic. There were some who thought that such a history should coincide with Celtic's Centenary. That Centenary, however, is ten years away and many voices that can still remember and recount the past may, by then, have lapsed into silence.

The writing of a Foreword to this book does not indicate that the sentiments expressed are my own. In fact, in some cases, I would have expressed the position differently, have dealt with other subjects in that same history, made different comment – but that said, I do believe that this is a worthy attempt to record the highlights of ninety years of Celtic history. Truth possibly is not what any one person says but is the combination of many voices and many beliefs.

In Chapter Six we have the old argument that in the middle 1890s the original concept for which the Club was founded – feeding the poor, particularly the children in the East End of Glasgow – had been lost from view. That according to the *Glasgow Catholic Observer* at that time 'the thing had become a mere business in the hands of Publicans and Others'. Whatever is the truth, the fact remains that those people who controlled the Club in the early days had produced a playing side to be proud of and a stadium at the turn of the century which was then one of the best in the world.

There is a quotation from the Bible which is perhaps apt – that, 'Man does not live by bread alone.' At that time those 'Publicans and Others' had given the Catholic and Irish poor of the East End something to cheer about. In the squalid, grey slums it gave them a cause, a relief from their surroundings and possibly a belief in the future.

Whereas perhaps not giving them full marks, I give a very high rating to those men who started Celtic on its long history. In any case, in the long term, more has gone to charity than would ever have been possible under the old concept.

Football has been progressively labelled by the media down through the years with descriptions of big business, commercialism, etc. Football is a sport which has survived, not by that materialism, but by the countless people in schools, amateur, junior and juvenile football, who give and have given long and unpaid services to this great game because of their love of it. Without these people football could not have grown or even survived. Today, club officials are termed amateurs by the Press as distinct from the professionals (managers). These people also give long and mostly unpaid hours in the service of our game.

No one in their right senses would invest in football as a commercial enterprise – to make money.

Football has lived chiefly by the fact that people loved this game and were prepared to serve it. The same is also true of the supporters. Football burst on the scene in Scotland because it had the support of the working man. It was his game, his sport, his involvement. He has stood on the terraces in driving snow and teeming rain. He has supported his team, carried their colours, sung their songs, the length and breadth of the land and he does so to this day because the same is still true – it is still his game.

Important figures have held the stage at Celtic Park. One of them was undoubtedly William Maley who, together with Bill Struth of Rangers, were the big management personalities in those far off days.

Willie had served the Club from the very beginning and had been Guest of Honour in 1938 when he received a gift of 2500 guineas from the Club, 50 guineas for each year of his service. Sir John Cargill, Chairman of Burmah Oil, and many other prominent businessmen were there that evening to honour William Maley. All was happiness and light.

It is sad that only months later a rift developed between the Directors and their Manager.

Willie Maley was a strong personality and liked his own way. In a tour of the United States he had requested that his brother Tom should be included in the official party. Rightly or wrongly this was refused. It was a rough crossing and Willie Maley, a bad sailor, was immediately confined to his cabin, in which he stayed until the ship docked in New York. Willie moved into his bed in the hotel, a sick man, and pleaded with the Directors that they should send for his brother Tom to take him back home to Scotland. Tom Maley set sail for the United States and miraculously Willie found an almost immediate cure and welcomed his brother at the docks on his arrival in New York. Needless to say Tom accompanied his brother Willie on the tour.

The heart of the trouble between the Club and their Manager was, I understand, taxation concerning the gift of 2500 guineas and the fact that we ate at the Bank Restaurant. The Directors, while admitting and agreeing that the food in the Bank Restaurant in Queen Street owned by Mr Maley was excellent, thought it was hardly the place to feed a football team, as it was really a glorified public house frequented by bookmakers and others.

It was sad that such a rift should develop after such a long and honoured service to the Club he loved but there was undoubtedly a lot of pride on both sides which we all know can, at times, be very difficult to overcome. However, an old era was dying and a new time in football was emerging.

Another strong personality who rose in football was George Graham, who owed a lot to Celtic in first obtaining the position of Secretary of the Scottish Football Association. Progressively over the years he controlled to a greater and greater extent the Committees of the Association by the power of his own personality, by freemasonry and by tickets. When away on official business in London and elsewhere he was not past informing Members of these same Committees, who were in fact his masters, that they would be sent home if they did not fall in with his own standards and requirements. He made power and he used it. In the end he used it against Celtic when he manipulated the flag controversy, using as a pawn Harry Swan, his President and Chairman of Hibernian Football Club. George Graham was a High Mason and Grand Master of the Orange Lodge who became a dictator and eventually went too far.

He opposed Celtic and its champion Robert Kelly. I can only have the highest praise for the Celtic Chairman's stand at that time. His theme was very simple; Celtic cannot be penalized if they have not broken a rule.

Out of the blue, in more ways than one, came strong support for Celtic's cause. John Wilson, Chairman of Rangers and father of the late Director of Rangers of the same name, supported Sir Robert's contention at an SFA meeting. Celtic were indeed grateful for that support, for there seemed at that time a strong lobby who would have been quite prepared to put Celtic out of football.

As you can read in the book that was the beginning of the end and sanity eventually prevailed. George Graham was later knighted for his services to football. There are some people who wonder why.

Fortunately for Scottish football he was succeeded not long after by a man of high ability and integrity – Willie Allan, whose Bible for the control of Scottish football was that same rulebook which Sir Robert had defied anyone to say the Club had offended.

I first really got to know Bob Kelly when he became Chairman of the Club. Bob was born into a football family. His father James had played in the original Celtic team in 1888, was attached to the Club as a player and as a Captain for a long time, had become a Committee man, then a Director and finally Chairman of the Club. Football played a very important part in that family and in the centre of it all was Celtic. It was talked about at breakfast, at dinner; when there were visitors in the evening, the topic of football and Celtic often lasted long into the night. Bob Kelly was a very religious person and was greatly attracted to the ideas and concepts concerning the foundation of the Club.

Bob Kelly became a Director on the death of his father and became Chairman on the death of my own father, Tom White, in 1947. He was a constant attender at Supporters Clubs functions the length and breadth of the land. As well as serving Celtic he became a double-term President of the Scottish Football League and a double-term President of the Scottish Football Association. As far as Bob Kelly was concerned, business took a very secondary place. His aim in life was the projection of the Club he loved – in fact football, Celtic and religion were his life.

He believed largely in the growth of our own young players ('The Kelly Kids' they were then called), and certainly believed that his players should carry with honour the image and colours of Celtic both on and off the field of play. He was equally concerned about that great family which are our supporters; that they should also be prepared to accept that discipline and good behaviour which would make Celtic supporters welcome everywhere. As Chairman he served

Celtic during the long period of semi-shadow when he took considerable abuse from some sections of our support, to that great high noon of success when he saw his team winning the European Cup in Lisbon in 1967 – the first non-Latin team to win this the greatest of all club football tournaments.

He was knighted by the Queen for his services to football and for the stand the Club made when the tanks of the Warsaw Pact countries swept into Prague. There were those who criticized us at the time – that sport should not interfere with politics. It was, in our opinion, at that time not a question of politics but an open invasion in which the liberty of a free people was crushed under the heel of tyranny.

At a Club Banquet in 1967 after the Lisbon triumph, he was presented with a gold replica of the European Cup and his Lady with a diamond brooch. Sir Robert was pleased. Celtic had put Glasgow and Scotland on the football map of the world. Our supporters walked tall.

If Sir Robert had a fault, it was that he believed that he could achieve the emergence of a great Celtic without a top flight football manager. It was only with the return of Jock Stein to Celtic Park that this final blossoming took place.

James McGrory will go down in Celtic history with all the glory of one of its greatest players. Gentlemen Jim, as he has been called so many times, was probably too gentle to fulfil a managerial role at the highest level.

That the emergence could have happened sooner is possible, but had it happened sooner, the Celtic history inside this book could well have been different – who can say for better or for worse.

When John, or as the football world know him, Jock Stein, arrived back home at Celtic Park, he had at his disposal a very promising group of young players – but he did not have a team. What was needed was something extra – something beyond the normal: Jock Stein supplied that need. By the strength of his own personality and his innate knowledge of the game, he inculcated into his players a belief in their own real ability, and in that united belief, created a great team.

Great as were our traditions and history in the past, nothing could match the success and glories of the years that followed. As his friend Bill Shankly once said to me, 'In writing the name of Celtic across the face of Europe, Jock also has become a legend in his own lifetime.'

That he was severely tempted, after the brilliance of his success, with the Club in Scotland and in Europe, to join Manchester United is true; but who in this life is not tempted? – and he is still with us today. That he made mistakes I believe also is true; but who but the gods make no mistakes? What undoubtedly is true is that for Celtic he was the right man, at the right place, at the right time.

Sir Robert Kelly had a special relationship with Jock Stein and Jock had undoubtedly some of his late Chairman's characteristics. Nothing relative to the game, to the Club or to his players was too much trouble – he was and is the master and the servant. One cannot tread those pinnacles of success without that absolute dedication.

Jock was a very lucky and unlucky man. Very unlucky to have a serious road accident in which he was in no way to blame. Lucky to be alive. There was a very considerable period after the accident when it seemed extremely doubtful to us all if he could ever return to the heat of the football management arena. It is only quite recently that those last shadows have disappeared. Today he stands firmly with Celtic.

Football is more than what happens on the field of play. It needs and demands a live support because it is live support that fires the enthusiasm of the players on the field of play to greater and greater endeavour, an endeavour that reacts on that same support to create the atmosphere and magic which makes football the greatest spectator sport in the world. In consequence, it is to our great bands of supporters that we, as a Club, must also say 'thank you' because our victories were your victories and your glory was our glory, and I feel certain that with your continued involvement we will see on that square of green at Celtic Park the colours of Green and White carried, once again, proudly on high.

To my Directors, Tom Devlin, James Farrell, Kevin Kelly, to Jock Stein, to our Players, to all those at Celtic Park, to those in the *Celtic View* and Development Offices and to our Wonderful Support – my thanks.

1 The New Era

A fairy-tale setting of golden-red sun, azure skies and a breathtaking amphitheatre fashioned on a hillside forest of evergreens is where Celtic's new era reached its pinnacle. If, therefore, the date 25 May 1967 seems an unusual one to begin the history of a club which officially kicked off on 28 May 1888, it is simply explained as being the most significant moment in ninety years of Celtic. The incredibly beautiful and unique setting was the Portuguese Estadio Nacional, a few miles along the coast from Lisbon towards the millionaires' playground of Estoril, and amidst scenes of great joy the team from Parkhead in Glasgow's deprived East End had just become the first British side to win the European Cup for Club Champions. What made it doubly satisfying was the fact that eleven home-bred Scots had won the victory – the first time it had been achieved by a team comprising players of one nationality. Until that twelfth European Cup Final only three countries had won the trophy – Spain, Portugal and Italy – all with multi-national teams built at great expense.

For most of Scotland Celtic's victory was an occasion of great rejoicing and emotion. The seemingly impossible task of breaking the Latin monopoly on the world's premier club tournament had been achieved by a team which cost virtually nothing when compared with the millionaire-backed clubs of Real Madrid, Benfica, AC Milan and Inter Milan, the previous winners. Real had brought Di Stefano from Argentina, Puskas from Hungary, Kopa from France, Didi from Brazil and Santamaria from Uruguay. Benfica, coached by Hungarian Bela Guttman, had brought Eusebio from Mozambique and Coluna from Angola. AC Milan had been bolstered by Hamrin of Sweden, Schiaffino of Uruguay and Schnellinger of West Germany while Inter were managed by Helenio Herrera who shot to fame coaching in Spain from where he plundered Suarez and Peiro.

Celtic on the other hand had bought goalkeeper Ronnie Simpson, a veteran with Hibs, for less than £3000 and striker Willie Wallace from Hearts for a then Celtic record fee of £30000. The rest had been reared by the club from Junior grade.

To many it must have seemed that manager Jock Stein had waved a magic wand in his short reign – and to a very great extent it was his magical ability in handling players and his intimate knowledge of the game which made Lisbon possible. But there was more to it than that. Long before his appointment on a wintry January day in 1965 the Celtic directorate of the late Sir Robert Kelly, Mr Desmond White and Mr Tom Devlin had, as their predecessors had done, embarked on a policy of raising their own players. Many fine performers from the 1950s had grown old together and a major rebuilding job was necessary. Traditionally, Celtic had always preferred to rear their own rather than brandish a chequebook in the transfer market and history had proved that their own were the most loyal servants to the club. But the birth of the Lisbon Lions, so named after their European Cup win, was a long and painful one. It meant years in the wilderness and no certainty of the promised land as young players struggled week after week. It brought the wrath of the supporters on the directors from time to time. Then, in the season of 1963–4, the first really hopeful signs appeared. Players like Gemmell, Murdoch, McNeill, Clark, Johnstone, Chalmers, Lennox and Hughes began to show great promise and reached the semi-finals of the European Cup Winners' Cup at their very first attempt. Despite that success in Europe and the valuable experience which came with it, the young Celts could not find the formula for trophy-winning at home. What they needed was orchestration and history provided the man in Jock Stein.

He was in his early forties and ambitious. Celtic had given him a great chance in life when they plucked him from the obscurity of non-League football in Wales where he was playing out a rather insignificant career with Llanelli after moving there from Albion Rovers. Celtic had turned to him in 1951 more as a reserve player who could use his experience in coaching their promising young players of the time. But he went one better, broke through to the first team and as captain led them to the Coronation Cup and a League and Cup double. Some fourteen years later, after a spell as manager of Dunfermline and Hibs, Celtic turned to him again and asked him to take the managerial reins.

Chairman Bob Kelly and his directors had been watching Stein's progress with interest. After leaving his coaching post at Celtic Park in 1960 he had won, at Celtic's expense, the Scottish Cup in his first full season at Dunfermline and had transformed them from a very ordinary provincial club into one of the country's leading sides. In his short spell with Hibs he had won the Summer Cup and built a very fine team at Easter Road. Bob Kelly had been very much the dictator of Celtic policy and over the years he had taken to dealing with team matters more than a chairman should, yet it must be stated that he firmly believed what he did was for the good of Celtic. He knew by those early days of 1965 that Celtic's future lay in the hands of younger men and eventually stepped aside and gave Stein total control of team matters. Jimmy McGrory, whose managerial career had never matched his playing achievements, was made the club's first-ever public relations officer at the age of sixty. With typical Celtic generosity McGrory was told by the chairman that it was a job for life – a wonderful gesture in a modern era when many managers find themselves, like used cars, on the scrapheap.

The story of Jock Stein's move back to Celtic has never been fully revealed until now. Bob Kelly had always been a father confessor figure to Stein who often sought the Celtic chairman's advice. It was on Kelly's advice that Stein had left his Celtic coaching post for Dunfermline in 1960 despite opposition from director-secretary Desmond White who felt that Stein's coaching ability could pay long-term dividends for the club. At that time Kelly had been grooming Sean Fallon for the manager's job in preparation for the day Jimmy McGrory retired.

When Hibs made their approach to Dunfermline for Stein he again sought Bob Kelly's advice before moving and it was during his short stay with Hibs that the most crucial of all their meetings took place. They met for lunch in Glasgow's North British Hotel where Stein told Kelly that he had received an offer from an English club. During their chat Kelly suddenly asked Stein if he would like the Celtic job. At this stage Kelly had not consulted his Board. Stein told him he was very interested and the following day Kelly called a Board meeting at the same hotel. He opened the proceedings by saying: 'Well, gentlemen, if you wish Jock Stein he is available.' The decision was instantly unanimous. But Bob Kelly had still not played all of his cards.

He shocked Stein by offering him a dual managership with Sean

Fallon. Stein was unhappy and a few days later he contacted Desmond White for advice. The advice given was not to accept the offer
and hold out for all or nothing. At their next meeting Stein told
Kelly he wanted to be in total control of team matters and Kelly
finally abdicated with the words 'It's all yours now.' The Board
settled all matters in the following days. Stein was their man and at
no time did they discuss the aspect of religion or what the predomi-
nantly Irish-Catholic support would think of the appointment. They
knew they were on a winner. The Press, however, had a field day with
banner headlines. The *Scottish Daily Express* front page was dominated by the heading 'First Ever Protestant Boss for Celtic'. It was
typical of the publicity which dominates the West of Scotland. In
some quarters a man's religion takes on more importance than his
talents. Jock Stein had the perfect qualification – his religion was
football. Stein, although he was appointed in January, did not take
up his new post until March and his last act as Hibs manager was to
inflict defeat on Rangers in the Scottish Cup quarter-finals at Easter
Road.

He then set about his task at Celtic Park like the professional
thoroughbred he had become with two former playing-day colleagues
in his backroom team. Sean Fallon became his assistant manager
and Neilly Mochan first-team trainer. In changing times the Board
had also taken on a new and younger look by inviting Glasgow
solicitor James M. Farrell to join them before Stein's appointment.

Celtic were out of the League race when Stein arrived and performances in that competition were poor although for the manager's
first game in charge on 10 March they thrashed Airdrie 6–0 at
Broomfield, Bertie Auld scoring no fewer than five. It took them two
games to overcome Motherwell in the semi-finals of the Scottish
Cup, but by Cup Final day Stein had the formula right and Celtic
beat his old team Dunfermline 3–2 in a dramatic game which ended
an eight-year trophy famine. It was their first major victory since the
famous 7–1 League Cup Final win over Rangers in October 1957
and it was the first Scottish Cup win in eleven years, Jock Stein having
been captain on the previous occasion. Suddenly there was a buzz of
excitement about the club which had been missing for too long.
Everyone, from the directors to the ball-boys, sensed things were
going to happen although no one could have guessed just how much
success was to come.

Most of Celtic's major honours had come in a terrific era which had stretched practically from the day of the club's foundation until the outbreak of the First World War. It was the kind of spellbinding success which would have merited the name bestowed on Celtic some eighty years later by a French soccer magazine. Because of the team's incessant attacking style the publication called them '*l'orage*' – 'the storm'. In their very first year of existence they had begun in whirlwind fashion by reaching the Scottish Cup Final. They won six consecutive League Championships between 1904 and 1910 and set up records in the Scottish Cup, Glasgow Cup and Charity Cup.

But the Twenties did not produce the same form, neither did the Thirties. Successes came but not often enough. Like the First World War, the 1939–45 War took a heavy toll of the club's playing resources but players like Tully, Fallon, Peacock, Stein, Evans, Mochan, Fernie and Collins brightened up the Fifties with the Coronation Cup, the Scottish Cup, a League and Cup double and two successive League Cups.

Then, towards the end of the Fifties, the club was to enter its worst era. It had never known such a bleak period in its peace-time history as it was to experience from October 1957 until that sunny April afternoon in 1965. By then there was a great hunger for success among players and fans and, just as the hungry boxer is the best boxer, the hungry Celts became the best players, technically as well as physically. Manager Stein had quickly assessed his playing staff and after the Cup win freed the unusually high number of twenty. Celtic had been running three teams but he felt the streamlining to a first team and reserve team would benefit the club. In the close season he bought only one player, the prolific goal-scorer Joe McBride, for a modest £22 000. The Motherwell player had an equally important credential in that he wanted to play for Celtic.

What few people know is that the shrewd Stein had influenced one of Celtic's greatest signings some months before he returned to Celtic Park as manager.

Bertie Auld had gone to the Midland Hotel in Birmingham the previous season after a Scottish League–English League match to have a chat with Jock Stein and found that Bob Kelly was with the Hibs manager. At no time was there any mention of Auld moving back to Celtic. In fact, it had been Bob Kelly who had insisted on Auld's transfer to Birmingham in 1961 because the young outside left had been a stormy petrel at Parkhead and Kelly had taken a dislike to his lack of discipline. The Celtic chairman seemed impressed with the more mature Auld, and Stein, who had coached him at Celtic Park before leaving to manage Dunfermline, had tremendous admiration for the skills of a player who was to become a midfield genius. The three parted and Auld continued to play for Birmingham. Then around New Year of 1965 Auld got a telephone call from a Celtic player to tip him off that Sean Fallon was travelling south to watch him play against West Ham United. He was told in the same telephone conversation that Jock Stein was about to be appointed manager of Celtic although it was over a month before that was to be made public. Auld jumped at the chance and was signed by Jimmy McGrory. He had signed for his old boss from Maryhill Harp, signed again after being farmed out to Dumbarton and completed a unique signing hat-trick in January 1965. Bertie Auld always maintained that Stein was behind his move back to Scotland – a move which Stein knew was vital if Celtic were to prove themselves in the greatest arena of all, the European Cup.

So by the beginning of his first full season in charge (1965–6) Stein had the players he wanted and suddenly Celtic could score goals – lots of goals. They won their League Cup section against Dundee, Dundee United and Motherwell and they crushed Raith Rovers 12–1 in the two quarter-final matches. The semi-finals almost saw the end of the run. Hibs were leading 2–1 at neutral Ibrox as the game went into injury time and with virtually the last kick of the ball Bobby Lennox kept Celtic alive. They won the replay 4–0 and faced the big test in the Final against Rangers. They had developed a complex about the Ibrox side during the years in the wilderness but the breakthrough came on the afternoon of 23 October 1965, thanks mainly to big outside-left John Hughes who had one of those days when he could run past a defence at will. He scored two penalty goals to give Celtic a 2–1 win. But the day was marred as the team did a lap of honour in front of their own fans at the King's Park end of Hampden. As they approached the half-way line – their intention was then to cross the field to the dressing-rooms and not parade the trophy at the other end also – thousands of Rangers fans invaded the pitch and tried to attack the players, who luckily got to safety in time thanks to the intervention of trainer Mochan. The Scottish League and SFA used the invasion as an excuse to ban all laps of honour, thereby depriving Celtic fans of many such enjoyable victory celebrations in the great years which were to follow.

The Celtic fans showed tremendous restraint that day. Had they decided to come over the wall to protect their own players it would have been a dreadful day for Scottish football. That they should suffer because of the League–SFA ban was most unfair. Many a time they had watched as Rangers paraded a cup.

That victory behind them, Celtic went on to win the League in exciting fashion. Their record was: Played 34, Won 27, Lost 4, Drawn 3, Goals for 106, Against 30. A 1–0 victory over Motherwell at Fir Park on 7 May 1966 gave them the title with fifty-seven points to Rangers' fifty-five. Although they lost 1–0 to Rangers in a replayed Scottish Cup Final and went out of the European Cup Winners' Cup, following a disallowed goal, at the hands of Liverpool, they had reached their number one priority. They were Champions and had qualified for the big one – the European Cup.

During the close season which followed a most important move was made in creating the kind of family spirit required of a club which has its sights set on the top. They embarked on a thirty-five-day 20000-mile tour of Bermuda, the United States and Canada. The players, after the strains of the season, were encouraged to enjoy themselves in surroundings where the Atlantic waters lapped gently against the coral shores. The paradise island of Bermuda, where every cigar has a millionaire on the end of it, was an ideal start and despite the high temperatures the team scored two victories.

They beat Bermuda Select 10–1 and Bermuda Young Men 7–0. Then it was on to the States and the serious opposition although the first game there against the local New Jersey All Stars provided no difficulty and a 6–0 win was recorded. The next match was against top English club Tottenham Hotspur. Again Celtic came out on top with a 1–0 win although their play should have brought them more goals. Canada was the next stop and to show they had not lost their scoring touch they hammered the Hamilton Select 11–0. The party then headed back to New York where they had a 0–0 draw with Italian team Bologna. In St Louis they beat CYC All Stars and then it was on to San Francisco where Spurs eagerly awaited revenge for their New York defeat. Auld and Lennox scored the goals that gave Celtic a 2–1 victory double over the London club. Eight games and still unbeaten, Celtic were the toast of the organizers. They finished the tour with a third game against Spurs which ended in a 1–1 draw, a 2–2 draw with West Germans Bayern Munich and a 1–0 win over

Atlas of Mexico in Los Angeles to return home unbeaten. The remarkable record read: Played 11, Won 8, Drawn 3, Lost 0, Goals for 47, Against 6. Bobby Lennox scored nineteen of the goals and struck up a wonderful partnership with Bertie Auld who had been carefully introduced to his midfield role for the first time.

It was a partnership which was to do great things for Celtic in the years ahead. Auld had the shrewd brain and Lennox had a speed seldom bettered and an appetite for scoring goals.

They returned to Scotland in the knowledge that they had encountered class opposition and emerged with great distinction. So they looked forward to the season which was to become the greatest in the club's history. Those who were privileged to see Celtic in the season of 1966–7 will never forget it. They were to win every domestic honour plus the European Cup – something never achieved by any club. The unbeaten tour had whetted the appetites of the fans who came rolling up in their thousands to Celtic Park on 6 August 1966 for a very glamorous start to the season. The visitors were the star-studded Manchester United with Denis Law, George Best, Bobby Charlton and ex-Celt Pat Crerand. Charlton and his English team-mate Nobby Stiles had played in the World Cup Final at Wembley in which England beat West Germany 4–2 only a week earlier. But the confident Celts were in no way overawed. They ran out 4–1 winners and showed signs of magic which could only have come from living, eating, and sleeping football on the tour. Lennox, Murdoch, McBride and Foulkes (own goal) made sure of victory against a team which was to win the European Cup the year after Celtic.

The League Cup provided an all-conquering run without a defeat or even a drawn game. The record read: Played 10, Won 10, Goals for 35, Against 7. The qualifying stages were won in great style with Hearts, Clyde and St Mirren all soundly beaten. Joe McBride scored thirteen of the twenty-three sectional goals.

Those seasoned cup fighters Dunfermline came to Parkhead for the quarter-finals and although they scored three goals they lost six and went down 3–1 in the return leg. Airdrie, who had shocked many by reaching the semi-finals, had been beaten 3–0 by Celtic in the League on the Saturday and a few days later went out of the League Cup by 2–0, Celtic's goals being scored by McBride and Murdoch.

A crowd of 94 532 people turned up at Hampden on 29 October 1966 to witness what was to be Celtic's first step towards the Grand

Slam to end them all. For the third year in succession it was an Old Firm League Cup Final and a 1–0 win put Celtic 2–1 up in that particular series. The only goal of a tense match came in the twentieth minute with Bobby Lennox finishing off a move which had begun with a long ball from Bertie Auld to the head of Joe McBride. Stevie Chalmers made history by becoming the first substitute in a Hampden Final, and in a typical gesture handed the winner's medal to the injured John Hughes.

The League Championship also began in great scoring form with thirty-seven goals in the opening ten games. But two teams, St Mirren and Dundee United, upset what at one stage was shaping to be a history-making run. St Mirren were in relegation trouble practically from the start of the season and had lost 8–2 to Celtic at Parkhead in the League Cup. But they came back for the ninth League match of the season and fought out a 1–1 draw thanks mainly to their goalkeeper, Denis Connaghan, who some years later was to sign for Celtic. A real fright came just two weeks later at East End Park, Dunfermline, in what must have been one of the greatest League games ever seen in this country. The 21 000 crowd gasped as Dunfermline went ahead 2–0, then 3–1 and in the second half by 4–2. With only twenty minutes to go Celtic fought furiously, backed by their fans, and Auld and McBride scored two in two minutes. In the very last minute McBride scored from a penalty to give Celtic the points.

But the run was still unbeaten and went on for a total of sixteen games – until New Year's Eve at Tannadice. The game had been brought forward an hour at Celtic's request so that the players could get back home in time to bring in the New Year with their families. Goals from Lennox and Willie Wallace, who had just joined the club from Hearts for £30 000, put Celtic 2–1 ahead in the second half but Dundee United fought back to win 3–2. As it turned out the same team were to complete a remarkable double seventeen games later at Celtic Park – and they could not have chosen a more vital game to establish their hoodoo. The date was 3 May 1967 and Celtic needed two points to clinch the League in front of their own fans – something they were never to achieve during their world-record nine consecutive Championships between 1966 and 1974.

The United double came after Celtic had just completed their finest week of the season by beating Dukla Prague to qualify for the European Cup Final. Three days later they had beaten Aberdeen

2–0 in the Scottish Cup Final so the game against United might well have been one of those nights of reaction to such a demanding programme. The pattern of the game was identical to the first meeting. Celtic were 2–1 up in the second half and again United came through to win 3–2.

That result only delayed the Championship victory but it was also responsible for a terrific climax against Rangers at Ibrox who still had an outside chance of the title.

About 78000 fans braved a day of driving rain and were rewarded with a memorable match. It was a game which had been postponed from New Year. In the stand was Inter Milan's manager, Helenio Herrera, an urchin from the streets of Casablanca who had risen to become the world's highest-paid football coach. In the stamina-sapping conditions he must have been unnerved at the show put up by both teams. It was nothing short of remarkable. Rangers had gone ahead in the first half but Jimmy Johnstone had shown Celtic's reserves of strength by equalizing in less than a minute and at half-time, with the score at 1–1, the Celtic fans were already singing their victory hymns. They knew even at that stage the Championship was won. In the second half Johnstone made a mockery of the heavy conditions and half the Rangers defence when he shuffled his slight frame inside from the wing and put Celtic ahead with a glorious 30-yard shot which went high into the net.

Rangers equalized near the end but Celtic had the point they needed for victory. It was the first time Celts had won the Championship in successive years since 1916–17 – exactly fifty years earlier.

Another highlight from that Championship run in which only one team had beaten them came at Firhill on 27 March when Bobby Lennox scored the hundredth League goal of the season in a 4–1 victory. The record read: Played 34, Won 26, Lost 2, Drawn 6, Goals for 111, Against 33, Points 58. Rangers were runners-up with fifty-five points and Clyde took third place with forty-six.

The Scottish Cup was also an all-conquering run with Clyde being the only team to put up any resistance in the semi-finals. It took two games to defeat them. Celtic were certainly fortunate in the calibre of opposition and did not have to leave Glasgow. On the day Berwick Rangers were defeating Glasgow Rangers in an historic occasion at Berwick, Celtic were taking care of Arbroath. Their northern neighbours Elgin fell in the next round and Queen's Park were victims in the quarter-finals although they gave a creditable performance in their 5–3 defeat. Goals by Lennox and Auld dismissed Clyde in the semi-final replay and Celts were into the Final.

Preparation for the game against Aberdeen could have been a lot better. There were those who feared a repeat of the previous season when Celtic had gone out of the European Cup Winners' Cup to Liverpool and lost the Scottish Cup to Rangers. But this time there was no reaction. Celtic were only forty-eight hours home from Prague and Jim Craig recovered from flu just in time to make the team. Jock Stein played Jimmy Johnstone through the middle of the field to upset the well-drilled Aberdeen defence and Celtic gave a highly professional display and a lesson to Aberdeen in possession football. Ten days earlier Aberdeen had held Celtic to a 0–0 draw in a League game at Parkhead but on Cup Final day Willie Wallace became the hero of the hour with two well-taken goals from crosses by Lennox and Johnstone.

Wallace had proved to be one of Celtic's best-ever signings. His two Cup Final goals came on top of another brace which had put Celtic into the European Cup Final. Seldom can a player have repaid his transfer fee so quickly. He did not just score goals for Celtic, he scored spectacular goals and hit 100 in less than three seasons. The wily Jock Stein had nipped in and bought Wallace while Rangers were still thinking about it. Stein had made his move while Rangers were in Germany playing Borussia Dortmund and made sure the Ibrox club, known to be interested, could not counter his bid of £30000 for the player. Wallace was the kind of professional who would have played anywhere for anyone. He was bought just in time too because a couple of weeks later Joe McBride got a knee injury which was to keep him out for the rest of the season. Towards the end of 1966 Joe was Scotland's leading scorer with thirty-seven goals and without kicking another ball after Christmas he still ended the season of 1966–7 as joint top scorer. One is left to ponder the records the man would have set that glorious year had that tragic injury not struck.

The Glasgow Cup, won earlier in the season, had shown Celtic at their consistent best. They accounted for Rangers, Queen's Park and Partick Thistle all by the same score – 4–0. The only other games of the season not already mentioned were two challenge matches against Dynamo Zagreb and Real Madrid. The Zagreb game had been arranged by Stein to give Celtic a taste of Yugoslav opposition before meeting Vojvodina in the European Cup quarter-finals. Stein, with all the aplomb of a circus ringmaster, advertised an outrageous plan which had most of his defenders in attack and attackers playing from deep positions.

It was outrageous enough to attract 50000 paying customers through the turnstiles but while it may have paid the Slavs their match guarantee it did not bring the expected victory. A last-minute goal by Zagreb made it all look a bit silly. However, it was still valuable experience for the team.

The other match, against Real Madrid, came just a couple of weeks after the Lisbon Final. Alfredo Di Stefano, the great White Arrow of Real, had approached Celtic in Lisbon even before they played Inter Milan to ask if they would provide the opposition for his benefit match. He said he wanted Celtic because of their attacking qualities. Celtic agreed despite such a long, hard season, and on 7 June lined up in front of 100000 fans at the Santiago Bernabeu Stadium in their first game as Champions of Europe. Thanks to a magnificent game by goalkeeper John Fallon and a Bobby Lennox goal, laid on after a superb run by Jimmy Johnstone, Celtic won 1–0. The game was slightly marred when Auld and Amancio were sent off for fighting. It was a result which could only consolidate Celtic's title in the eyes of Europe as Real had won the European Cup for the sixth time the previous season.

Their commitments fulfilled, the Celtic players and backroom team took a well deserved, if short, break.

Between 6 August 1966, when they kicked off against Manchester United in the challenge game at Celtic Park, and 7 June 1967, when they played Real Madrid, their fabulous record read, Played 65, Won 53, Lost 4, Drawn 8, Goals for 201, Against 50. It is a record which will surely never be beaten.

Other honours for Celtic that season were that nine of the team were capped by Scotland and eventually all eleven were to become full internationalists. Bobby Lennox scored a vital goal in Scotland's 3–2 victory over England at Wembley, the first defeat for England after their World Cup win, and Jock Stein was named Manager of Britain for the second season in succession. Jimmy McGrory was made a Freeman of Kearney, New Jersey, while there as a guest of the Kearney Celtic Supporters' Association and Sean Fallon was made a Freeman of his home town Sligo.

Celtic won a sixth trophy when the Reserves won their League

Cup. Jock Stein maintained it should have been seven but there had been no time to enter Bobby Lennox for the Derby.

One Cup Final from the season 1966–7 has not yet been discussed in detail – the European Cup Final in Lisbon. It was a day to remember. . . .

2 Lisbon, Day of Glory

Dawn on the morning of 25 May 1967 broke in most unusual fashion for Lisbon at that time of year with grey, overcast skies and a slight chill in the air. The cold wafting in through a small, top-floor pension window was enough to stir your writer from his sleep but it was a cold which was quickly dispelled by the gradual, warming realization that this was to be a very special day in Celtic's history. The club was just three days short of its seventy-ninth anniversary, having played its very first game on 28 May 1888, and this was the day they could – and surely would – win the European Champions' Cup. Out on the streets of the Portuguese capital many of the 15000 supporters from Scotland were already on the move. The beautiful seaport has much to offer the tourist with sights such as the Ponte Salazar which spans the winding River Tagus, the giant white statue of Christ the King overlooking the harbour, or a stroll on the tree-lined Avenida da Liberdade, one of Europe's great avenues.

But the great majority of Celtic fans were Catholics and it was the feast of Corpus Christi, a holiday of obligation. So their priority was to seek out the city chapels and they streamed in, some accompanied by non-Catholic friends. The prayer from every lip was the same. Lisbon had never seen anything like it as the greatest-ever football exodus from Scotland descended wave by wave on a city already in festive mood. The airport took the main strain as throngs of singing, banner-waving Scots swept through.

How Brother Walfrid and his co-founders of the club would have smiled. They had founded Celtic to feed the poor in Glasgow's East End. Now, a few generations later, the descendants of those same poor were flying abroad in astonishing numbers to support the club. The Scots found the Portuguese very much on their side, thanks to some good public relations by manager Jock Stein in a television interview the previous week in which he had pitted his attacking philosophy against the defensive tactics of Inter Milan. The Portuguese had bitter memories of those Milan tactics from two years earlier. Their own Benfica had gone to Milan for the European Cup Final to face Inter on the field of San Siro. The Benfica goalkeeper was carried off injured yet the Inter team had defended in depth after snatching one goal despite having home advantage for a Final.

So the citizens of Lisbon shouted a warm '*Bem Vindo*' ('Welcome'), and sought Celtic souvenirs. On the wide avenues hundreds of Celtic fans were climbing out of cars, buses and other less conventional forms of transport after an 1800-mile-long odyssey under the searing skies of France, Spain and Portugal which was crazy, sometimes courageous and certainly incomparable. Many were still en route and some, unfortunately, were not to arrive until after the game.

The Celtic headquarters, the magnificent Hotel Palacio in Estoril, a half-hour journey from the city, proved a great attraction for many of the supporters on the morning of the game.

Players were glad to spend the time chatting, signing autographs and posing for photographs. If any nerves were showing they were all from the supporters. One well-known Glasgow garage-owner was in such a state about it all that he took Tommy Gemmell aside and promised him thirty gallons of petrol if he scored a goal! Jock Stein seemed to be the most relaxed man in Lisbon and was at the hotel's luxurious swimming pool until shortly before the official party left for the stadium. He joked with local priests, saying that their chapels were getting their best 'gates' in years and would Celtic get a 50–50 share? Yet underneath it all there must have been great tension. During the day he had warned his players to keep out of the sun – 'I don't even want to see you near your bedroom windows' – and in the afternoon he sent them all to bed for a couple of hours. Earlier they had been out on the hotel lawn for a loosening-up session but all the serious work had been done back home at Seamill on the Ayrshire coast, including a film of the epic Real Madrid–Eintracht Frankfurt European Cup Final of 1960. That was how Stein wanted his men to play.

Suddenly it was time to leave for the Estadio and the bus roared away at high speed. If the friendly Portuguese had one weakness it was in organizing things and they had sent a driver who did not know his way. After a while it was realized that the bus was heading in the opposite direction and absolute panic set in among the party. The driver could not get the bus turned because of the thousands travelling in the other direction to the stadium. Eventually it was all sorted out and the Celtic party roared up to the stadium with a police escort. If the Celtic players had needed any reassurance of support it came when they appeared to inspect the playing surface. They were still in green blazers and grey trousers yet they got the type of reception normally reserved for a winning goal. The entire stadium seemed to erupt with the chants of 'Celtic, Celtic'.

The entire terracing at the 'Estoril End' was a mass of green and white banners with other clusters of ebullient Scots around the rest of the gleaming white arena. It was a majestic scene with all the pomp of a Roman amphitheatre and a fitting setting for the gladiators of Celtic. They had won every major honour on the domestic scene – League Championship, Scottish Cup, League Cup and Glasgow Cup. No other club in Scotland had ever matched such achievements. Now was the hour for achieving what no other club in Europe had done – the winning of the European Cup in addition to every domestic honour.

But there was highly formidable opposition to be overcome first in the form of Internazionale Milan, a team brought together at a cost of millions of lire. They were under the Svengali influence of Europe's high priest of football, the small, swarthy Helenio Herrera, the world's highest-paid coach. His message was simple. He preached defensive football on a scale never before known and had revolutionized European football thinking.

They had won their previous two Final appearances against Real Madrid in 1964 and Benfica in 1965 – both former winners. In contrast, this was not only Celtic's first Final but their very first appearance in the competition, although this was a situation in which Celtic teams had often triumphed in the past. And there was a new trophy for the winning, the original having been presented to Real Madrid for their feat in winning it six times.

Celtic, over the years, had made a habit of collecting new trophies so all the signs were right. But they were very much the underdogs – the inexperienced against the experienced.

The road to Lisbon had been long and hard, starting the previous September against Zürich of Switzerland at Celtic Park. Celtic won a bruising match by 2–0 and went one better in the return leg with a 3–0 win. They beat Nantes of France 3–1 home and away in the second round. Then came the long winter break until March and the quarter-finals against the unknown quantity of Vojvodina Novi Sad of Yugoslavia. They proved to be a hard nut to crack. They defeated Celtic by 1–0 in Novi Sad, inflicting the only reverse of the campaign. But in a lung-bursting effort in the return at Celtic Park two weeks later, Stevie Chalmers put Celtic level in the second half. It was the prelude to perhaps the greatest-ever finish seen at Parkhead. With the seconds ticking away into injury time and the threat of a play-off in Rotterdam, Charlie Gallagher took a corner kick out on the right – the last chance of the match. Captain Billy McNeill had started his run from the half-way line and rose to meet the ball right in the middle of his golden forehead and Celtic, to joyous scenes on the terracing and field, were through to the last four.

They beat the Czech team Dukla Prague 3–1 in the first leg of the semi-final at Parkhead with Willie Wallace making his European Cup début for Celtic. He scored two vital goals which turned a disappointing 1–1 draw at half-time into a solid victory. With a place in the Final at stake Celtic settled for a safety-first game in Prague. Billy McNeill was outstanding in the 0–0 draw which saw Stevie Chalmers as the lone attacker for most of the game. Manager Jock Stein admitted some months later that he got embarrassed every time he looked back on his tactics for that match. Such defence in depth was totally foreign to Celtic. But on that one occasion they could be excused. Reaching the Final had justified the means.

Inter Milan also had a far from easy route to Lisbon. They defeated Moscow Torpedo 1–0 and drew 0–0 away from home; Vasas Budapest (h 2–1; a 2–0); Real Madrid (h 1–0; a 2–0). The semi-finals proved the biggest headache of all, taking them three games to dispose of the little-fancied but well-organized CSKA Sofia of Bulgaria. The scoring rate of the Italians was not high. On the other hand Celtic had been scoring freely all season. Their record for 1966–7, excluding the European Cup Final, was: Played 63, Won 51, Lost 4, Drawn 8, Goals for 198, Against 49. Following the European Cup Final, of course, they added to this record by defeating Real Madrid, European Cup winners the previous year, by 1–0 in the Alfredo Di Stefano benefit match in Madrid. But all that glory was history as the players got stripped in the Estadio dressing-rooms for the most important match in Celtic's history. A curious thing about the placc was thc situation of the dressing-rooms, an old house on the perimeter of the Estadio.

In order to reach the pitch players had to walk through a little courtyard, about 200 yards along a tree-lined path, into an underground passage and up a flight of stairs. As both sides lined up and began their walk manager Jock Stein, quickly followed by Bertie Auld, struck the first psychological blow for Celtic. The Italians looked absolutely baffled as at the top of their voices they began to sing the Celtic song, 'Sure, it's a Grand Old Team to Play For . . .' The others joined in and in the semi-darkness of the underground passage it echoed even louder. The men from Milan knew that they were in for more than a mere game of football against these bold, adventurous men from Glasgow.

Just before the kick-off time Inter boss Herrera tried to pull one of his tricks by claiming the trainers' bench nearest the dressing-rooms but Stein beat him to it. The Celtic manager had already encountered the wiles of the little Milan fox. Herrera had come to Scotland the previous month to watch Celtic in action against Rangers. Through the Press he had offered Stein a seat on the private Inter Milan jet so that he could return with Herrera and weigh up the Inter team. It was all very friendly stuff until at the last minute Herrera stated there would be too much weight for the plane and left Stein to make his own way to Italy. Once there Stein was told by Herrera that he could travel to the stadium on the team bus and that he personally would arrange accommodation for the match. Stein waited patiently in the hotel lobby and when he eventually went outside he was just in time to see the bus vanish into the distance. He had to get a taxi and borrow a Pressman's ticket to get into the game.

The twelfth European Cup Final kicked off at 5.30 p.m. in over 80° F of heat. Celtic's immortal line-up was: Simpson, Craig, Gemmell, Murdoch, McNeill, Clark, Johnstone, Wallace, Chalmers, Auld and Lennox. Inter's team was: Sarti, Burgnich, Facchetti, Bedin, Guarneri, Picchi, Domenghini, Cappellini, Mazzola, Bicicli and Corso. Within seven minutes Celtic found themselves a goal behind. Right-back Jim Craig clashed with Italian forward Cappellini and referee Kurt Tschescher of West Germany awarded a penalty kick. Sandro Mazzola scored and the fear of every Scot was realized. Inter were famous for grabbing a quick goal then shutting the doors. When they attacked they still had a spare man behind two centre-backs who in turn had four men strung out in front of them. So when they defended in depth they were practically impregnable.

But they had not reckoned with the superbly fit young Celts who seemed unaffected by the intense heat. And anyway, Lisbon was not going to be robbed of its fairy-tale ending by a penalty kick. Just as Mazzola's goal had been scored other dramas were taking place elsewhere. A planeload of fans from Glasgow had just touched down at the airport and before the aircraft had finished taxi-ing they had opened the doors, 'dreeped' onto the runway and headed for the Estadio. They made it just before the half-time whistle was blown but another group had not been so lucky. They had left Glasgow by bus, a bus which had undergone major surgery in the days before. It broke down in France but most of the fans piled into taxis and made incredible efforts to reach the stadium at tremendous financial cost. Some arrived at the stadium just after the final whistle and others had to be content with watching the game through the window of a television showroom in Lisbon itself.

But for the fortunate fans who had been there from the start this had never been a mere game of football. In more ways than one it had become a pilgrimage and if faith and hope had anything to do with it Celtic would be victorious. Yet for so long after that penalty kick blow, one wondered if the happy ending would come. Every man in green and white was playing to his peak but the German referee seemed not to notice many of the strange goings-on in the Inter Milan penalty area. If he was convinced that Craig's tackle on Cappellini was a penalty, what could possibly have been going through his mind when Inter goalkeeper Sarti grabbed Willie Wallace round the ankles with both hands to prevent him scoring? Sarti, apart from such unorthodox habits, was a brilliant keeper on the day and stood between his team and a real thrashing. As one newspaper reported the following day: 'Lisbon, Thursday – Celtic annihilated Inter Milan by two goals to one here this evening.' The Inter keeper was in the kind of inspired mood which normally breaks the hearts of the opposition. He had fabulous saves from a Johnstone header and shots from Gemmell, Chalmers, Murdoch and Lennox. On the occasion he missed the ball in the first half, Bertie Auld's shot came crashing back off the crossbar.

At the other end of the field Celtic goalkeeper Ronnie Simpson was in an unenviable position of having touched the ball on only a couple of occasions, one of those being to lift it out of the net after the penalty. He was virtually unemployed, a dangerous situation for any keeper's concentration. Inter's penalty had been the result of a quick break upfield after a Celtic corner kick. Ronnie knew he had to keep on his guard yet it did not prevent him from having a heart-stopping moment while Inter were still a goal ahead. Another quick break by the Italians saw him having to race about thirty yards from goal to get to the ball before the Inter strikers. As they closed in he seemed to panic for a second. Should he lift the ball and concede a free kick or should he boot it clear not knowing exactly where it would go? The crowd gasped as he stooped to pick it up then, cool as you like, he backheeled it to safety.

Inter survived until the half-time whistle but found no respite in the burning heat of the second half. Tommy Gemmell at left-back became the hero of the day with his swashbuckling runs down the left flank, shooting with that awesome power of his at every opportunity. Then, in the sixty-second minute, came the big breakthrough. A long clearance from the Inter defence was stopped near the half-way line and a couple of passes saw the ball despatched across field to the overlapping Craig on the right.

He bore in on the Italian penalty area with, no doubt, the half-time instructions of Jock Stein running clearly through his mind. In the first half Celtic had been too predictable with the high cross ball so Stein had told them to angle it low and hard across goal. As the Inter defenders awaited a high cross, Craig, without even lifting his head, simply drew back his foot and rolled the ball into the path of the onrushing Gemmell who met it twenty yards out without breaking stride. The goalkeeper never saw the ball, although he no doubt felt the breeze as it passed him. It was a superb goal, fit to win any European Cup, and must rank with the greatest scored in the competition. The Celtic players went mad, the fans danced in ecstasy. The score was only 1–1 and the actual winning had still to be done. But there was nothing now which could stop the Celts and Inter knew it.

They were on their knees and the match was entirely one-sided. There was one nasty incident just after Celtic's equalizer when Cappellini booted Simpson on the shin after the keeper had safely gathered the ball. Amazingly, no action was taken against the Italian. Simpson recovered and with only six minutes to go Murdoch surged down the left and hit a low, angled shot towards goal. It was good but not good enough until quicksilver Stevie Chalmers intercepted it and prodded it into the net. The Inter defenders were still rooted to the spot as Stevie turned away to receive the embraces of his mates.

This was the signal for thousands of Celtic fans to mass around the wall and moat which had been designed by some optimist to keep supporters off the field. The ground seemed to be under an umbrella of green and white as the victory songs and dances began. Yet those last few minutes seemed an eternity as Bertie Auld used his great experience to keep team-mates calm. He called for possession and then proceeded to take the ball for a walk out to one of the corner flags. As the Inter players tackled, all they did was concede throw-ins. With the tension becoming unbearable and many a Celtic head buried in Celtic hands, one man slipped quietly away from the trainers' bench unable to take any more. The burly man with the slight limp headed off down the red ash track in the direction of the dressing-rooms. It was Jock Stein. He had within his grasp football immortality. He would be the first British manager to win the European Cup. He and his players would become household names to the hundred million television audience from every corner of the world . . . if only that final whistle would sound.

Before he reached the stairway to the underground rooms the whistle sounded. He was nearest to Ronnie Simpson and Billy McNeill. The three hugged each other and danced as John Clark sank to his knees and kissed the turf. Within seconds the pitch was a mass of people. A great cavalry charge of Celtic fans like some giant catherine-wheel of colour enveloped players and officials and produced some of the most emotional scenes in football history.

They dug up the turf for souvenirs and kissed it. They embraced the goalposts and refused to go home. It was more than half an hour before Billy McNeill could climb the imposing marble stairway to collect the giant, gleaming European Cup. He had to be helped through the crowd and lost two jerseys en route. After the presentation Billy could not face the arduous journey back through the jubilant mob and was relieved when the Chief of Police pointed towards his car and said: 'Come.' But Billy found himself mobbed again, this time by the Chief and his men. He had to pose with the Chief and the Cup and then just about every policeman there insisted on doing the same before he was driven back to join his colleagues in the dressing-room. Although the fans deserved their moment, it was a great disappointment that the players did not get the chance to do a dignified lap of honour. McNeill felt it was unfair that he should get all the limelight after the performances given by every member of the team.

Outside the Celtic dressing-room the world's Press clamoured to see Stein while just a few feet away Herrera sat totally ignored.

Before that game they had beaten a path to his door but the Estadio Nacional had been the catafalque of his football teachings. The little dictator was dead, Stein was king. The dressing-room scenes were unbelievable. Stein was sitting in a corner muttering: 'What a performance, what a performance.' Then he emerged from his daze to jump into the bath with his players. Bertie Auld hugged Ronnie Simpson and asked: 'What are we, what are we, son?' Then flashing his white teeth between parched lips he answered his own question with the roar: 'We are the greatest!' Champagne bottles popped open and Celtic songs were sung but above all the din came a gravel voice which was instantly recognizable. With all the sincerity of a man who believed football was a religion it boomed, 'John, you're immortal.' It was the legendary Scot Bill Shankly, manager of Liverpool, the only English-based manager who thought it worthwhile to make the journey and to congratulate the man who had made history.

Outside the dressing-rooms stood that great Celt Charles Patrick Tully who had flown to Lisbon with a planeload of Glasgow fans from the Gorbals. As usual he was surrounded by a group of supporters. One shouted to him, 'Hey, Charlie, would you have got a place in that team?' Quick as a flash the bold bhoy replied with that impish brogue: 'Sure now, I could have taken the corners.' Charlie, of course, was referring to that famous occasion at Falkirk in the Fifties when he had twice in succession put the ball into the net direct from the corner flag.

As the players eventually emerged to board the waiting team bus, the cheers reached a crescendo and this was well over an hour after the match. Ronnie Simpson still looked in a dazed condition. At the age of thirty-six, when most people had retired from the game, he had won the greatest club honour. Perhaps, too, he was reflecting on what had happened to him at the final whistle. While he was celebrating with manager Stein and Billy McNeill a fan had grabbed his cap as a souvenir. In it were his dentures and those of Bobby Lennox and Jimmy Johnstone! So confident had they been of victory that they wanted to make sure they had their teeth with them for the Cup presentation and lap of honour. Luckily Lennox and Johnstone had managed to retrieve them. The team bus drove into Lisbon for the prearranged banquet but when Celtic got there they discovered that Inter Milan had not turned up. There was a delay as officials of UEFA ordered Herrera and his men to attend.

At one stage Celtic chairman Bob Kelly had become very impatient and said he wanted the meal to start without the Italians. But they eventually appeared, ate, listened to the speeches and then left. It took nothing away from the Celtic celebrations and as the players wined and dined the fans took Lisbon and Estoril by storm. Their behaviour was in keeping with their new responsibility now that they were supporters of the Champions of Europe. Later that night many gathered in the Hotel Cibra just a few yards away from the Celtic headquarters and were joined by manager Stein, the directors and former manager Jimmy McGrory. The players, after the greatest day of their lives, had gone to bed. In the room shared by Billy McNeill and John Clark, the magnificent European Cup sat on the cabinet between their twin beds as they dreamt of glory.

Chairman Bob Kelly seemed to be in a daze and Jimmy McGrory wept with joy. In more than forty years with the club as player and official he had seen it all, but only this occasion had moved him to tears. Bob Kelly had still been gazing out over the playing field long after the final whistle, earlier in the evening, like a man who had at last come to the end of a great and trying journey. He had been totally convinced that Celtic would win. In the weeks leading up to the game he spoke only of going to see Celtic win the European Cup. Defeat was not a word he allowed to enter his head.

He had turned to his nephew Kevin before the game and said: 'There is more to being here than just ability. Celtic Football Club deserves to win for what the club has done and stood for in the past. They deserve this place in history.' Mr Kelly was no doubt referring to the club's charitable acts over the decades, plus the tremendous struggle against the forces which on several occasions had tried to put them out of football.

He was, of course, a deeply religious man with tremendous faith. When Kevin Kelly had pressed him to elaborate on what he had said, Mr Kelly replied: 'I am sure there has always been a special guiding influence over Celtic Park looking after our club.' But he would not be drawn further.

Bob Kelly had his critics. He was a dictator and he passionately believed that everything he did was for the good of Celtic. Had he altered course in the early Fifties then perhaps the barren years which were to follow could have been avoided. He was loyal to Jimmy McGrory even to the extent of allowing Jock Stein to leave Celtic Park for Dunfermline when Stein could have ended the trophy famine. For his single-mindedness and his loyalty he took much stick from the supporters but never at any stage felt bitter. On the evening of 25 May 1967 he felt vindicated. Although the youth policy had taken a long, long time to reach fruition it had done so and his beloved Celtic had reached the pinnacle.

As the celebrations went on that night Bob Kelly turned to his colleagues and said: 'Well, I don't know about you, but I'm away to my bed.' Those colleagues said later that he was just brimming with inner joy. He had nothing else to say. It had all been said for him and the club on the green acres of Lisbon's Estadio Nacional.

Jock Stein was deep in thought later when Bertie Auld said to him: 'What about our team, boss? Do you think anyone will ever beat us now?' Stein's reply came in a manner which left Auld in no doubt that the Big Man was already looking ahead. Stein said: 'No one will ever beat that team, no one.' Auld recalled later: 'I got the feeling there and then that the boss would make sure we were never beaten and in retrospect he played the Lisbon team only on a few occasions after that.' Auld recalled another incident with the manager in Portugal. He was teetotal and some of the players persuaded him that if they won the European Cup he would have to take a drink with them. With a talent for never committing himself he did not say no and the matter was left at that. Then, on the night of 25 May when the celebrations were at their height, Auld said to Stein: 'Will you take that drink now, boss?' Stein replied: 'I'll take it, Bert, if in your eyes it makes me a bigger man.' Needless to say he never had that drink.

Back home in Glasgow the scenes were incredible. At 5.30 p.m., normally the peak of the rush-hour, Sauchiehall Street, like everywhere else, had been deserted. A newspaper photograph showed only a woman and her dog on the street corner with not a car or bus in sight. Everyone was in front of a television set. Corpus Christi was also a holiday of obligation in Glasgow but evening Masses in most parishes had been put back to a later time, allowing clergy and congregations to watch the match.

Places like the Gorbals and George Square had become a riot of colour following the final whistle as people poured out of their houses desperate to share their elation with neighbours and any strangers who happened to be passing. Just about every street in the city saw people embrace, dance and wander down to the local pub for a drink. Those who had witnessed VE Day were experiencing the same feeling again some twenty-two years later.

Even people who had never been to a football match in their lives acted a bit daft as they got caught up in the emotion. Many an area echoed to the sound of accordions and the dancing went on in the streets until a late hour.

The city awoke with a great collective hangover on the morning of the 26th – just as Lisbon did. For those in the Portuguese capital it was a matter of getting home. For those in Glasgow the preparations were getting under way for another great night. The team was due to arrive back in Glasgow by early evening so offices and factories were deserted that bit earlier and 200 000 people lined the route from the airport to Celtic Park where another 60 000 erupted as the players and manager began a lap of honour on the back of a decorated lorry. An accordion band led them round the track and the scenes were unforgettable. Grandmothers were there, as were women with babies in their arms and some pushing prams. One fan risked life and limb to scale an electric pylon for a better view. Glasgow had never seen a football crowd like it.

Back in Lisbon the scenes at the airport could have rivalled those at Parkhead. The Inter players looked horrified when they arrived and discovered they would have to share the same departure lounge as the Celtic fans. But they were soon at ease when they got a warm round of applause. Plane after plane took off for Glasgow but some fans were certainly *hors de combat* and passed unfit to fly. In the event, travel agents banded together and sent back a special flight to pick them up once they had sobered up! The stories are legion but your writer's favourite concerns the Portuguese lad who had fallen in with some Celtic fans and went to see them off at the airport. They were all so drunk that he ended up on the plane with them and was waved through because he was wearing a Celtic scarf and hat. It must be remembered that the usual formalities were not in force because of the large numbers travelling.

Luckily, a last-minute count of heads discovered the error and the Portuguese was escorted from the aircraft. Another fan woke up just a few miles from touchdown at Glasgow Airport, only to remember to his horror that he had driven to Lisbon in his own car! Several dozen supporters had to be repatriated after the most exuberant occupation any city had ever known. Little pockets of fans had held out in the unlikeliest corners, noisily defending their own carnival atmosphere against the returning tide of normality. The British Embassy was under siege for several days but through everything shone a sense of humour and a standard of behaviour which was a credit to the club.

Perhaps the final memory of Lisbon should go to a little Glaswegian who died just a few years after seeing his team's greatest triumph. He was seen approaching customs officials at Glasgow Airport laden with parcels. His big pal was seen clutching a bag in a manner which suggested that he was in possession of the Crown Jewels. When opened it was discovered to contain small, neat pieces of turf from the Estadio. When the little gentleman, who had obviously been sampling the delights of duty-free alcohol, was asked if he had anything to declare, he unloaded his parcels on a desk, raised his arms in the air and with a serene, smiling expression replied: 'Have you no' heard yet? Celtic 2, Inter Milan 1. That's all I've got to declare.' And picking up his booty he breezed past the bemused customs men into the night.

3 Cry With Shame, Argentina

The history of the World Club Championship is a most iniquitous one. It has provided an arena for some of the ugliest facets of football, and in recent years European teams like Ajax Amsterdam and Bayern Munich have declined to play in it and later took part only after receiving cast-iron assurances against violence. Celtic's conquerors in the 1970 European Cup Final, Feyenoord of Holland, won the World title in Rotterdam after surviving the trip to South America. But their manager said later that, despite the fact any necessary play-off would have taken place in Madrid, he would not have allowed his players to take part because of the South Americans' attitude over the two games. The competition, which had its inception in 1960, was primarily brought about to find new competition for Real Madrid who had won the European Cup every time out. Formerly named the Inter-Continental Cup, it was an unofficial tournament until and including Celtic's ill-fated participation in late 1967. It was, in fact, the happenings of the matches between Celtic and the Racing Club of Argentina which at last brought about intervention by FIFA, the world ruling body on football. Its President in 1967 was Sir Stanley Rous, an Englishman, but although Celtic were the first British team to qualify for the tournament there was no official presence. Yet the following year, when Manchester United took part, the competition had been taken under FIFA's wing and officialdom was there in force. Even the rules had been changed.

For the first time, teams scoring away from home could count goals as double in the event of a draw over the two games. Had that been in force the previous year then Celtic would have taken the title. In the event, Manchester United also fell at the hands of the Argentinians and not without some violence being shown on the field, although nothing like the scale of the Celtic–Racing matches.

Before the World Club Championship Celtic had let their European crown slip. Because the withdrawal of an Albanian team left an even number of teams in the competition, the reigning champions were made to play in the opening round for the first time. The champions had previously always received a bye into the second round. As luck would have it, Celtic drew Dynamo Kiev of the Soviet Union, an excellent team, and were shocked in the first leg at Celtic Park on 20 September – the day the *QE2* was launched at Clydebank. Celtic were sunk by two quick Russian goals although Lennox pulled one back before the end. In the second leg Celtic put up a fine attacking show and went ahead, again through Lennox. But the Italian referee sent off Murdoch for no apparent reason, disallowed another Celtic goal which would have won them the tie and, just to rub it in, the Russians scored in the very last minute. The high-quality French magazine *Miroir du Football*, by far the best of its kind in Europe, commented after the second match: 'The scandalous comportment of the referee, who, as everyone knows, sent the Scottish half-back Murdoch off in the fifty-fifth minute, refused, in fact, in the sixty-sixth minute a perfectly legal goal for Celtic, who would have led 2–0 at that moment and would therefore have qualified. It is the first time in the European Cup that we have seen a team attacking against 100 000 and 11 adversaries. It was something poignant and dignified all the time.' It concluded: 'The referee was mainly responsible for the elimination of Celtic; who could seriously deny it?' And it made the further claim that despite the set-back Celtic were still the European champions of attacking football.

On the domestic front Celtic had still been going well and reached their fourth consecutive League Cup Final. The opponents were Dundee and a crowd of 66 000 turned up on 28 October to see Celtic win comfortably by five goals to three. They had eliminated Rangers, Aberdeen and Dundee United in a very tough section without losing a game and scoring fourteen goals for the loss of four. They beat Ayr United 8–2 on aggregate in the quarter-finals and Morton by the famous score of 7–1 in the semi-finals.

That League Cup Final had come the day before Celtic flew out to South America for the second game against the Racing Club. Earlier in October the men from Buenos Aires had come to Hampden and given due notice of their tactics in front of 90 000 Scots. They tripped, kicked and spat on the Celtic players. When Jimmy Johnstone returned to the dressing-rooms at half-time his hair was matted with spit from his callous opponents. The Celtic players discovered that they did not have to be in possession of the ball to qualify for such treatment. The Argentinians would do their thing in passing – and when the referee was looking the other way. Their number 10 was the main man for dishing it out but the minute he struck he would get off his mark and his team-mates would rush into the fray and cause as much distraction and confusion as possible while he made his getaway.

It is a long-held belief of Celtic director Mr James Farrell that the Racing tactics stemmed from a reserve match at Celtic Park six nights before the Hampden game. Some of the Racing Club directors had left South America before the team and toured Paris and London. They had arrived in Glasgow early and decided to watch the reserves. They admitted afterwards that they were amazed at the standard of the young Celtic players and by the looks on their faces they were not spinning the usual Latin platitudes.

They knew that night there was only one way to beat Celtic and the Racing players got their instructions when they arrived. Your writer, who witnessed the game, tried to leave Hampden at half-time that night through sheer disgust at the cynicism of the Argentinians but could not get out because of the force of the crowd in the North Enclosure.

The Celtic players managed to keep their heads despite the great provocation and it paid off when skipper Billy McNeill headed the winning goal from a John Hughes corner kick. As well as the goal, he had got an elbow in the eye as he rose to meet the ball and he sported a right 'keeker' for days afterwards. The final score was 1–0 and few Scots in Hampden thought much of Celtic's chances in the return – not through any lack of ability but in what they had witnessed from the Argentinian players. Yet they had seen only the tip of the iceberg. Buenos Aires and neutral Montevideo were to bring a lot worse.

It was the opinion of many that Celtic should have withdrawn immediately after the final whistle at Hampden and made public their reasons. They had defeated a team of villainous and treacherous players. In the eyes of the world they would have been acclaimed champions. Certainly, chairman Bob Kelly had misgivings about travelling to the Argentine but he made no concrete moves to cancel the trip although he was desperately worried about what would happen to his players and the long-term consequences for Celtic.

The journey to Buenos Aires lasted about twenty hours for the team who flew out on an Aerolineas Argentinas jet which had called specially at Prestwick to pick them up. A plane-load of fans in a turbo-prop Britannia took twenty-nine hours and certainly lived up to their title as the greatest supporters in the world. At £200 a head they flew to South America via the Canary Islands, Sal in the Cape Verde Islands, Recife in Brazil and then into Buenos Aires – some 7000 miles in all. Among the 106 fans on what was the longest flight ever to leave Glasgow were six priests, a minister and two doctors, more than enough to look after the spiritual and medical needs on the journey. Some people had cashed their life assurance policies to raise the cash and there was also a recent pools winner on board. It was an eventful journey with a certain amount of refreshment-taking and all went well until the approach to Ezeiza International Airport. About three miles from touchdown a terrible thunderstorm blacked out the entire city below – including the runway lights. So the fans had to go on a mystery tour of the heavens above Buenos Aires for about half an hour until the storm died and the lights below flickered back to life.

The fans were staying in the city centre, but the team and officials had been accommodated at the Hindu Club, an American-style country club about an hour's drive from Buenos Aires. Lisbon Lion Bertie Auld recalls the club as being something of a hostel – with a very hostile staff. It was far from ideal for a football team as it was shared with holidaymakers. The players were scattered over a considerable distance and because of the atmosphere had to be on their guard at all times.

They were constantly warned to check their rooms before settling down for the night in case they were compromised by local women. It was an atmosphere completely foreign to them. They were cooped up most of the time and could only go out in groups. It was hardly the right kind of preparation for such an important match and it showed in everyone – including manager Stein who had been very unhappy at the accommodation which had been fixed by the Argentinians. Stein was always the man who lifted the party on occasions like this but Buenos Aires saw him in sombre mood.

On match day armed police arrived in trucks and on motorcycles to escort the team to the stadium. Even the fans had to travel in a police convoy and many felt fear on the swift journey to the giant concrete Avellaneda Stadium which rose out of acres of dilapidated shacks. The Argentinian capital is a gay, wonderful sun-drenched city which, apart from its untold riches, has abject poverty. The Racing fans had emerged from tin shacks, ghettoes without running water or any form of sanitation. Racing were very much the team of the poor and their fans had been whipped up into a frenzy of nationalism to the extent that they *were* the Argentine. So for Celtic it was to be no ordinary match. They were playing a nation.

The games against Racing came, of course, just over a year after England had helped themselves to the World Cup at Wembley and angered the Argentinians in the process. Their captain, Rattin, had been ordered off, they had been denied training facilities at Wembley and England manager Alf Ramsey had called them 'animals'. They had left for home in a rage and the first 'Britishers' on whom they could take their revenge were Celtic. Not for the first time was Scotland to be confused with England in foreign lands – and to Scotland's usual disadvantage.

The Celtic fans, clutching their £8 stand tickets, found that their seats had been taken by Argentinians. When they protested some were urinated upon from the top tier of the stadium. What they witnessed for the next couple of hours was sheer terror. The directors of the club left the players and Stein in the dressing-room and were ushered to an enclosure a good distance away where it seemed seating had been installed for the occasion. Such was the siting of it that they had to stand during the match to see what was going on!

A riot of noise met the teams as they came onto the park. Rockets, streamers and banners were everywhere. The hard-core fans behind the goals wore only loincloths and beat huge drums. Bands played on the field but could not be heard in the cacophony of bedlam. It was not so much a show of support for their team but intimidation of the opposition. The war cry of '*Ya lo ve, ya lo ve, el equipo de José*' ('They are here, they are here, José's team') echoed around the stadium threatening to split its high concrete walls. Following it came the battle-cry 'Argentine, Argentine'. But if the Celtic players, fans and officials thought that was bad they had no idea of the worse experiences which lay ahead.

During the kickabout goalkeeper Ronnie Simpson was seen to clutch his head and fall to the ground. He had been struck by a piece of metal with such force that his head was split open right along the top. Manager Jock Stein and his assistant manager Sean Fallon ran onto the field. There was pandemonium with photographers and radio and television reporters trying to get close to the keeper who was surrounded by his team-mates. Stein gestured in the direction of the directors' box and shouted for advice but his voice could not be heard above the din. The directors could do nothing. To get onto the field they would have had to leave the stadium, cut through a school playground, get through the main stadium door, down into the underground dressing-rooms, along a tunnel and up onto the field. They themselves knew that it would be too risky a business.

Many people said after the whole sad affair was over that Celtic should have withdrawn at that point. They could not be expected to play without their goalkeeper. But that was easier said than done. Everyone in the Celtic party realized that in that stadium such action would have resulted in a riot and they would have been lucky to escape with their lives. John Fallon quickly stripped and took over in goal. What must have been running through his mind is anyone's guess. He was a brave man indeed that day and did not let his side down.

Simpson's injury, like the assassination of John F. Kennedy, has never been solved and probably never will. There is a belief at Celtic Park to this day that it was done by someone on the field. Such was the force of the blow a catapult must have been used. The fans were separated from the playing field by a massive wire-mesh fence and although some of them were on high vantage points where they should not have been it would have taken a feat of marksmanship to hit Simpson. Having seen what Racing were capable of there is no reason to disbelieve the theory that they put someone up to this footballing atrocity.

What would have happened had Fallon been injured during the match? Would it have become illegal? Had such an incident occurred in Scotland Celtic would have immediately withdrawn from the tie and conceded the title. But not Racing Club. There was not even an apology after the match. All that was said by their directors was that Fallon played very well.

The match itself was a farce. Celtic took the lead when Johnstone was pulled down by the goalkeeper. The referee had no alternative but to award a penalty kick and Gemmell scored. A good-looking second goal by Johnstone was disallowed and the wild men of Racing were allowed to dictate the game by Esteban Marino of Uruguay who got weaker with each passing minute. In the thirty-fourth minute the stadium erupted when Rafo equalized, and again three minutes into the second half when Cardenas scored the winner. It was the greatest frame-up ever perpetrated on any team, but a blessing also.

Had Celtic won there is no telling what would have followed and even after defeat they were still in danger. The dressing-rooms were invaded by all kinds of people at the end after a rumour spread that Celtic would not play a third game. Outside the stadium a pitch battle broke out between Argentinian fans and fans from Uruguay who had travelled to support Celtic and again a heavily armed police escort was necessary to take the team back to the Hindu Club. Everyone was shattered and the great debate began about the advisability of playing a third game in neutral Montevideo. Chairman Bob Kelly wanted to fly straight home. His worst fears had been realized. But secretary Desmond White wanted to stay. He felt that to go home immediately after a 2–1 defeat would let Celtic's enemies call them cowards. James Farrell, who had just joined the Board, was left in an invidious position but he too eventually decided on playing the third game. Celtic's fourth director, Tom Devlin, had not gone to South America because of illness. Jock Stein wanted to play because he believed his players were good enough and the thought of getting out of the Argentine before a neutral crowd eventually won the day.

So a few days later the team, followed by their faithful 106 fans, flew the short journey across the magnificent River Plate to Montevideo which was to play host to another famous battle.

For the play-off on 4 November thousands of Racing fans made their way across the River Plate on every conceivable type of craft. It was a sort of Dunkirk in reverse as home-made rafts and rowing boats formed into the most amazing flotilla. It was a holiday weekend in Buenos Aires and few services were running to Montevideo in Uruguay. But the Racing supporters were not going to be denied. This time, however, they were very much in the minority and controlled by a police force which was standing no nonsense. Celtic had won the hearts of the neutral Uruguayans, historic enemies of the Argentinians. Uruguay sits in the shadow of the vast lands of the Argentine (a sort of Scotland–England situation) and they were backing Celtic to put one over on their foes. On the day before the match, when Celtic were training at the stadium, the Penarol players, who had visited Celtic Park at the beginning of the season, began telling the Celtic players some of the tricks they used against the

Argentinians. From what they said it was obvious they had a great hatred of that country's football.

On the day of the game Celtic players went out shopping and bought the biggest Uruguayan flag they could find and paraded it around the stadium before the kick-off. They were a bit baffled by the lack of response from the crowd until they found out later that the Racing players had been out on the field ten minutes earlier with an even bigger flag.

The atmosphere was much more relaxed for the first twenty-five minutes of the match and it seemed that the Racing players were going to behave themselves. But a shocking waist-high tackle on Johnstone ended the uneasy truce and yet another weak referee failed to take action. Instead, with just four minutes to half-time, Johnstone was sent off for using an elbow to free himself from a jersey-pulling opponent. Johnstone had shown great restraint despite the dreadful treatment and his ordering off was the point where Paraguayan referee Dr Rodolfo Perez Osorio lost all credibility.

His next move was the one which finally cracked the Celtic players. They had taken everything Racing could throw at them but the dismissal of Bobby Lennox, one of the game's greatest sportsmen, was the final straw. He had been some forty yards away from a clash between Murdoch and a Racing player, yet when the referee sorted things out Lennox got his marching orders. It was one of the worst-ever cases of mistaken identity and Lennox was later exonerated.

John Hughes was next to go, leaving Celtic with only eight men. Bertie Auld, who had missed the Buenos Aires match because of injury, took part in the infamous third game and he too, according to the referee's report, was sent off. Yet Auld had still been on the field at the end of the game!

Tommy Gemmell was involved in the most publicized incident of the game which the referee missed completely. He lost control of himself and went after a Racing player and kicked him on the back-side. It was an incident which the television cameras saw and the BBC took a great delight in showing it in the days to follow. Racing won the match by 1–0, thanks to a goal by Cardenas in the fifty-sixth minute, and they had won the trophy they wanted so much. They managed to do to a Celtic team what no other side had ever managed to do – rob them of their self-respect.

One cannot condone the action of the Celtic players yet it is difficult to blame them in the face of such provocation. Bertie Auld recalled later: 'At one stage in the game I was jogging back towards my own half after an attacking move when I got a vicious punch on the back of the head. I turned round and one of their players was just two feet away grinning in my face. No one had seen it and the ball was at the other end of the field. He was obviously hoping that I would hit back and get caught by the referee. That was the kind of thing we were up against.'

Mr Willie Allan, secretary of the Scottish Football Association for many years, prepared an excellent report on the three matches which he sent to FIFA, the European Football Union, and the SFA. This is what he had to say about the third match in Montevideo on 4 November:

The FA of Paraguay appointed the referee, Dr Rodolfo Osorio and his linesmen. Dr Osorio was by far the poorest in every respect of the three referees. His conception of what constituted an infringement did not compare with that of Señor Gardeazabal or that of Mr Marino. Nevertheless it did not appear for a time that he would be put to the test. For 25 minutes of the first half, and although play had not been lacking in incident or infringements, the ill-feeling which had been generated in the two previous matches was held in check. However, by his own weakness in failing to dismiss a player guilty of a brutal infringement half-way through the first half he set in train his own downfall and the downfall also, in the sense of discipline, of the Celtic players mainly.

From this moment onwards his outstanding weakness, lack of control, was exposed for all to see. The occasion turned out to be too much for him and he was totally incapable of dealing with subsequent events.

Underlining his incompetence is the report on the match which he himself completed and submitted and in which he referred to the dismissal of four Celtic players – Lennox, Johnstone, Murdoch and Auld. Murdoch was not involved in the incident in the 61st minute. He has been wrongfully accused. The player whom Dr Osorio dismissed and who left the field was not Murdoch. The following questions immediately arise:

1. In view of the circumstances and because of mistaken identity, was the player who left the field dismissed unjustifiably?
2. Had he not been mistaken for Murdoch would he have been dismissed on the strength of the incident in which he was involved?
3. Was he dismissed, following the incident, in the belief that he was Murdoch – not for the incident alone but because of previous infringements committed by Murdoch?

Dr Osorio also reported the dismissal of Auld. If he did in fact dismiss Auld certain questions arise, because Auld did not leave the field. He continued to play until full-time.

The questions:

1. Why did the referee re-start play while Auld remained on the field?
2. Why did he allow Auld to engage in the game from the time of his dismissal until full-time?
3. Was he aware that Auld had not left the field?
4. Did he err in saying he had dismissed Auld?

Players

Although infringements had been numerous in the first 23 minutes of the game the expected 'battle' had not materialized. The explosion followed the referee's decision to which reference has been made. The Celtic outside-right who had suffered shamefully at the hands of his opponents in the two previous games, and who had been denied protection by the referees concerned, was at that stage of the game fouled brutally. Had the referee dismissed the guilty player the subsequent events might not have occurred.

However, from this point onwards the Celtic players lost their heads. Only their goalkeeper was beyond reproach. The conduct of many of the others was more befitting a boxing ring than a football field. Several others were fortunate not to have been ordered off – a fate which would have befallen them had a stronger referee been in charge.

The players of Racing Club were less indisciplined in this match than in the two others. In spite of that, much of their conduct was to be deplored, and again with a stronger referee others would have been dismissed.

Spectators

The spectators, including a large contingent of Argentinians, were well behaved. Mostly, the Uruguayans lent their support to Celtic. The FA of Uruguay are to be complimented on their arrangements. The playing field was kept clear at all times and proper facilities were provided for the visiting officials.

Conclusions

A. Dr Osorio could have been spared an ordeal for which he was not fitted had the two previous referees made full use of the powers conferred on them by the Laws of the Game to eliminate – at least to curb – the indiscipline of the Racing Club which was rife in Glasgow and Buenos Aires. Had they done so the match in Montevideo would have developed along different lines.

B. The happenings in Montevideo need never have occurred.

C. They would have been avoided if (1) the players of Racing Club in the first two games had elected to play football rather than pursue the obviously calculated policy of provocation already described, or (2) the referees had measured up to their responsibility.

D. Nevertheless the Celtic players must accept responsibility for their actions in Montevideo. However, this report may have advanced a reason or reasons why a normally well-disciplined team conducted themselves as they did.

E. The playing of three matches within such a short period is undesirable.

F. Although it is not the function of this report to make recommendations on the organization of this competition one suggests in all sincerity that if it is to be continued along its present lines the competing clubs should be declared joint winners of the trophy if, after the second game, the result is still a draw. In order to avoid as far as possible such an outcome, a rule similar to the one in present European competition, whereby a goal scored when playing away from home counts double, could suitably be introduced.

Celtic also received support from *Miroir du Football*, which was the only non-British publication to send a staff correspondent. Under the banner headline 'Racing of Buenos Aires, Champions of the World of Violence, Treachery and Theatricals' he reported: 'The Johnstone ordering off was disgraceful. The player who had been the constant target of all the aggressions perpetrated from the start of the match in Buenos Aires and from the start of the match in Montevideo was the victim of the man who was supposed to protect footballers from butchers and actors. For my part, I have never seen such a stupefying decision.'

On the journey home the players were subdued. The directors were edgy and upset. They knew they had been responsible for sending them into that third match. The result was a long and weary Board meeting at Celtic Park on their return home at which chairman Bob Kelly stated he wished to see the players fined for their actions. He felt such a move would go some way to restoring the club's battered image.

An announcement was made to the Press that every member of the team – including goalkeeper John Fallon – was to be fined £250. The first the players knew about the amount was when they read about it in the papers. The fines were deducted from bonus money due for that season.

In addition to that financial loss, Bertie Auld and John Hughes were each fined £50 by the SFA for their part in the Montevideo affair. Jimmy Johnstone, who had created a bit of history by having a suspension lifted which allowed him to play in South America, was severely censured. The procedure at that time was that suspension in domestic competition also ruled a player out of European and international matches. In view of the fact that it was a World Championship the SFA had allowed Johnstone to go. He must have been the first player ever to be sent off while under suspension!

Bobby Lennox, whose ordering off was a case of mistaken identity, was exonerated.

One director said of the decision to fine the players: 'We sympathized with them but they had let the club down and themselves down. We have to constantly remind our players about discipline because a Celtic player going for justice usually faces a different set of rules than others. It is a point which has been proved over and over through the years. Celtic players can never afford to relax their discipline.'

Perhaps the only amusing incident of the whole sorry affair came at Prestwick Airport on the return home. Secretary and treasurer Desmond White was seen carrying a huge, battered suitcase through customs. What was unknown to everyone except the directors was that the case was crammed full of Uruguayan pesos – twelve million of them! It was Celtic's share of the gate money from the third game.

Following the match Mr White had gone to the Uruguayan FA treasurer to collect the usual cheque. But he was informed there could be no such thing. Inflation, explained the treasurer, was at the country's throat. He instructed the Celtic director to get hold of a large suitcase and meet him at a bank in town some time later. Mr White returned to his hotel, borrowed the black tattered case and headed for the bank. It was after normal hours but it was specially opened as all the gate money had been taken there from the stadium.

To Mr White's horror the bank staff began loading money into the case. In his own words, it was like something out of a James Bond film. Both he and the Uruguayan treasurer had to sit on the case to get it shut! 'You would probably be advised to take a taxi,' someone said to him. Mr White readily agreed and set off back to the hotel in fear of his life. He sneaked into the premises and up to the room containing the club hamper. He removed the strips and training gear, put the case in, covered it up with the gear, locked it and the outside door and went for a well-earned meal.

He and his fellow directors discussed ways to get the money back to Scotland. There was a suggestion that perhaps they should buy precious stones with it. But it was then realized that such a move could cause even more trouble at customs both in South America and back home in Scotland.

There was only one thing to do and that was take a bold gamble. Mr White, firmly clutching the case, approached customs and just as firmly said he had nothing to declare. He boarded the aircraft still carrying the case which he put under his seat and kept there on the 7000-mile flight home.

But that is not the end of the story. When he took the case to the bank in Glasgow no one wanted to know about Uruguayan pesos. So the money, still in its battered suitcase, was shipped to London where the reaction was exactly the same. It had to be sent on to New York for clearance and by the time Celtic received their cheque inflation had cost them about £3000! Desmond White later recalled saying to his fellow directors before leaving Uruguay: 'My God, imagine living in a country with inflation like this.' He had been horrified when told inflation was running at about 16 per cent. It is amusing in view of what has happened in Britain in recent years.

It is the firm conviction of the Celtic directorate that certain assurances would have to be given before Celtic would again travel to the Argentine or play hosts to one of their teams. The lesson of South America was a cruel one, but a lesson learned. Scotland's South American tour of 1977 took them to Buenos Aires and yet again the Argentinian players showed little regard for the laws of the game. They showed a callousness in chopping down opponents and in successive games with Scotland and England had players ordered off. Shortly after the publication date of this book the 1978 World Cup Finals are scheduled to be played in Argentina. If the Argentinians have mended their ways by then it will come as a great surprise to many.

4 A Family at War

If ever proof was needed that Celtic are a family club then that proof must come from the fact that the Parkhead directors have on only a handful of occasions taken issues to a vote. Certainly there have been differences of opinion and in the case of the late Sir Robert Kelly, chairman for quarter of a century, and present chairman Mr Desmond White, they had from time to time very divergent views. A story untold until now perhaps sums up how the Celtic Board works. Around 1950, five years after Jimmy McGrory had become manager, Desmond White felt that while Jimmy had been a wonderful servant on the field of play, he was not satisfying the conditions of management as football evolved and he approached Bob Kelly about appointing Matt Busby as manager of Celtic. Desmond White did not wish to see Jimmy McGrory sacked but given some other position at Parkhead, perhaps in administration.

Busby, a Lanarkshire man, and later to manage Manchester United, had been a Celtic fan from boyhood and one of his ambitions had been to play for the club. He had in fact been denied pulling on the green-and-white jersey during the Second World War while stationed in Scotland. A policy decision by the Board prevented players guesting for the club although everyone else took advantage of good players on their doorsteps. By 1950 Busby's playing career was over and he was a free agent.

Desmond White's move had not come at Board level. He had approached Bob Kelly privately but the chairman was against it and said that the supporters would not stand for a change in the set-up involving a loyal servant like Jimmy McGrory. Desmond White felt that Busby would be a better manager because he would be more independent of Bob Kelly who often interfered with team selections. The two men were in opposite camps but the issue never went to a vote. Desmond White's attitude was that such a matter involving such a respected man as Jimmy McGrory should not be treated that way.

He had been hoping for unanimous backing so that a civilized approach could then have been made to Jimmy McGrory. In the event he dropped the matter and Jimmy McGrory stayed in the position of manager for another fifteen years until the arrival of Jock Stein.

The image of the Celtic Football Club has always come first among the men who have been charged as custodians. At the end of the day and following full discussion every decision has been 'unanimous' and the Board has shown a united front to the supporters and the public in general.

At a specially convened Board meeting in the summer of 1968 there were no differences of opinion. Chairman Bob Kelly and directors Desmond White, James Farrell and Tom Devlin like the rest of the free world had a common enemy – the forces of the Warsaw Pact. In the dawn of an August morning their tanks and armoured divisions had crossed into Czechoslovakia and once more snuffed out a nation's right to chart its own course.

Later that morning a telephone call between Bob Kelly and Desmond White set up a meeting, the result of which must go down in history as the most courageous stand ever taken by a football club. Even after a study of all the great sporting names in Europe one somehow cannot imagine any club other than Celtic taking the course of action they did. From the day of their birth they had been the team of the people and in 1968, eighty years after their foundation, they were yet again to justify that title. Had the same Celtic Football Club, in the cause of peace and freedom, not seen its ranks decimated by two world wars? Those wars had taken a terrible toll of their resources, broken up wonderful teams and left major rebuilding jobs on hand. The year 1968 was no different. Freedom had been challenged once more and Celtic felt it was their place to give moral support to the Czech nation.

During the Board meeting much thought went into their action and the outcome was a decision to send a telegram of protest to the headquarters of the Union of European Football Associations (UEFA) in Berne, Switzerland. Before that decision had been taken Jock Stein had been summoned to the meeting and asked for his views.

He expressed worries about Celtic interfering with the running of the European Cup. As manager he was obviously concerned about the possibility of his players losing contact with the world's number one club competition. It had been twelve months since they had last played in it. If Celtic were to withdraw it would mean at least another year in the wilderness as there was a chance UEFA would suspend them for a season or two if they refused to take part in the 1968–9 competition.

The Board, however, sent the following telegram to Hans Bangerter, secretary of UEFA: 'In view of the illegal and treacherous invasion of Czechoslovakia by Russian, Polish and Hungarian forces and in support of the Czech nation, we, the Celtic Football Club, do not think that any Western European Football Club should be forced to fulfil any football commitment in any of these countries.'

It was a bold move because Celtic had already been paired in the European Cup first round with Ferencvaros of Hungary. Had UEFA refused to entertain the Celtic stand then Messrs Kelly, White, Farrell and Devlin would have had little choice but to withdraw. But news of their telegram – the first of its kind ever received by UEFA – brought backing from other clubs and the Swedish Government and a swift decision was taken in Berne to re-make the European competition draws to keep East and West clubs apart. This brought immediate protests from the Iron Curtain countries and Bulgaria, East Germany, Hungary, Poland and Russia all withdrew. In the rearranged draw Celtic's opponents were St Etienne, champions of France.

Enemies of Celtic, jealous of their stand and subsequent victory, implied that they had been afraid to play Ferencvaros. Yet before the invasion, when both clubs were arranging dates, Celtic agreed to bring the Parkhead game forward by a day to allow Ferencvaros the services of no fewer than three players who were representing their country. Hardly the action of cowards.

Celtic, of course, had already fought a notable off-the-field battle with the Soviet Union in 1966, when drawn against Dynamo Kiev in the European Cup Winners' Cup. As Celtic were soon to find out, no dealings took place with the club but with the Soviet Sports Ministry. That body informed Celtic that the match could not take place in Kiev because of weather problems at that time of year and it would have to go on at Tbilisi which would add several hundred miles to the journey. But the shocks did not end there.

Celtic were told that they would have to use a Russian airliner.

It was at this stage that the Celtic Board dug in their heels. They insisted on using their own charter flight although at that time no Western charter had ever penetrated Russian airspace. Knowing that the Russians wanted the games played quickly, director-secretary Desmond White began negotiations with the Soviet Sports Ministry and offered early dates in return for permission to use a Western charter. Normally the quarter-final ties were played in March but White offered early January, which suited the Russians. Most airlines told him he was wasting his time over the charter and only Royal Dutch Airlines and Aer Lingus showed any interest. In the days ahead the Russians agreed to the Celtic demands and got their dates while Aer Lingus promised to make available one of their brand-new BAC 1–11 jets and Celtic gave the Irish airline the contract.

Dynamo Kiev arrived in Glasgow for the first leg on 12 January and lost 3–0. By this stage, despite telephone calls and letters to Aeroflot in London and letters and cables to the Ministry of Sport in Moscow, Celtic still had not been given the required landing per-mission, although the Tbilisi game was due to be played the following week and Celtic to fly out on Sunday first. Celtic asked the Kiev officials to contact the Sports Ministry by telephone on their behalf, but which Russian wants to telephone Moscow? Still nothing happened. The final ultimatum from Desmond White to the Sports Ministry in Moscow was that unless landing permission was granted by 10 a.m. on Friday Celtic would call off the game. This went by special cable. Aer Lingus also contacted Aeroflot in London. At 11 a.m. on Friday, just forty-eight hours before they were due to fly out and having received no reply, Celtic sent the following cable to Moscow: 'Regret match cancelled. Reporting all matters to UEFA.' Only four hours later Desmond White received a call from Moscow and the gentleman on the other end of the line was no less a person than the Minister of Sport. In broken English he inquired: 'What is the meaning of your cable?' Desmond White replied he thought it was rather obvious. The Minister said that thousands of tickets had been sold and Celtic must travel. He was told by the Celtic secretary that Celtic were anxious to travel but had received no landing permission. After pointing out all the cables which had been sent and telephone calls which had been made there was total silence at the Moscow end of the line followed by an apologetic: 'Someone here has made a big mistake.'

The Minister then asked if Celtic could still travel but by that time Aer Lingus had withdrawn their plane. Desmond White told him that if landing permission was granted Celtic would consider travelling and playing the match the following week on 26 January, to which the Minister replied: 'Landing permission is herewith granted and will be communicated to London inside one hour.' This was done and Celtic flew out the following week via Moscow. They fought out a quite magnificent 1–1 draw against the very physical Russians who had thirty-one fouls given against them although the occasion was marred by the sending off of Jim Craig and one of the Russian forwards.

Little could Celtic have realized after their difficulties in getting into Russia that getting out would be even more of a problem. The brand-new Aer Lingus jet developed all kinds of trouble. When the players were climbing aboard after a refuelling stop in Moscow, a fault developed in the aircraft. The Celtic party had given up their visas and were, in consequence, regarded by the Russians as stateless people and had to stay on the aircraft while the repair job was going on. Armed soldiers stood at either end of the cabin.

Before they finally left Moscow, news was flashed to the pilot that Amsterdam was closing down because of heavy snow, and the plane was diverted to Stockholm. At the refuelling stop in Sweden there were again difficulties in getting the plane started. Twice the Celtic party had climbed aboard only to return to the airport lounge. On the final call, they marched out onto the tarmac full of hope. It was now snowing hard and they were not surprised when an airport official dashed out, waved his hands and shouted that all flying was cancelled. It was now ten o'clock at night and the Celtic party had no option but to stay in Stockholm overnight on the promise that everything would be in order in the morning. They returned to the airport at 9 a.m. on the Friday. At half past nine they were aboard the aircraft. At quarter to ten they were back in the airport lounge. At half past ten they were once again aboard the aircraft and at quarter to eleven they were finally being offered more coffee and biscuits in the lounge.

Mr Stein, who had been commendably restrained up to that moment, told the Aer Lingus officials what they could do with their aircraft. A meeting was held with these same officials. Celtic demanded that a substitute aircraft be flown in as they had no intention of climbing aboard the first aircraft again. This was eventually set up by

Aer Lingus. A Boeing was being diverted from Brussels to touch down at Stockholm at five o'clock that night. Manager Stein, in the meantime, telephoned the Scottish Football League, informed them of the Celtic party's plight and of their considerable doubt as to when they would eventually arrive in Scotland. He asked that the match be postponed. Mr Fred Donovan, the League Secretary, said he would telephone around the Members of his Committee and that a message would be waiting for the party on their arrival at Prestwick Airport. At 5.30 p.m. the substitute Boeing flew into Stockholm. It was refuelled and reserviced, and the Celtic party climbed aboard. They flew into Prestwick at 7.50 on Friday night, and as the party cleared customs, they found a message waiting for them from the Scottish Football League which stated: 'If the Celtic party arrive on or after 8 p.m. the match against Hearts, Edinburgh, tomorrow Saturday will be postponed.' Celtic had beaten the deadline by ten minutes. Stein took the players straight to Celtic Park, where they began a training session at 11 p.m. which lasted almost to midnight. About 500 fans had gone to the Park to cheer them on after hearing of their ordeal.

Not surprisingly Celtic lost to Hearts the following afternoon by 3–2 although they still went on to win the Championship.

That incident with the Scottish League, which had shown a total lack of sympathy for the Celtic position, coupled with other such decisions, was to bring about a famous and justifiable outburst from manager Jock Stein some ten years later which is discussed in the final chapter of this book. To expect a team which had undergone such a marathon journey, and arrived home twenty-nine hours late, to play football and give of their best was an absolute nonsense.

Those shattering experiences behind the Iron Curtain had, of course, nothing to do with Celtic's stand in 1968. The club deplored the invasion and wished, at any cost, to put on record their moral support for the people of Czechoslovakia. It was also felt that Western players and officials could be at risk behind the Iron Curtain in view of the upheaval.

In examining Celtic's circumstances around that period one can only have the highest admiration for the directors. Following the South American shambles against the Racing Club the previous November and their early exit from the European Cup, Celtic went crashing out of the Scottish Cup at the hands of Dunfermline in the very first round played in January 1968.

C

The Grand Slam team of only twelve months earlier had held on to the League Cup for the third successive year and there was still a chance of the League and the Glasgow Cup. In the Championship race Celtic were to give so much entertainment that it would have been a tragedy if they had been forced to withdraw from the European Cup the following season.

Yet just after the turn of the year Championship chances began to look black. Trailing Rangers by two points, Celtic met the Ibrox side at Parkhead in the New Year match. The previous day Celtic had lost Ronnie Simpson through injury and John Fallon deputized in the Old Firm game which was to be a nightmare match for him. Twice Celtic took the lead and were by far the better team. But twice Fallon let simple balls slip by him and Rangers held their vital two-point lead. Now they could only lose the League. Celtic had to wait, hope and start scoring a lot of goals if they were to get back into the European Cup. Unlike the present Premier League set-up, there was no chance of Celtic meeting Rangers again in the Championship that season. There were only two meetings which meant that the New Year match was always a vital encounter. The team which emerged from that game in front always took a lot of stopping.

It was around this time that a vitally important and somewhat unusual talk-in was held by manager Stein and his players. Stein asked them if there was anything they wanted changed; anything bothering them. He wanted to know, and if necessary he would completely alter the training schedules. He told the players that if they wished a bit of variety they could suit themselves about training either in the mornings or the afternoons. He knew also that they were missing the European scene and promised to do all in his power to fix up some attractive matches with top-class opposition. The heart-to-heart seemed to work because the following Saturday Celtic went to Stirling to face the Albion – who under former Ranger Sammy Baird in the seasons around that time strangely donned orange strips for the visits of Celtic – and won 2–0. It had been something of a bogey ground to Celtic with Albion players who seemed to reserve all their energies for that particular fixture.

That win marked the beginning of a six-match League run which saw Celtic score 24 goals for the loss of only 1. With goals piling up the pressure was very much on Rangers, who were holding their lead but playing not half as convincingly as Celtic.

While the heat was on Rangers made what must go down as one

of the worst decisions of their history. Celtic had beaten Partick Thistle 5–0 in the Glasgow Cup and were drawn to meet Rangers in the semi-finals. Incredibly Rangers scratched, saying that they had too many commitments.

The simple fact was that they were terrified at the prospect of playing the rampant, high-scoring Celts. The Rangers hierarchy knew that defeat at the hands of Celtic at such a vital part of the season could be catastrophic for morale as they were chasing the League, Scottish Cup and Fairs Cities Cup (now UEFA Cup). Yet their decision to withdraw seemed to have as much effect on their players as a defeat from Celtic would have had. Everyone with any knowledge of football knew the real reasons behind their refusal to play and within weeks they had been beaten by Hearts in the Scottish Cup quarter-finals and eliminated from the Fairs Cup at the same stage by Leeds United. Meanwhile Celtic had taken 4 goals from Aberdeen, 4 from Airdrie, 3 from Falkirk, 5 from Raith Rovers and 6 from St Johnstone at Perth. The game at Muirton Park saw Celtic go back to the top of the League for the first time that year. They were there only on goal average (now goal difference) and had played a game more than Rangers, but it was a morale-boosting situation. It let Rangers clearly see the position if they dropped their two-point lead. There was no way they could live with Celtic's scoring rate. A 5–0 win over Dundee United at Tannadice really turned the screw on Rangers and the first crack came the following midweek when the Ibrox team travelled to the same ground and dropped a point.

Then came another dramatic night in this eventful title race.

With only a handful of League games to go and that one-point gap still in Rangers' favour, Celtic lined up at Hampden Park for the Glasgow Cup Final against Clyde. At half-time Celts were leading 7–0. But it was another half-time score which had the Parkhead faithful delirious – Morton 2, Rangers 0. Because of the tense situation in the League, fans had become accustomed to carrying transistor radios and soon word filtered through that Morton were leading 3–1. It was too good to be true.

As nail-biting minutes passed Rangers pulled back to 3–2 and then equalized near the end. But Celtic were back on top and by an avalanche of goals. Incidentally, Celtic won the Glasgow Cup by 8–0!

The following Saturday brought the most dramatic day of the

entire season. Rangers were at Rugby Park playing Kilmarnock and Celtic were at home to the same Morton who had badly dented Rangers' hopes. On form it should have been another big win for Celtic and everything looked good when Willie Wallace got an early goal. But Morton equalized, nerves set in among the Celtic players and with just a minute to go it was still 1–1. Through the transistors everyone knew – including the players on the field – that Rangers were winning 2–1. Surely such a valiant fight by Celtic – they had not dropped a single point since the New Year game – was not to end in such a cruel fashion and in front of 40 000 home fans. Into injury time and Celtic continued to launch almost frantic attacks. Bobby Lennox ran over to the touchline to take a throw-in and a fan shouted that the final whistle had gone at Rugby Park and Rangers had won. Bobby told your writer years later that it acted like an electric shock on him. He ran about shouting the score to his team-mates as the final effort was made. Then came a cross from Bobby Murdoch on the right. The ball glanced off the head of John Hughes who was surrounded by defenders. Every Morton man was back. It broke to Willie Wallace who swung at it right in front of goal but missed his kick. But before the fans could gasp Bobby Lennox jabbed out a foot and the ball crossed the line and into the net. The whole place went mad. Tommy Gemmell, in true extrovert fashion, ran towards a policeman on the track and was about to borrow his helmet for the celebrations until he saw a big sergeant wag a warning finger!

Before the ball could be centred the final whistle blew and Celtic were still ahead on goal average with just one game left – against Dunfermline at East End Park. The strain and then the sheer excitement that afternoon had really taken its toll on the fans and many looked in a state of exhaustion afterwards.

No one knew it then, but Celtic were to be crowned Champions before kicking another ball. The following Saturday Dunfermline, conquerors of Celtic, and Hearts, conquerors of Rangers, met in the Scottish Cup Final which meant Celtic had a free day. Rangers went ahead with their game against Aberdeen at Ibrox knowing that a win would really put the pressure on Celtic who were scheduled to meet Dunfermline on the Wednesday night. Incredibly, Rangers lost to Aberdeen on their own ground by 3–2, their first League defeat of the season in the very last match. How ironic it would have been had they remained unbeaten yet lost the Championship to Celtic on goal average. The Celtic players, who had watched the Cup Final, were just boarding the team bus outside Hampden when a delighted Jock Stein rushed out to them with the result.

What a setting for the midweek match at East End Park – the Champions versus the Cup Holders. It was purely academic but the new Cup winners had a reputation to defend and Celtic knew that a victory would give them an incredible 64 points out of a possible 68 and a post-war record.

It was reckoned that 35 000 people had travelled from Glasgow and about 5000 were locked out. Fans had to be accommodated around the touchlines and others were on top of the enclosure roof or perched on the floodlighting pylons. Despite the crowd pressure and the game having to be stopped on a couple of occasions it was a good-natured night. Both teams did a lap of honour before the kick-off and it was a night of great sentiment.

Celtic were a goal down at half-time but fought back to win 2–1 with Lennox scoring both goals. It meant Celtic's incredible record in the 1967–8 Championship read: Played 34, Won 30, Lost 1, Drawn 3, Goals for 106, Against 23. They had gone thirty-two games without defeat and taken a full thirty-two points from the last sixteen games. Truly remarkable.

It had seemed that night in Dunfermline that half of Glasgow had travelled, despite all the problems associated with getting away from work to midweek matches. And there can be no doubt that the reason so many travelled was because they knew they had witnessed a very special League campaign – surely the most exciting Scottish football has ever known. Even the great 1953–4 victory which had seen Celtic, with games in hand, pull back an eight-point lead by Hearts could not compare with the finish of 1967–8.

So, out of a season which had started badly, Celtic had retained the Championship, League Cup and Glasgow Cup. Rangers, who had been in contention for the Championship, Scottish Cup, Fairs Cup and Glasgow Cup until their decision to opt out of playing Celtic, won nothing for the second year running. Following Celtic's Grand Slam of the previous year Rangers had sacked manager Scot Symon in the autumn of 1967 although he had the Ibrox club leading the League. They appointed David White, a former Clyde player, in his place yet within two years he was to go the same way after Rangers had spent more than half a million pounds on players in the hope of breaking the Celtic domination.

It had been a difficult season for Celtic and they had done well to retain three trophies out of five. Manager Jock Stein, in his annual *Celtic Football Guide* report for the season 1968–9, was to say that he knew things would be tough for his men after achieving the Grand Slam.

When Celtic set out at the start of 1967–68 [he stated] as European Cup holders, Scottish League Champions, winners of the Scottish Cup, League Cup and Glasgow Cup, all of us knew that a tremendous task lay ahead. Was it reasonable to hope for another season so full of success; was it fair to assume that Celtic players would again be so outstandingly triumphant? I do not believe that even the most optimistic, enthusiastic Celtic supporter was confident of yet another series of great victories.

Personally I thought that season 1967–68 would be for us very, very difficult indeed, and right away I must say that when it ended I was not only very satisfied but very delighted. We won the League Cup in a public-pleasing high-scoring 5–3 win over Dundee and at the end of the season we kept possession of the Glasgow Cup, having beaten all the clubs eligible *and prepared to play us*. Best of all, we kept up our pursuit of the League leaders and finally retained the Championship.

In the close season Celtic headed across the Atlantic once more to play matches in the United States, Canada and South America, but first of all the players were given a week-long break in sun-kissed Miami. That holiday showed up in their first match against AC Milan of Italy with the unusual sight of Celtic players tiring in the second half. But they still managed a creditable draw considering they were without Jim Craig and Jimmy Johnstone, who had been allowed to stay at home because of the pressures of the season and his dislike of flying, Bertie Auld, who had been out injured most of the season, John Hughes and Tommy Gemmell. An aggravated injury meant that Gemmell had to return home early from the tour. On the other hand AC Milan had been playing competitive football right up to their arrival in America, having won the European Cup Winners' Cup in Holland and their own Championship.

Celtic played a second game against the Italians in Toronto for a trophy named 'The Cup of Champions' and in front of a record crowd of 31 000 won by 2–0, thanks to goals by Charlie Gallagher and Bobby Lennox. Gallagher had been a wonderful player to Celtic that year. With Bertie Auld missing for months the subtle Gallagher had been drafted into Auld's midfield role and was behind many of Celtic's goals with his fine passing. So valuable was he that when Stein thought Celtic had a particular game won, Charlie would be taken off rather than risk injury. That 1967–8 Championship was very much Gallagher's Championship.

Celtic waved goodbye to AC Milan although they were to meet them again much sooner than they thought. The next stop on the tour was Mexico City, 7500 feet above sea-level, where the high altitude posed all kinds of problems for Celtic. In a massive concrete pressure-cooker called the Aztec Stadium, with a capacity to seat 105000 spectators, Celtic found themselves three goals down to FC Nexaca. But a whiff of oxygen at half-time saw them fight back and end the game with a 3–2 defeat. The match had been a marvellous experience considering the World Cup Finals were to be held there in 1970.

While the first-team men were showing the flag on that side of the world, younger members of the club were doing likewise in a youth tournament in Italy. Names which were not yet familiar to the Celtic supporters were entertaining the Italians so much that they were awarded a trophy for being the most attack-minded team in the competition. And the names? Kenny Dalglish, Danny McGrain, Paul Wilson, Lou Macari, David Hay and George Connelly. So successful were they that they were offered four more tours on the spot! Those young men used to call themselves 'The Quality Street Kids' and there was not a trace of big-headedness about it. They all were to go on to prove their talent in higher company.

The season of 1968–9 kicked off to a new-look Celtic Park. During the close season the east terracing was covered for the first time, which meant that practically the whole of the stadium was under cover. It was to be a strange season on the domestic front with all three major trophies – the League Cup, Scottish Cup and League Championship – not being decided until the very last month of April.

In qualifying for the League Cup in the early part of the season Celtic made a superb start. More than 80000 fans packed into Ibrox for the opening match in which Celtic defeated Rangers by 2–0.

Rangers' skipper John Greig blundered twice and Willie Wallace scored the goals. In the return match at Celtic Park Wallace scored the only goal and Celtic virtually had the section wrapped up. They won their other matches against Morton by 4–1 at Celtic Park and 3–0 in Greenock, and Partick Thistle were beaten 4–0 at Parkhead and 6–1 at Firhill for a clean sweep of 12 points. In the quarter-finals Hamilton Accies were crushed 10–0 at Celtic Park and 4–2 at home despite a liberal sprinkling of reserves in the Celtic side. A nervy 1–0 win over Clyde in the semi-finals set Celtic up for their fifth consecutive League Cup Final and the players went off to Seamill to prepare for the big game scheduled for 26 October. But while there Hampden was ravaged by fire and the fixture against Hibs was postponed until the end of the season.

On the League front Celtic took nine points from the first six games, their only defeat being at the hands of Rangers in a controversial match at Celtic Park. As was quite common at that time, a referee called Bobby Davidson of Airdrie was at the middle of the dispute. Rangers had scored two early goals but Wallace pulled one back for Celtic.

Then, just before half-time, Bobby Lennox got the ball, beat Rangers defender Roger Hynd and slipped the ball past the goal-keeper only for an astonishing offside decision to be given against him. A Celtic team which had roared back into the game and looked capable of going on to win were shattered by the decision, lost a third goal and in the end were beaten 4–2. Manager Stein was reported to the SFA afterwards by Davidson for a remark made to a linesman at time up and the manager was censured.

Just four days later Celtic were in France playing the Champions St Etienne in the re-drawn European Cup first-round tie. Prices had been doubled for the 35 000 capacity crowd with top seats costing £4.

Without Bobby Murdoch, suspended for one match for having been sent off the previous year against Kiev in Russia, and Tommy Gemmell, who was injured, Celtic went down 2–0 in a match which saw them have a shocking first half but recover well in the second period. It was that second half which gave Stein some hope for a comeback.

Your writer remembers an amusing incident on the way home from St Etienne immediately after the match. Two plane-loads of fans had flown from Glasgow to Lyons that same afternoon and were scheduled to return home about midnight. The first flight was just about ready to leave with everyone in their seats and the cabin doors sealed. Everyone was fairly silent because of the defeat and all that could be heard was the soft music and the slight whine of the engines as the pilot got things warmed up. Then, to everyone's amazement – especially the air hostesses' – came a loud knock at the rear door! The pilot was informed and the door was opened.

Standing outside, despite pleas from ground control staff, was a huge Glaswegian decorated in green and white complete with duty-free carry-out! While they had been trying to get the steps away from the plane he had insisted on climbing up to the door. Having had a refreshment or two he demanded a seat, saying: 'I flew out here in this b—— plane and I'm going back on it.' His ticket was checked and he was reassured that he was booked on the second flight due to leave about half an hour later. It was an incident which brought a lot of laughs and put everyone in good heart for the journey home. After all, it's not every day you sit in a plane awaiting take-off and hear a knock at the door! It was only one of many amusing incidents involving the intrepid travellers. Celtic fans travelling in Europe have through the years been a credit to the club with their singing and non-belligerent joviality. In victory and defeat they have behaved with dignity and this has given the club as much satisfaction as anything achieved on the field by the team.

On the home front in recent years Parkhead has been virtually trouble-free but a young element among the support disappoints the club from time to time with certain songs and chants which are no part of Celtic. One can only hope that in the years ahead influences like the club's newspaper *Celtic View* will educate these misguided souls and point out the error of their ways.

In the return match with St Etienne at Parkhead Celtic faced the stark reality of another first-round knock-out, having suffered such a reverse the previous season at the hands of Dynamo Kiev. They were without the injured Lennox and knew that the loss of even one goal would mean that they needed four to stay in the competition.

The match had an unusual twist in view of Celtic having been responsible for the draw being re-made because of the invasion of Czechoslovakia. The referee for the match was Zdenek Vales of that same country. He gave Celtic a penalty just a minute from half-time from which Gemmell scored and Celtic went on to record a 4–0 victory with further goals from Craig, Chalmers and McBride. Even at 3–0 the Celtic players knew that the loss of a goal would eliminate them from Europe so it was a tightrope situation right up until McBride scored the fourth. The St Etienne players were furious after the match with some offside decisions given by the referee and his linesmen and at the after-match banquet a couple of players stuffed franc notes into the referee's top pocket in a gesture that he had taken a bribe from Celtic! That made the referee furious and he reported the St Etienne club to UEFA. Your writer would not disagree that the St Etienne players had a grievance over some of the offside decisions. But for once Celtic had been given a few breaks and they marched forward to the second round to face Red Star Belgrade of Yugoslavia. They had already beaten Dynamo Zagreb and Vojvodina from that country in European competition so hopes of success were high.

But in the weeks leading up to the match Celtic's mercurial right-winger Jimmy Johnstone caused several storms of controversy which tended to overshadow the forthcoming event. Three days after the St Etienne game he was substituted in a League match with Dundee United at Parkhead. As he left the field he was seen to shout something in the direction of the dug-out which brought the amazing sight of manager Jock Stein leaping out onto the track and pursuing the little winger up the tunnel and into the dressing-rooms.

A Board meeting was held immediately after the game and the manager reported Johnstone's indiscretion which brought him a one-week suspension. Full of remorse, Johnstone apologized but in attempting to patch up that row he caused further uproar when he said that all his energies should be devoted to playing for Celtic as they paid his wages and he did not wish to play again for his country. That too was smoothed over and he did play again for Scotland. Yet the saga was far from over.

The strangest story of all came a few days before the Red Star game at Parkhead. Johnstone took his passport into the manager's office and they got talking about the trip. Johnstone had always hated flying and it was a fear which seemed to get worse each time he stepped onto an aircraft. It was a genuine fear because in the close season he would think nothing of getting into his car and driving the family to the Continent rather than fly. During the meeting he struck up with the manager one of the strangest-ever bargains in football. Stein told him that he could miss the Belgrade match if Celtic won the first leg by four clear goals. The wily Stein, of course, knew just what a match-winner Johnstone could be!

A crowd of 67000 turned up at Parkhead for the first leg and Bobby Murdoch got Celtic off to a dream start with an early goal which just about burst the net.

But by half-time the Yugoslavs had equalized and things were not looking too bright. Whether or not the fear of flying was on his mind, Johnstone took the game by the scruff of the neck right from the kick-off in the second half and gave probably his greatest display in a Celtic jersey. He put Celtic 2–1 ahead and began mesmerizing the Red Star defenders. He cut inside, doubled back, played back-heelers and one-twos and had everyone chasing shadows.

He laid on a third goal scored by Lennox and then Wallace added a fourth – courtesy of Johnstone – and to keep the manager happy Johnstone scored a fifth. Celtic had won by four clear goals and Jimmy ran from the field wiping tears of joy from his face. Some of his team-mates, however, thought that he should still travel because some of them were not too keen on flying either. Manager Stein tried to coax the wee winger to go to Belgrade but Jimmy held him to the terms of the bargain. In front of 40 000 fans in Belgrade Willie Wallace, on as a substitute for Stevie Chalmers, put Celtic one goal ahead and although the Yugoslavs equalized near the end they had been given a comprehensive beating over the two ties.

In the quarter-finals draw Celtic's name was paired with AC Milan, the team they had met on their close-season tour the previous year. They had drawn 1–1 and then beaten the Italians 2–0 so confidence was again high although the class of the Italian Champions was well known. There was, however, a three-month wait until the quarter-finals so all eyes once more turned to the Championship race at home. Celtic had led since the middle of October but dropped three points in drawn games with Falkirk, Kilmarnock and Airdrie and then lost the New Year game to Rangers at Ibrox by 1–0, Rangers having been awarded a penalty kick. Yet New Year was still a time for celebration as chairman Bob Kelly was knighted – the first such honour ever to go to a club side in Scotland.

There is no doubt that Sir Robert Kelly received the honour not just for his club's achievements at home and in becoming the first British team to win the European Cup, but also because of the club's stand against the invasion of Czechoslovakia. It was an honour to be shared by the directors, staff and supporters.

A 3–1 win against Dunfermline and two excellent away wins at Aberdeen and Tannadice saw Celtic consolidate their position and put the Rangers result behind them. With everything in order on the domestic scene they travelled to Milan for the first leg of the European Cup ties on 19 February and as usual encountered all the ballyhoo which is so much part and parcel of the Continental build-up. Milan coach Nereo Rocco announced that he was calling in a psychiatrist to talk his players into scoring more goals as they had managed only sixteen in sixteen League matches. If he did call on such services they did not work because in freezing conditions at the snow-covered San Siro Stadium, Celtic fought out a no-scoring draw. It was a match which should never have been played. But once started in front of 75000 volatile Italian fans the referee had no option but to let it continue. Twice before the kick-off the centre-circle had been swept clear of snow and twice the swirling snow, falling through a slight mist, covered it over again. Long before the end most of the lines had been obliterated and the frustrated fans began throwing snowballs to pass the time. The fact that a white ball was being used by the teams meant that they had great difficulty in following its path. Bearing in mind that conditions favoured neither team, it was a result of significance. It was the first time a Scottish team had gained a draw at San Siro.

For the return game at Parkhead two weeks later on 12 March all 75000 tickets had been snapped up and there was a black market operating, so valuable were the briefs. There was a great feeling after the result in Milan that this could again be a European Cup year.

But the game was only twelve minutes old when Billy McNeill failed to control a simple throw-in from Jim Craig and in a flash the Italian striker Prati had snatched the ball away. He sped in on goal with the Celtic defence caught square and lashed the ball low and hard past John Fallon.

It was the signal for the Italians to bolt the door and the signal for furious attacks by Celtic. Bertie Auld, who had been out of action for the best part of a year, was sent on as a substitute in the hope that his wiles would open the Italian fortress. Although not fully fit he managed to make a few openings, only to see them squandered and the Italians held out to win. It was a bitter defeat but the Celtic players came away with great credit and were later highly praised by Italian officials for having stood at the end to applaud their conquerors from the field. If there was any consolation for Celtic it came from the fact that AC Milan went on to win the European Cup in Madrid two months later, defeating Manchester United in the semi-finals and Ajax of Amsterdam in the Final. How Celtic would have loved that semi-final joust with Manchester United, the reigning European Champions. But it was not to be.

Normally such a defeat would have knocked the bottom out of the remainder of the season. But not in the season 1968–9. Celtic suddenly found themselves with a League Cup Final to play, a Scottish Cup

Final to play and a Championship to be won. Bertie Auld began easing himself back into the side and the little master's touches began to show in the team's overall performances. Celtic began playing in their old fashion and one was left to ponder the fate of AC Milan had the crafty Celtic general been ready just a month or two earlier.

For the League Cup Final against Hibs on 5 April 1969 Celtic sent out the following team: Fallon, Craig, Gemmell, Murdoch, McNeill, Brogan, Johnstone, Lennox, Chalmers, Wallace, Auld, with John Clark as substitute.

The Hibs team was: Allan, Shevlane, Davis, Stanton, Madsen, Blackley, Marinello, Quinn, Cormack, O'Rourke, Stevenson, with Hunter as substitute.

Both sides were loaded with talented footballers and the crowd of 75000 roared in anticipation of a close match as the teams had drawn 1–1 in the League just a week or two earlier. Lurking in the minds of the Hibs players, however, must have been a match played at Easter Road earlier in the season. They had been leading 2–1 with just ten minutes to go when Celtic provided one of their greatest-ever finishes. Those who were there that day will never forget it. Celtic hit four goals in those last ten minutes to win 5–2. Could it happen again?

The Final was twenty-eight minutes old when Wallace gave Celtic the lead. Only four minutes later Auld added a second and Lennox scored a third just a minute from the interval. The procession continued in the second half with two further goals from Lennox for his hat-trick and one by Craig. It had been a brilliant exhibition of attacking football to win the trophy for the fourth consecutive year and even two late goals by Hibs failed to take away any of the gloss. John Clark had come on for Gemmell with the score at 6–0 and smiled later at the thought of playing sweeper, losing two goals and getting a winners' medal!

But the day was not yet done. Just as the Cup was being presented word spread around Hampden that Rangers had lost to Dundee United at Tannadice, which meant that Celtic had virtually won the Championship. In fact they still needed a point from their remaining two games and gained it with a 2–2 draw against Kilmarnock at Rugby Park.

Trailing 2–0 at half-time, Celtic fought back with goals from Murdoch and Gemmell, the latter scoring in the final minute to give

Celtic their fourth consecutive Championship. It was a Championship which showed that games can be lost to Rangers without affecting the end result.

So there was one outstanding fixture to come – the Scottish Cup Final against Rangers.

In the days leading up to the game there was such an amazing Press campaign on Rangers' behalf that any Celtic follower travelling to Hampden would have been excused feeling that he was only going there to enjoy the April sunshine. Rangers, too, got caught up in the heady atmosphere and announced a few days before the Final that a banquet had been arranged to take place at Ibrox immediately after the match and that they would open the gates for their fans and have a lap of honour with the Cup! Celtic were without wingers Jimmy Johnstone, suspended for having three bookings, and John Hughes who was injured. In the event it made no difference. Celtic sent out: Fallon, Craig, Gemmell, Murdoch, McNeill, Brogan, Connelly, Chalmers, Wallace, Lennox, Auld, with John Clark as substitute. Rangers' team was: Martin, Johansen, Mathieson, Greig, McKinnon, D. Smith, Henderson, Penman, Ferguson, Johnston, Persson, with Jardine as substitute. The referee was Mr Jim Callaghan of Glasgow, a man who was to fall foul of Rangers just a few months later.

With only two minutes gone Rangers' dreams of the after-match banquet, lap of honour and the ending of a three-year trophy famine had taken a distinct knock when Billy McNeill rose unchallenged to head home a Bobby Lennox corner from the left. Billy's mistake against Milan was forgotten in that magic moment as players and fans went wild with delight.

At the other end, John Fallon, who the previous season had lost bad goals to Rangers in the New Year match, also atoned by making some very brave saves as Rangers fought hard to get back into the match. Two of the Rangers players, Willie Johnston and Alex Ferguson, seemed to feel they had more than football ability to prove and took it upon themselves to agitate Celtic defenders. It was a tactic which brought about their downfall and the downfall of their team. In the ugliest scene of all Ferguson made as if to butt Murdoch in the face but the Celt remained cool and showed the character which had brought him the Player of the Year trophy.

That example was followed by his team-mates although Brogan had managed to get himself booked in only fourteen minutes for a foul. At the end of the game, however, he could count himself unlucky to be the only player to have his name taken.

Celtic continued to build their play from the back and through the midfield and in two devastating minutes scored two goals which put the result beyond doubt with the half-time whistle still to sound! Young George Connelly, just twenty years of age and playing in his first Cup Final, dispossessed the Swede Persson and sent Lennox away. His speed left the Rangers defence helpless and he shot low and hard into the net. Before the celebrations from that goal had died down Celtic had struck again. This time Connelly caught Rangers' skipper Greig trying to control a throw-out from his keeper. Young George got the ball, strode forward, and with all the authority of a veteran, rounded the goalkeeper and stroked the ball into the net. The scenes at half-time were unbelievable. One end of the ground was in ecstasy and the other totally numbed.

Even with their commanding lead Celtic continued to take the game to Rangers in the second half. Lennox hit the crossbar with a fine header and Auld brought out a great save from keeper Martin. Then, in the seventy-seventh minute, Chalmers scored a fourth goal and a cheeky one at that. With the goalkeeper and centre-half McKinnon closing in on him he stabbed the ball between them into the net. It brought thousands of Rangers fans pouring over the boundary wall although police managed to keep them off the field and in the end they trooped sadly away. There were few left to witness the scenes of Celtic jubilation at the finish. Billy McNeill and Jim Craig turned to congratulate goalkeeper John Fallon on his shut-out only to find John swinging on his crossbar whooping with delight.

Celtic went off to celebrate their record twentieth Scottish Cup win while Rangers' banquet turned to an evening of humble pie. Bearing in mind that there have been only a few Old Firm Scottish Cup Finals, it was the first time that Celtic had beaten Rangers at the ultimate stage since 1904 and the first time Rangers had been beaten in the Final since 1930. In the earlier rounds Celtic had beaten Partick Thistle 8–1 at Parkhead following a 3–3 draw at Firhill in the first round. In the second round they defeated Clyde 3–0 at Parkhead following a 0–0 draw at Shawfield. It was after only three minutes of the Shawfield game that Celtic lost Ronnie Simpson through injury. Ironically he dislocated a shoulder blocking a shot from Jimmy Quinn, a Celtic player on loan to Clyde. Tommy Gemmell took over in goal and Celtic played a very defensive game for the next eighty-seven minutes. That injury to Simpson was to end his fabulous career just a few months later. Celtic had beaten St Johnstone 3–2 at Celtic Park in the quarter-finals and Morton 4–1 in the semi-finals at Hampden before facing Rangers.

In that month of April 1969 Celtic created a record which could well stand for all time. The Hampden fire had given them the unique opportunity of winning the three major trophies in one month and they had taken that opportunity in exciting fashion, inflicting absolute hidings on both Hibs and Rangers while also taking the Championship.

Although they had been disappointed in the European Cup they knew that with just a little more luck they could have gone on to win it. But they had still taken a lot from that particular competition because of the stand against the Warsaw Pact invasion of Czechoslovakia. It had strengthened more than ever the bond between directorate, staff and supporters. Because of it the Celtic 'family' could walk with their heads that bit higher. They were in good heart for the season 1969–70, a new decade and another European Cup campaign.

Brother Walfrid, the Marist Brother who founded Celtic.

The Celtic team in 1888.
Left to right, back row: J. Anderson (trainer), J. Quillan, D. Malloy, J. Glass, J. McDonald (committee members); *second row:* J. O'Hara, W. McKillop (committee members); *third row:* W. Groves, T. Maley, P. Gallacher, W. Dunning, W. Maley, M. Dunbar; *front row:* J. Coleman, J. McLaren, J. Kelly, N. McCallum, M. McKeown.

Celtic Park in 1900. The small pavilion on the left was burned down later, destroying club records.

Belgian War Relief Funds Game. Celtic (League Champions) *v*. Rest of League, Hampden Park, 20 May 1916. (See Appendix for identification.)

Celtic team of 1908, the first Scottish team to win four trophies in one season.
Left to right, *back row:* Directors T. White, J. Kelly, T. Colgan, J. McKillop, J. Grant, M. Dunbar.
middle row: W. Maley (secretary), Young, Somers, McMenemy, Adams, Mitchell, Weir, R. Davis (trainer).
front row: Hamilton, McLeod, Loney, Hay, Quinn, McNair.
Left to right: Charity Cup, Scottish Cup, Glasgow Cup. The League Championship trophy had still to be presented. The Glasgow Cup had been won for the fourth successive year. The previous year they had won three trophies – the Championship, Scottish Cup and Glasgow Cup.

The all-conquering players of 1966-67, the first to win five trophies in one season.
Left to right, *back row:* Gemmell, Chalmers, Craig, Fallon, Hughes, Simpson, Murdoch, O'Neill, Clark.
front row: Johnstone, Wallace, Gallagher, McNeill, McBride, Auld, Lennox ; *trophies:* Glasgow Cup, League Championship Cup, European Cup, Scottish Cup, League Cup.

John Thomson.

John Thomson, head swathed in bandages, is stretchered off.

Moment of impact. The ball runs wide after the clash between John Thomson and Sam English. Willie Cook chases the ball with Jimmy McStay following up.

Above: The famous, talented Scottish Cup winning team which defeated Motherwell in 1931.
Left to right, back row: W. Maley (Manager), Geatons, Cook, J. Thomson, McGonagle, Wilson, W. Quinn (trainer); *front row:* Napier, Scarff, McGrory, J. McStay, R. Thomson, A. Thomson. This is also the side which took the field at Ibrox on 5 September 1931 when John Thomson died.

Above: Patsy Gallagher showing his skills against Airdrie at Celtic Park.

Below: Jimmy McGrory scores the winner against Motherwell in the 1933 Scottish Cup Final.

Celtic captain John McPhail, who scored the winning goal in the 1951 1–0 Scottish Cup Final win against Motherwell, holds aloft the cup which ended a thirteen-year trophy famine.

Celtic goal-scorers against Rangers in the 7–1 League Cup Final of 1957. *Left to right:* Willie Fernie, Billy McPhail, Neilly Mochan and Sammy Wilson.

Scottish Cup Final *v*. Dunfermline, 24 April 1965. Bertie Auld beats full-back Willie Callaghan and goalkeeper Jim Herriot to head Celtic's first goal. Watching are Tommy Gemmell and Alex Edwards, the Dunfermline winger.

Skipper Billy McNeill (in centre) scores the winning goal with a header and goalkeeper John Fallon shows his delight at the other end of the pitch.

Skipper Billy McNeill holds aloft the Scottish Cup after Celtic's win over Dunfermline in the 1965 Scottish Cup Final ended an eight-year trophy famine.
Left to right are: Ian Young, John Hughes, John Clark, Stevie Chalmers, Bertie Auld, Tommy Gemmell, Bobby Lennox, Charlie Gallagher and goalkeeper John Fallon. Missing is Bobby Murdoch who was saluting the supporters at the far end of the ground.

In the 1967 Scottish Cup Final Celtic beat Aberdeen 2–0 with the team which was to play in the European Cup Final the following month. *Left to right:* Bob Rooney (physiotherapist), Willie Wallace, scorer of both goals, Jim Craig, Stevie Chalmers, Bertie Auld, Jimmy Johnstone, Billy McNeill, Jimmy Steele (assistant physiotherapist), John Clark, Tommy Gemmell, Sean Fallon (assistant manager); *front, kneeling:* Bobby Lennox, Bobby Murdoch, Neilly Mochan (trainer).

5　Milan – the Reason

Jock Stein has proved for nearly two decades that he is one of the finest managers in the world. He is the Merlin – the wizard – who breathed life into ailing clubs and blew them to giant stature. His achievements with Celtic have made him a legend in his lifetime and his performances with other clubs are also worth noting. It is more than a coincidence that when he was with Welsh non-League club Llanelli their crowds doubled as the team enjoyed success under his influence on the field and that with the moderate resources available to him at Dunfermline and Hibs he created an exciting atmosphere, gave players extraordinary faith in their ability and produced winning teams. It is also more than a coincidence that when he left East End Park and Easter Road the magic wore off and things were never quite the same again.

Ask any player who has been privileged to share a tactics talk with Stein what he thinks of the man as a manager and the answer is always one of the highest regard. Many a player has said: 'When you actually go onto the field it is like watching the re-run of a movie you have already seen. He has already told you the strengths and weaknesses of the opposition and how they are likely to play.'

Stein is a communicator. One of his great attributes has always been an ability to express himself in footballing terms. He uses his big, powerful hands in much the same way as an orchestral conductor uses his to get the message across to his particular players. Those same hands once helped knit strands in a carpet factory in his native Lanarkshire and later helped extract energy-producing coal from the pits. It could be said that in a way they still do both jobs.

With that pedigree behind him it is difficult to imagine that he could make the kind of mistake which in one terrible night at the San Siro Stadium in Milan brought his – and Celtic's – world crashing to the ground and heralded a period which almost saw his departure from Parkhead. It is no exaggeration to say that only in the past few years have both Celtic and Stein, despite continued domestic success, emerged from the shadow of 6 May 1970. It was a night which took the club to its lowest ever ebb and began so many rumours about the manager's future.

Since Stein's arrival in 1965 Celtic had won the League for five consecutive years. The League Cup had sat on the Parkhead sideboard alongside the Championship trophy all through those five years. The Scottish Cup had been won in 1965, 1967 and 1969, the latter being a spectacular 4–0 thrashing of Rangers. In addition, the 1967 European Cup had been won and a few Glasgow Cups provided the icing on the cake.

The fifteenth European Cup Final against Feyenoord of Rotterdam saw Celtic as overwhelming favourites amongst most people outside Holland. It was to be the crowning glory on five fabulous years, the final seal of greatness and ultimate proof to some biased scribes south of the border that the men from Parkhead were no flash in the European pan.

But it turned into a nightmare occasion which shattered Stein's confidence and hastened the break-up of the Lisbon Lions, seven of whom played in the match. Worst of all, it disillusioned many of the 20 000 Celtic fans who made supreme sacrifices to get to the Final.

Following the match that disillusionment grew as the soccer gossip mills of Glasgow churned out rumours of which some had a semblance of truth while others were totally unfounded. What really happened was that for the first time the Midas touch had deserted Stein. He had not lost his ability as a manager but like many others, he had fallen into that most lethal of football traps – over-confidence. In the following pages the real story of what actually happened in Milan will unfold itself. It is a catalogue of carelessness and to some extent callousness. It is told not to cause recrimination or bring criticism on any individual or individuals but because the many thousands of fans who spent hard-earned money to travel on that fateful trip deserve to know just what went on behind the scenes before, during and after Milan.

Stein, born in the mining village of Earnock, Lanarkshire, in 1923, had come up the hard way. Even his football life had been tough, playing for unfashionable Albion Rovers and Llanelli. But the grim years had forged an iron man who never took anything for granted.

Never, that is, until after two particular performances against the mighty champions of England – Leeds United. The happenings in those European Cup semi-final ties convinced him that his team would take the trophy for the second time.

He travelled to Amsterdam following the semi-finals to weigh up Feyenoord, a job at which he had always excelled. Unfortunately for Stein the match was played in the Ajax Stadium which holds only 25000 spectators and is not unlike Shawfield in appearance.

Ajax, who had reached the European Cup Final the previous year, played their European ties at the large Olympic Stadium in Amsterdam. Feyenoord, on the other hand, were a rich club and had a 65000 capacity stadium in Rotterdam. Seated in that insignificant Ajax ground Stein watched an end-of-season match finish in a 3–3 draw. The atmosphere was distinctly small-time and the standard of play pedantic and uninteresting. He could not have chosen a worse match or setting for his vital mission.

As a result he returned in confident mood and on his return to Glasgow left people close to the club in no doubt that the Final was past the post. The confidence spread among the directors and players and the general feeling was that the Final had been won against Leeds. Now it was a matter of winning the semi-final. The normal meticulous planning before a big European encounter went right out of the window.

It was probably the first time Jock Stein had been wrong with a football assessment. His inescapable air of confidence was summed up in one comment from him: 'If the team plays as well as they did against Leeds I will have no complaints.'

The confidence also spread through some ranks of the supporters who began thinking in terms of a four-goal victory. What had seemingly escaped the notice of many was that Ajax had hammered Liverpool 5–1 in Amsterdam a couple of years earlier and drawn 2–2 at Liverpool in the return after manager Bill Shankly had made the confident remark: 'We'll take eight off them at Anfield.' No one had learned from that ill-fated forecast that Dutch football was not to be taken lightly. As already mentioned, Ajax had reached the 1969 European Cup Final before losing 4–1 to an AC Milan team at its peak – a team which had come to Glasgow that year and beaten Celtic 1–0 at Parkhead. That Final was the beginning of a five-year spell in which Holland was represented at the ultimate stage of the competition. In 1970 Feyenoord had beaten the highly rated Poles of Legia Warsaw in the semi-finals. That too seemed to have gone unnoticed.

Those semi-final performances against Leeds United had probably been the worst possible thing for Celtic. They had often scaled the heights in European football but against the men from Elland Road they reached a new pinnacle of exciting attacking football. But they possibly reached their peak too soon. The second game at Hampden must rival Lisbon for sheer excitement. Even the first-leg win at Leeds, thanks to a goal scored in forty-five seconds by George Connelly, was not enough to impress English journalists that Celtic were Britain's best. But then English sports journalists have often been proved to be shocking bad judges. Outside-right Jimmy Johnstone had reduced the much vaunted Leeds defence to chaos and Connelly scored a second goal which the French referee disallowed but later admitted should have stood. Those who were at the return match at Hampden on 15 April experienced the most incredible atmosphere that famous ground has ever had, including the most partisan of Scotland–England affairs. The crowd far outnumbered the tickets which had been sold. Such was the clamour to see this 'Battle of Britain' that thousands more turned up and charged the huge gates.

They were successful in gaining entry and the crowd must have swelled to more than 140000. The official attendance of 136505 stands as a record for the European Cup.

Leeds captain Billy Bremner, so often their inspiration, pulled back Celtic's one-goal lead from the first match in the thirteenth minute with a long, swerving shot against the run of play. But it did not deter Celtic who continued to play all-out attacking football. Their reward came just two minutes into the second half when John Hughes, never noted for his heading ability, glanced a brilliantly placed header past centre-half Jackie Charlton and goalkeeper Gary Sprake.

Just four minutes later Hampden went wild with delight when Bobby Murdoch put the tie beyond doubt with a tremendous low shot following a dazzling run by Johnstone who had torn the Leeds left flank to shreds. Terry Cooper, the fine England full-back renowned for his attacking flair, spent both matches chasing Johnstone's shadow. It speaks volumes for his sportsmanship that during the two games, sorely tried as he must have been, he did not stoop to dirty play. The scenes at the end were fabulous. Bertie Auld, mastermind of the side, donned a trilby hat given to him by a supporter as the team began a victory lap of honour – the first at Hampden since

1965 when Rangers fans attacked Celtic players as they displayed the League Cup. The outcome of that had been a ban by the SFA on laps of honour. But ban or not, this occasion demanded that the Celtic players salute the crowd which they did to the strains of 'You'll Never Walk Alone' which split the night air. They had outplayed the pride of England so much that at times it had been almost embarrassing!

The road to Milan had started nine months earlier against Basle of Switzerland in the trim St Jacob Stadium. Switzerland had also been the first stepping stone for Celtic on their way to Lisbon so it was a good omen. They drew 0–0 in Basle and won 2–0 at Celtic Park with goals from Harry Hood in sixty-five seconds and from Tommy Gemmell. Neither performance had been of a high standard.

But the second round was to produce all kinds of fireworks. Out of the champagne bucket in a Swiss hotel came together the names of Celtic and Benfica, the star-studded White Eagles of Lisbon who had twice won the European Cup.

It meant a highly nostalgic build-up with many fans booking for the second leg in Lisbon. For some it would be the chance to re-visit hallowed places and for others to make a pilgrimage to Lisbon they had missed in 1967. But on the eve of the first game at Celtic Park came a shock transfer request from left-back Tommy Gemmell, a man whose name and spectacular goals were synonymous with the European Cup. It had all stemmed from an international match in West Germany the previous week. Gemmell had been upset by German forward Helmut Haller and repeated his infamous Montevideo party piece by kicking Haller on the backside. Again it happened on television in front of millions of viewers and the referee had no alternative but to give him his marching orders. The Celtic directors and manager were furious with the player.

As it turned out, Celtic were due to play in their sixth consecutive League Cup Final on the Saturday against St Johnstone. It was a game which was won by a Bertie Auld goal, giving Celtic a 1–0 victory. It was only Bertie's third game of the season after a long spell out because of injury and it also marked the return of his great midfield partner Bobby Murdoch who had spent some time at a health farm losing weight. Gemmell had travelled to Hampden on the team bus and spent some time outside the main door chatting to friends and relatives before heading for the dressing-room. When he opened the door he got the shock of his life. Davie Hay, who had just broken into the first team at right-back, was pulling on the number 3 shorts – Gemmell's shorts! Gemmell, who had not been informed that he had been dropped, got the message and walked out. Smarting over the loss of a fifth consecutive winners' medal in the tournament he promptly put in his transfer request after a meeting with Jock Stein.

Yet after only seventy-six seconds of the first-leg match with Benfica everyone had forgotten the request – including Big Tam himself who scored one of his greatest-ever goals. Bertie Auld, some thirty yards from goal, began his usual free-kick antics of carefully placing the ball and pretending to kick it. He moved forward as if for a shot or cross but instead rolled the ball sideways just a couple of feet into the path of the onrushing Gemmell. His shot rocketed high into the net for the most sensational of beginnings. It was a wonderful night as Benfica had all their big names on view including Eusebio, Coluna, Simoes and the tallest striker in world football, José Torres, at six feet four inches. Every time a corner kick or high ball flew over the Celtic penalty area there were gasps from the home crowd. But the defence stood firm against all threats and further goals by Willie Wallace before half-time and one in the sixty-ninth minute by Harry Hood gave Celtic a commanding lead. They had another goal disallowed and also struck the crossbar. It prompted Jock Stein to say: 'I thought we were worth another two goals but going to Lisbon with three is good although you can never have enough goals.' How right those words were to be!

Celtic prepared for the return match at the Hotel Palacio in Estoril, their headquarters for the 1967 Final, and there was much nostalgia about the trip. Everyone was in good heart on the journey to Benfica's Estadio da Luz (Stadium of Light) but not long after the kick-off one had the feeling that Benfica could do to Celtic what Celtic had done to them at Parkhead. The great Eusebio had not recovered from injury but made a morale-boosting appearance for his team despite one of his legs being heavily strapped up. He showed his greatness by opening the scoring in the thirty-seventh minute and just two minutes later Benfica got a second goal.

Eusebio went off and Celtic hung on by their fingernails right until the last minute when Benfica scored the equalizer. The referee had run straight from the park when the ball had gone into the net and left the entire stadium in uproar. But he reappeared five minutes later to begin extra time. Until that point no one was quite sure whether the goal had been allowed to stand. Celtic amazingly held out and both captains were taken into the referee's dressing-room where a coin was tossed to decide the outcome of the tie. Billy McNeill called 'heads' and his guess was correct. But he was then informed by the referee that this gave him the right to call for the tie. Billy called 'heads' again and the Dutch 2½-guilder piece spun into the air. Referee Van Ravens managed to miss the coin on its descent. It struck his boot, rolled across the floor, hit the skirting board and landed 'heads'. McNeill decided not to hang about and tempt fate a third time. He ran off down the corridor shouting to his mates that they had won. John Clark had run outside to inform the 1000 Celtic fans of the result. The match had started at 9.30 p.m. on the Wednesday but with extra time and the coin-tossing episode it was into the early hours of the Thursday before it was all settled – surely the first time a match ran for two days!

After the initial elation a more sober mood set in. It had not been a satisfactory way to win such a major tie and Celtic immediately tabled a motion to the European Football Union asking for a change of rules. Chairman Bob Kelly said afterwards: 'Had we lost we would have said nothing but in winning it strengthens our argument.' UEFA took heed and at the end of the season decided to introduce penalty kicks as a decider rather than the toss of a coin. Once more Celtic had shown the way and although penalty kicks may not be the complete answer they at least introduce an element of skill rather than a dependence on luck.

With their Lisbon fright behind them Celtic went forward to the quarter-finals where they faced the highly talented Italians of Fiorentina. Again, the first leg was at Celtic Park and again Celtic took a three-goal lead. Bertie Auld, so valuable against the tight Italian defences, opened the scoring in the thirty-first minute after John Hughes had got behind the rearguard and cut the ball back to him. Bertie was about twenty yards out, but where others might have wasted the chance he surveyed the scene unhurriedly then serenely placed a low, crisp shot just inside the keeper's left-hand post. His arm was raised in acclaim before the ball had crossed the line. An own goal by an Italian defender and a third by Willie Wallace in the last minute sent Celtic confidently – but carefully – to Florence for the return leg. They lost 1–0 there without making the mistakes of Lisbon and so qualified for the semi-finals with Leeds United. Between the Leeds games Celtic had lost 3–1 in the Scottish Cup Final to Aberdeen despite being red-hot favourites. The opening goal that day, a penalty, caused great annoyance in the Celtic ranks. It was awarded by Bobby Davidson of Airdrie, a man certain newspapers insisted was equally hard on Rangers over the years!

The penalty was awarded after a full-blooded shot hit Bobby Murdoch on the shoulder. Those listening to television and radio broadcasts of the incident heard astonished commentators exclaim: 'It surely can't be a penalty!' But penalty it was, according to Mr Davidson, and Celtic never recovered their composure. In another incident in the first half, Aberdeen goalkeeper Bobby Clark amazingly dropped the ball as Bobby Lennox stood in front of him. Lennox immediately prodded the ball into the net but Mr Davidson, half the field away, felt he was in a position to disallow the goal and of course took refuge in that antiquated SFA rule which gags referees and linesmen.

There is no way Mr Davidson could have seen an infringement had one been committed. Perhaps he was acting on knowledge from a previous game after which Clark claimed that Lennox had punched the ball out of his hands. Mr Davidson booked Jimmy Johnstone for showing dissent and turned down a glaring penalty when Lennox was fouled by Martin Buchan in the box. Despite that disappointment Celtic could take much pride in the fact that the Championship had been won for the fifth consecutive year and by a massive 12 points from second-place Rangers. They had also beaten Rangers in the quarter-finals of the Scottish Cup at Parkhead in a bad-tempered game which flared up when Rangers' Colin Stein and Willie Johnstone mocked Jim Craig after an own goal. Celtic's goals in the 3–1 win came from Lennox, Hay and Johnstone, and afterwards both captains were ordered to appear before the SFA and censured for lack of example to their teams. With the other tournaments settled all eyes turned to Milan but Celtic's build-up to the Final with Feyenoord can be conservatively described as casual. Training was kept to a minimum and the preparation bore no resemblance to those before the Lisbon match of 1967. A decision was taken to play matches at Fraserburgh and Stenhousemuir. As one director was to say after Milan: 'What were Celtic doing in such places before a European Cup Final?'

They went straight from those games to their country retreat in Varese some twenty-five miles north of Milan, a place more suited to Trappist monks than footballers. Unlike Lisbon it meant that the fans could not see the players because of its isolation. The players therefore never really got the feeling that they were there for a European Cup Final. The place lacked atmosphere and they had little to occupy their time. Unfortunately a business agent, appointed after the Leeds matches, was allowed to hold meetings with them in the days before the game when they discussed plans for a big financial killing on what they regarded as a certain victory. They had committed the cardinal error of counting chickens before the eggs had hatched.

It was an ill-timed situation and had their loyal fans known what was going on in that mountain retreat many would not have travelled. The supporters were making great sacrifices and treating the occasion with the respect it deserved while some of the players were showing as much interest in the financial rewards of victory as in the game itself. That dreadful Scottish trait which gives us such a conceit of ourselves when things are going well seemed to permeate the entire club to the extent that an open-top bus had been ordered to meet the team on its return to Glasgow. That had never been the Celtic way. In Lisbon the players had been constantly warned to keep out of the sun and even to keep away from their bedroom windows. In Varese they walked about stripped to the waist.

In the tactical summing-up before the game the Feyenoord players were practically written off as second division material. One player was told his opposite number would cause problems for twenty minutes and not be seen again. That player was to say later: 'I didn't see him again because after twenty minutes he was going past me so quickly.' Another Celtic player was to say when it was all over: 'We had been given the impression that all we had to do was turn up and the rest would look after itself.'

The teams for the Final were:

Celtic – Williams, Hay, Gemmell, Murdoch, McNeill, Brogan, Johnstone, Wallace, Hughes, Auld, Lennox, with Connelly as substitute.

Feyenoord – Graafland, Romeyn, Israel, Laseroms, Van Duivenbode, Jansen, Van Hanegem, Hasil, Wey, Kindvall, Moulijin, with Haak as substitute.

The referee was Concetto Lo Bello of Italy.

Just after the kick-off the thousands of Celtic fans in the vast stadium sensed there was something wrong. The players in green-and-white far below them were struggling to put their game together.

They were disjointed and not the usual free-running side. They were surrendering possession and finding it very difficult to get the ball back from a clever, methodical Feyenoord team who played the game at their own pace, were uncompromising at the back, fluent in midfield and very nippy on the attack. Players like Hasil and Van Hanegem played with a skill and arrogance which showed that they were above average. Jimmy Johnstone was the recipient of some hefty and illegal tackles and Jim Brogan chipped a bone in his leg in the opening minutes. He bravely played on but really would have been better leaving the field. Despite those early setbacks it was Celtic who took the lead with half an hour of the game gone.

A quickly taken free kick by Murdoch saw Gemmell hit one of his thunderbolt shots. It was so quickly taken that referee Lo Bello had to jump over the ball after Gemmell hit it and several Feyenoord players complained bitterly that he had unsighted the goalkeeper. So Celtic were one ahead. Could this be the break they needed? Could this restore the missing confidence? The answer came within two minutes when Billy McNeill only partly cleared the ball with his head. Rinus Israel met it quite far out and floated in a header which beat the entire defence and dropped into the back of the net. It was a bad, unprofessional goal for any defence to lose. Had Celtic been able to hold their lead until half-time and get the Dutch used to being a goal behind they might have gone on to win. But here were the Feyenoord players right back in the game and their morale sky-high.

The second half was an even greater disaster for Celtic. Their play got worse as the game went on and they began chasing shadows as the Feyenoord players realized the initiative had passed to them. Almost with ease they ran through the Celtic defence but amazingly they kept failing to score. Shots zipped past the posts and over the crossbar. One came crashing back off the bar. The terrible din of the Dutch fans' horns drowned out the Scottish chants and songs and it was obvious that it was not to be Celtic's night. The game went into extra time, which was more than Celtic deserved, and John Hughes, at centre-forward, almost put Celts ahead in the opening minute with a powerful run which saw him take on the entire defence single-handed only for keeper Graafland to block the ball with his legs.

Graafland, like Ronnie Simpson before him, was a bit of a Peter Pan character. He had not played for the first team all season but had been dramatically recalled for the Final because it was felt that Feyenoord's other keeper had lost his form. That save from Hughes vindicated the manager's decision, although had Celtic been at their best and tested him properly they might have been able to exploit his lack of match practice at that level. In the event, Graafland, in his mid-thirties, retired after the game.

For the extra-time period George Connelly came on in place of Bertie Auld who had been a great disappointment. The extra time went into its second period and it began to look as if Celtic might hang on for a replay. Surely they could not play as badly again. Just as that thought was going through the minds of their fans, Celtic lost a second goal.

There were just three minutes left when a high ball through the middle was beating Billy McNeill. He threw up his hands but only partly stopped it. Before the referee could give a penalty kick Feyenoord centre-forward Ove Kindvall, the Swedish internationalist, had toe-ended the ball over the advancing Evan Williams and into the Celtic net. There was no time for a fight-back even had Celtic been playing well. The haven of full time which had been such an attractive thought had suddenly become an enemy to be avoided. The black-clad arm of referee Lo Bello signalled the end of the match and the Dutch went wild with delight as Celtic players wept.

In Lisbon they had lost the first goal but never stopped running. In Milan they had scored first but never started.

The build-up and the briefing had seen Celtic kick off in casual fashion and, as every sportsman knows, when you begin at that pace and discover you have seriously underrated your opponent it is very difficult, in fact practically impossible, to alter course.

As the Feyenoord manager Ernst Happel congratulated his players he felt a tug on his sleeve. It was Jock Stein with a quiet word of congratulations and a handshake before limping along the track back to the dressing-room. Stein and his players looked like the survivors of an atomic war. Their eyes were glazed, they were shattered. They could not believe it had happened to them. The scoreline on the giant electric board read 2–1 but it could easily have been 6. In the dressing-room afterwards Stein, surrounded by journalists, would say only: 'I know what went wrong. It is between me and my players.' His remark took on all kinds of sinister meanings and rumours swept Glasgow about the players being split into two camps in the dressing-room before the kick-off. Certainly there had been some players who felt that Connelly should have been in the team from the start.

The following day, as thousands of fans were badly delayed – some up to twenty hours – by an airport strike, they were hit by a blow even worse than the loss of the European Cup. Before leaving Varese the players and their business manager held a Press conference at which they announced they hoped to make several thousands of pounds from reaching the Final. It was added that the loss of the European Cup had probably cost their venture about £40000. It was bizarre that a Celtic team could hold such a mercenary meeting at such a time. Unfortunately, neither the directors nor the manager seemed aware of the extent of the business dealings.

There can be no doubt that it sickened many supporters. Yet those supporters were magnificent in defeat. Milan had been such a contrast to Lisbon but despite shocking treatment by the airport staff they behaved with dignity and caused no trouble.

Eighty-three years earlier to the month Celtic had played their first game to provide money for charity. The players who took part in that match had three ambitions – to play good football, entertain their supporters and thereby raise money for the poor and needy of Glasgow's East End.

In the early days of May 1970 it seemed, for a while at least, that some Celtic players cared only for themselves and had forgotten their club's high ideals and the people who supported them.

6 In the Beginning

The story of Celtic's beginning must be the most wonderful of all club origins because they were born to the cause of charity. Of the three virtues of Faith, Hope and Charity, St Paul tells us 'the greatest of these is Charity'. And whilst the men who have guided Celtic's fortunes over ninety years have, at times, had to show an abundance of Faith and Hope, it is gratifying that their original cause still burns brightly today.

It was a combination of Edinburgh Hibernians' success and newly acquired leisure time among the working people of industrial Scotland in the 1870s and 1880s which helped bring about Celtic's formation. The game of football already held a great fascination for the masses and with many factories introducing a one o'clock closure on a Saturday instead of 6 p.m. the sport had ready-made audiences.

Until the coming of Celtic, Hibs had enjoyed tremendous success, winning all the eastern honours and, in 1887, being the first team to take the Scottish Cup to Edinburgh when Celtic were still but a twinkle in the eyes of some forward-looking men. Energetic officials had recruited many of the Hibs players from western clubs such as Lugar Boswell, Cowlairs, Vale of Leven and Airdrie, so their West of Scotland supporters always turned out in great numbers when they travelled to Glasgow. The Scottish Cup win was a source of tremendous pride for their western fans who after that game wined and dined them at a special function in St Mary's Hall, East Rose Street, which was to be the birthplace of Celtic.

The famous Renton team who were in their prime in those years had played a charity match in Glasgow with Hibs for the benefit of the Poor Children's Dinner Table of the East End. Hibs, who had been formed in 1872, in fact played quite a number of such matches.

Those games plus the scenes which had followed their Scottish Cup win inspired the ambitions of a group of Glasgow Irishmen.

In those times the Catholic parish played a prominent part in organizing social activities such as winter concerts and summer outings and, in the deprived area of Glasgow's East End, school-teachers were particularly active in the provision of free dinners and clothes for needy children at a time when the Welfare State did not exist.

From the three Catholic parishes of St Mary's, St Andrew's and St Alphonsus there emanated a desire to have a football team right in their own midst which could be a source of income, and several meetings were held to see what course of action should be taken to put the proposed club on the right lines. But as in all things Irish jealousies arose and various good men drew out rather than submit to being shoved aside by the more pushing sort always to be found. The St Mary's representatives, who showed the greatest amount of enthusiasm for the scheme, eventually forced matters to a head and at a big meeting held in their hall it was decided to proceed with the formation of the club and look for the necessary ground.

The then Archbishop of Glasgow, Archbishop Eyre, gave his patronage to the new club because of its charitable aims. Its first honorary president was Dr John Conway, a local MD, and he was partnered by John Glass, a joiner, who took on the role of first president,

With these two men came the real inspiration, Brother Walfrid, a Marist Brother born in Ballymote, Co. Sligo, Ireland, on 18 May 1840, by the name Andrew Kerins. He was the head of the Marist Teaching Order in Glasgow at the Sacred Heart parish, an offspring of St Mary's, and probably the most enthusiastic Celt who ever lived.

It is to him that Celtic owe their very special name. Despite strong moves to name the new club Glasgow Hibernians he stuck to his guns and eventually persuaded the committee to accept one of the most magical and stirring names in football. So on 6 November 1887 he was in a position to declare the formation of 'The Celtic Football and Athletic Club' although it was to be six months before they officially kicked off.

A stretch of half a dozen acres of ground running east of Janefield Cemetery on the Gallowgate was secured only a week later for an annual rent of £50 and a throng of voluntary workers helped a handful of craftsmen to prepare it. By the end of the month a publication of the time – the *Scottish Umpire* – could write: 'We learn that the efforts which have lately been made to organize in Glasgow a first class Catholic club have been successfully consummated. We wish the Celts all success.'

In those embryonic days of the club when money was very scarce, one cannot estimate how much it owed to the hard work of the men who volunteered their services in building the old ground and later the new Celtic Park which came after practical eviction. There was much to contend with in those early times with antipathy, distrust and jealousy. Celtic found the same Press antagonism which had at first threatened to swamp Hibs. But it faded quietly away before a resolute body of men who plainly had come to stay.

In addition to Brother Walfrid, Dr Conway and John Glass, the following committee was formed to further the cause: J. M. Nelis, Joseph Shaughnessy, M. Cairns, J. H. McLaughlin, W. McKillop, T. E. Maley, Daniel Malloy, John McDonald, Joseph McGrory, David Meikleham and P. Welsh. The match secretary was William Maley, later to become manager the treasurer was Hugh Darroch and the secretary John O'Hara.

In January 1888 the following circular was issued in a bid to raise funds. Under the heading 'Celtic Football Club' it read:

The above club was formed in November 1887 by a number of Catholics in the East End of the city. The main object of the club is to supply the East End conferences of the St Vincent de Paul Society with funds for the maintenance of the 'Dinner Tables' of our needy children in the missions of St Mary's, St Michael's and Sacred Heart. Many cases of sheer poverty are left unaided through lack of means. It is therefore with this principal object that we have set afloat the 'Celtic', and we invite you as one of our ever ready friends to assist us in putting our new park in proper working order for the coming football season.

It was fairly successful and among the donations was one from Mr R. F. Barr, of the firm now known as A & G Barr & Co. Ltd who make our other national drink – Irn Bru. Their present-day factory beside the Gallowgate lies on the ground east of Janefield Cemetery which was the original Celtic Park.

Weekly committee meetings were held and there was also a general monthly meeting when new members were enrolled, donations accepted and sub-committees made their reports. Within six months a level pitch 110 yards long by 66 yards wide had been laid, surrounded by a track 19 feet wide intended for cycling events. There was also an open-air stand to accommodate nearly 1000 people. A rough mound around the track provided basic terracing and under the stand was the pavilion consisting of a committee room and two dressing-rooms. Nine gates provided admission, which was sixpence, with women – and later soldiers in uniform – admitted free.

In the early days of the club's history players were classed as amateurs although wages, amounting to about thirty shillings a week, were quietly paid except in the case of Queen's Park. It was good money considering that the wages of a male labourer between 1850 and 1900 ranged from twelve to twenty-two shillings. In England they had voted for professionalism in 1888 but the Scottish Football Association, with that stupidity which has often marked their actions, muddled along sternly against what a leading writer of the time described as something which would be 'the utter ruin of the game'. By dangling financial carrots both Hibs and Hearts had benefited from the many good players they enticed from the west. But under-the-table payments meant too that England had an open door to the north and came and took away what she wanted as the famous Preston North End team of the time – with eight Scots – proved. It was obvious that the game in Scotland would suffer badly if players were not allowed to earn an honest living.

Like Hearts and Hibs, Celtic also managed to attract the men needed including James Kelly of Renton, father of the late Sir Robert Kelly. Although he had promised to join Hibs the new Celts proved too much of an attraction and he decided his place was at Parkhead. It began a Kelly connection with Celtic which lasts to this day. Kelly's change of mind and club was not an unusual thing in those times. The Scottish League had not yet been founded so players were not tied to particular clubs and could move as their fancy – and finance – dictated.

With preparations complete and the new ground handselled on 8 May 1888 by Hibs and Cowlairs who played out a goal-less draw in front of 3000 spectators, the great day was on the horizon. And on Monday, 28 May, Celtic, in white shirts with green collars and a Celtic cross in green and red on their right breasts, presented by the well-known Penman Brothers, Drapers of Bridgeton Cross, played their first match on their home ground before 2000 people. The opponents, as history would have it, were Rangers. It was a friendly match and the new Celts ran out winners by 5–2. That first Celtic team was: Michael Dolan (Drumpellier), Eddie Pearson (Carfin),

J. McLaughlin (Govan Whitefield), William Maley (Cathcart), James Kelly (Renton), Phil Murray (Blantyre), Neil McCallum (Renton), Tom Maley (Cathcart), John Madden (Dumbarton), M. Dunbar (Busby), H. Gorevin (Govan Hibs). The Rangers side, already well established, was: Nicol, McIntyre, Muir, McPherson, McFarlane, Meikle, Robb, McLaren, McKenzie, Souter, Wilson.

For a team which had been brought together by men of no football or athletic knowledge excepting the Maley brothers, the new Celts seemed to be on the right track.

After the match both teams drove to nearby St Mary's Halls where they were entertained to supper. Toasting and music filled the evening and one of the toasts was to the referee, a Mr McFadden of Edinburgh Hibernians, and the umpires. It is worth pointing out that until 1895 there were no neutral linesmen.

Each team put up its own umpire and the referee carried a flag as well as his whistle and was the final court of appeal. He was paid on a sliding scale depending on the distance he had to travel. The rate began at five shillings for under five miles reaching a maximum of £1 7s. 6d. for ninety to one hundred miles. It was not until 1894 that the SFA laid down a fixed rate for the job and the Scottish League Committee of 1898 raised the tariff to one guinea and by paying it themselves made referees absolutely independent of the clubs. It was quite a while before referees discarded their high collars and best walking-out suits for a rig more in keeping with their task.

Celtic's second game at Parkhead brought out a crowd of 6000 who saw them beat Dundee Harps by 1–0. After their first match Celtic joined the Glasgow and Scottish Football Associations. Though the Scottish League did not come into being until the season of 1890–1 friendly games and national and local cup ties provided a full list of fixtures.

Celtic's first season was highly successful with a 6–0 defeat of Airdrie, a 5–1 defeat of Clyde, who incidentally were the first team to beat Celtic by 4–1 in that opening month of May, an 8–0 defeat of Cowlairs, 11–1 against Shettleston, 7–1 against Dundee Harps, a 6–1 Glasgow Cup win against Rangers, a 9–2 win over Clyde in the Scottish Cup and an 8–3 win over Motherwell. Like the Celts of to-day the early Celts were attack-minded. In fifty-six matches they scored an amazing 197 goals and lost 85. Just the stuff to bring in the crowds.

The ground, being held on a yearly basis, brought trouble in 1892

D

when the landlord decided that the rent should be increased from
£50 to £500! At one stage the club thought of moving to Possilpark
or Springburn but as Cowlairs had a sort of unofficial right to the
north of the city it was decided not to go there although the land was
very cheap compared with other places. A seemingly impossible site,
a quarry hole between the old ground and London Road, was to
become the Celtic Park for all time. More hard work from the pioneers turned it into a fine stadium and as one smart chap said: 'It's
like leaving the graveyard [Janefield] to enter Paradise.' That title
was immediately seized upon by Pressmen and has stuck to this day.
The club got a ten-year lease on the ground and later bought it outright. Part of it had been a brickfield half-filled with water to a depth
of forty feet and it took over 100000 cartloads of material to level
it with the surrounding surface. When completed it was much in
advance of anything seen in Scotland, with two spendid tracks for
foot running and cycling, and in later years was to house the World
Cycling Championships.

On Saturday, 20 March 1892, the famous Irish patriot Michael
Davitt laid on the centre of the field a fresh sod of turf with shamrocks
growing from it. It had been brought from Donegal and to commemorate the occasion the following poem appeared in one of the Catholic papers:

> On alien soil like yourself I am here;
> I'll take root and flourish, of that never fear;
> And though I'll be crossed sore and oft by the foes
> You'll find me as hardy as Thistle or Rose.
> If model is needed on your own pitch you'll have it,
> Let your play honour me and my friend Michael Davitt.

But a souvenir hunter or vandal carried off that Donegal sod, so its
shamrocks never bloomed. What befell the thief no man knows. He
carried, however, for the rest of his life the weight of the poet's wrath,
as when the theft became known the following verse was published:

> The curse of Cromwell blast the hand that stole the sod that Michael
>   cut;
> May all his praties turn to sand – the crawling, thieving scut.
> That precious site of Irish soil with verdant shamrocks overgrown
> Was token of a glorious soil more fitting far than fretted stone.
> Again I say, may Heaven blight that envious, soulless knave;
> May all his sunshine be like night and the sod rest heavy on his grave.

Like all things Irish, the new club found there was always contention and plenty of room for argument amongst the newfangled membership, and with a big committee of twenty duly elected there was much vying for position although thankfully there was the guiding influence of Brother Walfrid who held the respect of all. But one leading paper felt compelled to write: 'The Celtic Football Club might well desire to be saved from their friends. We know of no public body whose acts are so freely or fiercely criticized. Despite giving over £400 to charity in their first year there were those who complained that Celtic had not issued a balance sheet, that not all players, committee men, etc., were teetotallers, and that they were stingy to Catholic charities.'

The in-fighting grew so rapidly that by the summer of 1889 one group of malcontents were negotiating with Hibs to move from Edinburgh and take up quarters in the East End of Glasgow under the title of Glasgow Hibernians, the name Brother Walfrid had successfully overcome at the founding of his beloved Celtic. Hibs toyed with the idea because they were not too happy at the new club. In those first few months the Celts had attracted several fine players from the strong Hibernian side and Hibs were resentful at what they considered to be a piece of sharp practice. But the Edinburgh side could not have been too confident of success in the west and stayed put. Celtic, however, did not get off scot-free. When they travelled to Edinburgh later in that very first season to play a 'friendly' game with Hibs they encountered a bitterly hostile crowd which invaded the pitch on three occasions. Celtic decided to cut the match short by ten minutes although the referee would gladly have called a halt to the proceedings long before that.

Hibs began falling on bad times and shortly afterwards ceased to exist as a club and were not resurrected for another three years during which time the Glasgow agitators made another attempt to found a Glasgow Hibernians, going to the extent of raising money and opening a ground in Oatlands. But their venture failed again.

Seldom can a new club have rocketed to fame as did Celtic. In that very first season they reached the final of the Scottish Cup and set the scene for becoming the most successful ever club in that particular competition. They beat Shettleston 5–1, Cowlairs 8–0, Albion Rovers 4–1, St Bernard 4–1, Clyde 9–2, East Stirlingshire 2–1 and Dumbarton 4–1. The fifth-round tie against Clyde was a protest game. Clyde had beaten Celtic 1–0 at Parkhead but Celtic protested that the late arrival of the Clyde team led to the last ten minutes being played in darkness. Clyde were so annoyed by the protest that they refused to use the Parkhead dressing-rooms for the replay. They stripped at their own ground and arrived in their football gear. Their annoyance at the end must have been even greater following the 9–2 hammering they received.

The new club began to be noticed for a style which was its own peculiarity and following a Glasgow Cup tie against Rangers at Ibrox on 27 October which they won by 6–1 the *Scottish Umpire* recorded: 'The Celtic came away with a brilliance which has seldom, if ever, been equalled at Ibrox Park. The dodging and dribbling of the entire forward quintette was a caution while their shooting was dead on.' Another publication of the time, following a match at Dumbarton, commented: 'To see five men working a ball with their feet as if they were handing plates across a table stamps the outcome of their work as due to a thorough understanding of each other.'

Celtic's first-ever Scottish Cup Final was played at Hampden Park against Third Lanark on 2 February 1889 and replayed the following Saturday. Although heavy snow hit Glasgow on the morning of the first game the refereee and umpires declared the ground playable. But as the crowd swarmed into Hampden a blizzard struck. Before the kick-off officials of both clubs, in the presence of a solicitor who happened to be at the stadium, drew up a legal form in protest to the SFA against playing a cup-tie under such conditions. The document, signed by the captains of both teams, was lodged with the referee. The agreement was a private one because it was feared that the spectators, who had paid one shilling instead of the usual sixpence, might invade the field. It was the largest amount of gate money ever taken to that date, coming to £920 6s. 8d. Third Lanark won 3–0 and in the replay again won, this time by 2–1, to stop Celtic getting off to the most incredible of beginnings with a national trophy in their first season.

The following year, 1890–1, Celtic took revenge by winning the Glasgow Cup and beating Thirds by 4–0. They also won it the following season beating Clyde 7–1 in the Final. Then on 9 April 1892 at Ibrox Park, they beat Queen's Park in a replayed Scottish Cup Final by 5–1 ensuring that their name would be engraved on the Cup itself – something Rangers and many other top clubs never managed.

The Scottish Cup Final had already been played on 12 March with Celtic winning 1–0 but as in the 'snow final' it was agreed at the interval to make it a friendly because of spectators spilling on to the

field. The crowd had been enormous for those days, numbering nearly
40000, some of whom had neglected in the confusion to observe the
formality of paying at the gate. In spite of 150 policemen – including
four mounted ones, a novelty at the time – it was estimated that 5000
jumped the barriers as train after train pulled into Ibrox Station in
quick succession. Roads leading to the ground had been jammed
since noon.

But there was no such problem with the replay thanks to the
bungling of officialdom. There were 500 policemen on duty, including
thirty mounties, but only 15000 spectators turned up because of a
decision to double the entrance fee to two shillings – a lot of money
in those times. Certain publications tried to play down Celtic's
victory with excuses that Queen's had been under strength. But the
Celtic team which goes down in history for that first Scottish Cup
win was: Cullen, Reynolds, Doyle, W. Maley, Kelly, Gallacher,
McCallum, Brady, Dowds, McMahon, Campbell. The £1900 taken
over both games showed the remarkable drawing power of the Celtic
Football Club.

Two months later, on 1 June, Celtic beat Rangers by 2–0 in the
Charity Cup Final, therefore winning three cups – the 'Glasgow',
'Charity' and 'Scottish' – in one season. They also set Charity Cup
gate records in a most successful year which saw them take second
place in the League, playing forty-three matches, winning thirty-three,
losing four, drawing six and scoring a massive 156 goals for the loss
of 58.

Within a year of their beginning there had been a rumour that
Celtic were planning an ambitious tour of America. Two years
later a Canadian team toured Scotland and the rumours began again.
The Press, in general, believed that Celtic, because of their energetic
officials, could organize such a trip. One commentator wrote: 'Their
peculiar racial name in a continent which is largely peopled by exiled
Celts would, we are sure, provide a great attraction.' But another
writer implored them to postpone it for a year or two and even went
to the trouble of detailing the financial magnitude of such an under-
taking for their sober consideration: 'Fifteen players and a manager;
steamship passage to New York and back – £250; Hotel, travelling
and incidental expenses at 20 dollars per man per week – £640;
arranging fixtures – £10; making a total of £900.' He pointed out
that it would be worthwhile waiting to see how the game was pro-
gressing there as each club would have to guarantee the Celts £75

to meet expenses. Whether or not that thorough journalist frightened the Celts or not is unknown. In the event, they did not reach America's shores for another forty years, although the rumour about a tour cropped up from time to time.

In 1893, just a year after moving to their new ground, Celtic played their first match under artificial light against Clyde on Christmas night but the experiment was not a success and was abandoned after just a few weeks.

The wires, fixed to a dozen wooden posts fifty feet high, were stretched across the field, with lamps attached, and along the covered enclosure additional illumination was provided by one hundred gas jets. Apart from the unsightly mass of wires and lamps, which distracted from the appearance of the ground, the structure was apt to sag and impede the flight of the ball. In fact, just a month later, St Bernard, beaten 8–1 by Celtic in such a match, entered a protest on these grounds. But the ball had only struck the wires twice during the course of the match and the appeal was turned down. Celtic had not been the first team to experiment with lights. Third Lanark had also made unsuccessful efforts a few years earlier, and as early as 1879 a rugby match between Hawick and Melrose at Hawick had been played under such lights. In keeping with their enterprise in those far-off days the Celtic committee bought tarpaulin covers to protect the playing field from frost and regularly covered it with straw during the winter months. They also toyed with the idea of protecting the spectators on the terracing with a covering of canvas sacking or other waterproof material.

The season of 1892–3 lacked the Cup glory of the year before although was by no means unsuccessful with appearances in the finals of the Scottish and Glasgow Cups, losing to Queen's Park and Rangers by 2–1 and 3–1 respectively.

On the other hand they won the League Championship for the first time and beat Rangers 5–0 in the Charity Cup Final.

The Scottish Cup Final at Ibrox, played on 11 March, was originally scheduled for 25 February but, as seemed to be the norm of the times, it was decided, after the spectators had arrived, to play a friendly on account of frost and Celtic won by 1–0. In the second match Queen's winning goal was a doubtful one. Maley headed out the ball but the referee adjudged that the ball had crossed the line. Celtic believed that the doubt could have been resolved if goal nets had been in use and one of the committee suggested to the SFA at a meeting that the Association should decree their introduction. By a slender majority of 41–35 the motion was carried but only for semi-final and Final ties as some thought nets – at £3 a time – might prove too expensive for the not-so-well-off clubs. Celtic had introduced nets to Scottish football in a friendly match with Dumbarton on New Year's Day in 1892. But they were not used by Queen's Park who, for the Final, requested that the SFA dispense with them as their players were not familiar with nets and they could give the goalkeeper a cabined, cribbed and confined feeling. They also claimed that nets could cause inaccuracies in their forwards' shooting!

In the same month as it had proposed an official ruling on goal nets, the Celtic club had also tabled a motion at the AGM of the SFA that professional football should be legalized in Scotland in a bid to halt the frequent raids north of the border by the English. Celts had also raised the matter the previous year only to be defeated by a small majority. But the second time round they got almost unanimous backing although one opposer moaned about players shooting for gold instead of goals. The Celtic *Handbook* of the following season (1893–4) claimed credit for the club in procuring the change. 'A new era' is how it was described and the writer attacked those clubs who had the audacity to pose as purists on the amateur question when in fact they had been paying wages to players.

It was around this time that the club began to go off-course from its original aims. Brother Walfrid, who had always been the guiding influence, had been moved by his superiors to London in August 1892. Certain people who had been voted onto the committee began having other ideas about the club's function and ignored the Poor Children's Dinner Table. The last contribution there had come at the end of season 1891–2 – a sum of £140 with another £77 going to other charities.

The Celtic *Handbook* the following season made reference to the fact that Celts had been greatly handicapped with their new ground debts and that some £40 to £50 went to charity. But from an income of £6696 2s. 9d. visiting teams had taken away only £1450 yet the Poor Children's Dinner Table got nothing – a situation which Brother Walfrid would never have tolerated. Celtic were in a comfortable position, so comfortable, in fact, that at the AGM of 1893 the committee put forward the motion that the club should be formed into a limited liability company. Honorary secretary J. H. McLaughlin moved the motion and was seconded by solicitor Joseph Shaughnessy, the honorary president. Part of the motion called for the re-election *en bloc* of the committee. But member J. M. Nelis opposed the motion and got a seconder. The arguments raged on all night with a pro-LLC man expounding that the club would be in a position to give more to charity if they took the proposed new move. But those against treated this as a smug prediction and, in the words of Bertie Wooster, 'just so much apple sauce, and Grade A apple sauce at that'. Mr Nelis and his amendment won the day and before the long meeting closed at one o'clock in the morning he carried eighty-six votes to thirty-one. The radical suggestion had been sprung too quickly on a membership which in reaching its decision combined fear of biting off more than it could chew with a sentiment for the club's original aims. The new move brought the following comment from *Scottish Sport:*

This is the first proposal of its kind in Scotland. The first thing to strike the outsider is that it affects the constitution of the club which was formed for charitable causes. If the interests of charity are safeguarded then there can be no objections. But if they are not safeguarded we have enough experience of the rapacity of mankind to warrant us in believing that dividends will gradually come to have priority.

At the AGM of 1894 200 members attended, some worried about what seemed to them a deliberate attempt on the part of those in office to bypass the object for which the club had been founded. One put forward a motion that 200 new members be taken on at a charge of ten shillings each and that the money be immediately handed over to the Poor Children's Dinner Table. And this in a year when the club's income was £7000! Perturbed by the absence of charities from the balance sheet, and dissatisfied with the manner in which the committee had been elected, some members signed a petition for an extraordinary meeting to inquire into allegations of irregularity in voting and inaccuracy in enumerating. The Glasgow *Catholic Observer* wrote:

The idea in the minds of those who began the Celtic Club was to do good to Catholic charities. That is all over now. The thing is a mere business, in the hands of publicans and others. Catholic charities get nothing out of the thousands of pounds passing through the treasurer's hands. Can we not get a club that will carry out the original idea of Brother Walfrid? The income of the Celtic Club is drawn mainly from our own people.

The half-yearly meeting in December 1895 brought a rebuke from Tom Maley that once more the Poor Children's Dinner Table had received nothing. At the AGM of 1895 it was again revealed that no money had gone to this charity.

In the four years that the arguments raged, many members went through a personal purgatory wondering which way to turn. But on the field of play the Celtic team was getting on with the real job of work and warmed the hearts of their supporters by winning the Charity Cup for the third consecutive year in the season 1893–4 and ending in style with the Championship to go with it. Celtic Park was so superior to any other ground in the country that it was awarded the 1894 international match despite an offer from Queen's Park that Hampden would be given free provided their own members got the good seats! Parkhead housed a 46000 crowd and the takings were £2650, a record then for an international football match in Britain.

The struggle between those hell-bent on making the club a limited liability company and the old faithfuls who wished to adhere to the original aims was finally resolved on 4 March 1897 in the same St Mary's Hall which had witnessed the birth of the club as a cause dedicated totally to charity. Now it was to witness the burial of that ideal. The articles of association for the club read:

1. That a limited liability company be formed to be called 'The Celtic Football and Athletic Company Limited'.

2. That the nominal share capital of the company be £5000 in 5000 ordinary shares of £1 each.

3. That each present member of the Celtic Club be entitled on application to one fully paid-up share in the company.

4. That every holder of ten shares in the new company shall be entitled to one vote, and every holder of more than ten shares to an additional vote for every ten shares over and above that number.

5. That each of the present members of the club be entitled to one vote for the fully paid-up share allotted to him, and that the annual subscription of such members shall not exceed five shillings per annum.

6. That the company take over the whole debts and liabilities of the club as at the first day of April 1897, in exchange for which the company shall be entitled to the whole assets thereof.

7. That after paying a five per cent per annum dividend, the directors shall have power to give for such charities as they may select such sum or sums they may think proper.

8. The qualification for directorship shall be the holding of one share in the company.

9. That the first directors of the company shall not exceed seven.

In the ensuing season, despite a British record profit of £16267, Celtic gave nothing to charity. Instead, that first directorate of Michael Dunbar, John Glass, James Grant, James Kelly, John McKillop, John McLaughlin and John O'Hara declared a 20 per cent dividend for shareholders, £105 in directors' fees and a gift of 100 £1 shares, an honorarium of £100 and a testimonial to president John Glass. The annual dividend over the next three years was 10 per cent. The goings-on brought the following comment from *Scottish Sport*: 'Though the vast majority of the old members are not at all satisfied with the selection, they have only themselves to blame, as in handing the club over to a few monied individuals they cut a rod to beat themselves and must endure their whipping with the best grace they can muster.'

Despite their lack of charity, there could be no denying the amount of enterprise shown by the new Board which in a very short time bought the ground outright from the landlord. New director James Grant, a Northern Irishman who was big, strong and plain-spoken, was largely responsible for the erection of the first-ever two-tier stand which was built in 1898 and known as the Grant Stand. He also had the idea of having large, sliding windows which could shut out the cold and the wet but he and the architects had overlooked the problem of 'sweating', caused by the breathing of the spectators. The windows had to be taken away and the stand became very unpopular. Spectators did not like having to climb up the steep flights of stairs and the stand was on the opposite side of the ground from the pavilion. Mr Grant lost a lot of money through his unsuccessful venture and sold out to the company at a small price. The stand was eventually burned down in 1927 while being demolished to make way for the present-day stand which itself has been vastly modernized in recent years. The old club pavilion, much like the one which still stands at Broomfield Park, Airdrie, to this day, had been set on fire in 1904 following a Celtic victory the previous day. It was generally thought at the time that the fire had been raised by someone unhappy with the result. That pavilion had been witness to many great Celtic innovations of the time. It was a busy hive for bookmakers during the famous Celtic Sprint Handicap.

The year 1898 saw the World Cycling Championships held at Celtic Park. The club had built a cement track for the occasion and for many years afterwards the finest cyclists in the world, both pedal and motor, delighted large crowds. Harry Martin, the famous cyclist of the time, thrilled the crowds with the then amazing speed of 45 m.p.h. Other famous names included Vogt, Killachy, McLaren, Flynn, Zimmerman, Arend, Bourillion, O'Neill and Barden.

The benefits of being a limited liability company certainly showed in the appearance of the ground. The coloured cement track really set it off on big sports days. At that time Celtic got the opportunity to buy all the ground right down to London Road where the school building is today. That would have enabled the club to build terracings as big as Hampden's. But it was felt that the cost of terracing, which was of wooden construction in those times and therefore very expensive, would be more than the club could afford.

Celtic Park, however, had its day as regards international matches and can lay claim to being the first club to build towards that end. Perhaps the most famous was the Rosebery International of 1900, named because of the attendance that day of the Earl of Rosebery, in which Scotland gave England a football lesson. During the First World War too, Celtic Park played host to several sporting occasions which were held in the cause of charity.

Among the many great occasions was a baseball game between two American Navy teams who were at that time stationed at the Tail of the Bank. A most unusual occasion was a touch of war games when soldiers, home on leave, or wounded, gave a display in trench warfare, preparatory for their return to action. They erected temporary dummy trenches which were defended and attacked by all kinds of harmless bombs which made great noise but caused no damage, much to the delight of the huge crowd.

Again it was Celtic Park which housed the first mass display of musical drill by schoolchildren, the idea of manager Willie Maley who had witnessed a similar display on a visit to the Chelsea FC ground. It was such a success that it was later copied at Hampden Park during the Coronation festivities. Another great day came in 1911 during those Coronation rejoicings. A great parade of colonial and home troops from every part of the Empire massed on the Parkhead turf and gave a display never forgotten by those privileged to witness it.

Celtic also tried to get boxing to their ground but it did not really catch on. Probably the most outrageous of their plans was in offering the sum of £500 to Graham White, then doyen of airmen, to fly in and out of the ground – this being in an era when aeroplanes were not so common. Everything seemed set until White arrived at the ground and declared it unsuitable because of iron railings round the playing pitch which would impede his flight. The railings, it was immediately agreed, would be taken down for the day but there was then an objection about the steepness of the terracing and Mr White felt that with only a clear run of 150 yards he could not be certain of clearing the field. The engagement was therefore called off.

Celtic's experience of ground building was to be a great help to Ibrox and Hampden when their day came, and by the end of the century Celtic had a stadium capable of holding 70000 spectators and was unrivalled in Great Britain. In the soft April light of an international day with its terraced slopes comfortably packed and its terracotta track standing out against the vivid green turf, its long covered stand with tip-up seating and enclosure on the north side gay with flags and bunting it lived up to the sobriquet bestowed upon it by the newspapers.

The ideals for which the club had been founded may have become sicklied over with the pale cast of gold, but the enthusiasm of the rank-and-file supporters remained undimmed. The Scottish Cup had graced the trophy room in 1891–2, 1898–9 and was won again in 1899–1900. In that period the Championship had been won on four occasions, the Glasgow Cup had also been won four times and the Charity Cup six times. On 26 October 1895 Celts had set a record Scottish League score by beating Dundee 11–0 at Parkhead. There was much to look forward to in the new century, a century which would demand the benefits of a limited liability company. When the change came it perhaps came just too soon and in a manner which did not show certain Celtic individuals in a good light. There can, however, be no doubting the long-term wisdom of that change, which has kept Celtic in the forefront of Scottish, European and world football.

7 Into the Twentieth Century

The new century opened with a squabble as the newly formed Scottish League argued about formations and eventually chose eleven teams to make up the First Division. It was a quite stupid arrangement as it meant one team having a blank Saturday. That very first League comprised the following teams: Celtic, Dundee, Morton, Hearts, Hibs, Kilmarnock, Partick Thistle, Queen's Park, St Mirren, Rangers, and Third Lanark. The Second Division had: Aberdeen, Airdrie, Ayr, Clyde, East Stirlingshire, Hamilton Accies, Leith Athletic, Motherwell, Port Glasgow Athletic and St Bernard. The following year saw Partick Thistle drop into the Second League leaving an even ten teams but they returned the following season in the company of Port Glasgow Athletic, giving the First Division twelve teams.

Season 1900–01 saw Celtic finish second in the Championship race and they were beaten 4–3 in the Scottish Cup Final by Hearts. They also lost in the final of the Charity Cup to Third Lanark by 3–0 after a replay.

But from these setbacks emerged a team which was to give Celtic a fabulous era and records which were to stand until the great side of the Sixties made its mark. In addition to many cup records they were to win the Championship for six successive years, a feat which stood until the same Celtic Football Club recorded nine Championships in a row from 1966 until 1974.

At the beginning of season 1901–02 a young man appeared on the left wing who was to become one of the all-time greats – Jimmy Quinn. Before the end of the match he had moved in to centre-forward, a position he was to make his own. As the young blood began flowing into the club the old warhorses who had served Celtic so well in the 1890s began to go. One of the best goalkeepers, Dan McArthur, was given a benefit match in recognition of his fine service.

The season was marred by two incidents, one of which concerned Celtic in an unpleasant situation with Rangers and the other being a calamitous situation affecting Rangers and the SFA.

In preference to the competing claims of Hampden and Cathkin, a previous home to Queen's Park, it was decided by the Glasgow Association to hold the Final of the Glasgow Cup between Rangers and Celtic at Ibrox. The result was a draw and Celtic insisted that the replay, in fairness, be played at Parkhead. But Rangers would have none of it and insisted that as the tie had been awarded to Ibrox it should be completed there. The Association sided with Rangers, and Celtic decided to scratch from the competition. The Cup was handed over to Rangers.

A couple of years earlier Rangers had started reconstruction after obtaining a lease on additional ground. They planned for an 80000 capacity and, as Celtic had done years previously, they formed themselves into a limited liability company. By the season of 1900–01 work was shaping well and the Rangers application for Greater Ibrox as the setting for the international of 1902 was upheld by the SFA against the claims of the old venue which was Celtic Park. Celtic, it seemed, got no support from officialdom in their off-the-field battles with Rangers. So on 5 April 68 114 people travelled to Ibrox and within five minutes of the start came the first Ibrox disaster when the top of the huge west terracing, a wooden structure of broadwalks erected on steel uprights, gave way and hundreds of spectators plunged forty feet to the ground. Twenty-six were killed and when it was all settled in the months ahead 587 people received compensation.

That disaster, coupled with several deaths at Ibrox in the early Sixties and the 1971 Ibrox disaster, in which sixty-six people died on stairway thirteen, brings the total deaths for that ground to around a hundred in the past eighty years.

As Celtic helped in 1971 with a generous £10000 cheque to aid Rangers, they agreed in 1902 to compete in a special tournament Rangers organized to raise money needed for compensation payments. And it was from this tournament that Celtic got a bit of justice against their great rivals. Celtic's fortunes in the Glasgow Exhibitions of 1888 and 1901 were not of the happiest, with bad feeling being generated in both because of the treatment handed out to Celtic by the authorities. In 1888 they were slighted to such an extent that they refused to take part. But as they were one of the prime attractions of Scottish football an eventual arrangement was reached and they competed. In the Final, however, they got a very raw deal and lost to a Cowlairs team which had been specially strengthened for the occasion. In 1901 Rangers defeated them in the Final where again the handling of the game caused extreme annoyance in the Celtic ranks. The trophy won by Rangers was the one put up by the Ibrox club for this special disaster tournament. Celtic took care of Sunderland and Rangers beat Everton. In the Old Firm Final Celtic were not to be denied a second time and won the very handsome trophy which has a proud place to this day on the Parkhead sideboard.

The season of 1902–03 was remarkable for the amount of chopping and changing of the team in an effort to get the right combination. Manager Willie Maley had embarked on a youth policy instead of replacing the ageing players of the 1890s with seasoned footballers which had previously been the case. From that youth policy, as was to happen in the 1960s, came a great side. From Dunipace came international junior goalkeeper Davie Adams and from Kilmarnock, after a year with Bristol Rovers, came fair-haired Jimmy Young who was to become known as 'Sunny Jim'. Willie Loney and Jimmy Hay joined him in a half-back line which is reckoned to this day to have been one of the finest-ever in football.

Rutherglen Glencairn provided international junior centre-forward Alec Bennett and one of the great inside-forwards, Jimmy McMenemy. Although the talent was there, the team ended the season of 1902–03 with the worst record since their foundation. They won nineteen matches, lost twenty-two with fourteen drawn out of a total of fifty-five games. Yet they managed to score 101 goals for the loss of 68. But the following season, with Jimmy Quinn established at centre-forward after trials on both flanks, Celtic were ready for anyone and reached the Scottish Cup Final. The team which lined up against Rangers on 16 April 1904 was: Adams, McLeod, Orr, Young, Loney, Hay, Muir, McMenemy, Quinn, Somers' Hamilton. Down 2–0 at half-time, Celtic came back to win 3–2 with Jimmy Quinn scoring all three. In the final League match of the season against Kilmarnock at Parkhead the following week Quinn had five of the six goals scored.

The season saw the introduction of the famous green and white hoops as Celts had mostly played from their beginning in a jersey of green and white vertical stripes. They became the first Scottish team to tour the Continent of Europe in that year of 1904, playing in Vienna where they got a wonderful reception from a people who were just beginning to appreciate the game. They travelled on to Prague and over the next few years they were to pioneer routes to Budapest, Berlin, Dresden, Leipzig, Hamburg, Copenhagen, Lille, Roubaix, Paris, Basle and Cologne. At the last-named town Celtic played a British Rhine Army Select which was stationed in that famous old cathedral town to hold the balance between France and Germany after the First World War. In that first tour to Vienna they played two games for a guarantee of only £150 and it was a credit to the men who represented Celtic that rather than squeeze the club for pocket money, they offered to forego their wages to allow them to make the trip.

In 1907 Celtic played three games for the same guarantee although by 1923 they got £1200 for three games in Prague. Austrian football owes much to Celtic for its origins because it was an old Celtic player, Johnny Madden, who went out there to do football missionary work and spent a great deal of his life in that country. The only complaint from those early days of Continental football was when Celtic won their first 'European Cup' but never received it. It all began in 1914 when Celtic played in a charity match against Burnley in Budapest. They had won the English Cup and Celtic had won the Scottish Cup. The local club, Ferencvarosi Torna, put up a beautiful trophy for the match which ended in a draw before a huge crowd.

Celtic were scheduled to return home next day although Burnley had another week to play out their list of engagements. It was decided that the Cup would be sent over to Britain and that the two teams play for it there. Burnley won the toss and Celtic travelled south in the September and in keeping with their wonderful record against English clubs on their own grounds beat the home side 2–0. A proportion of the gate money was sent out to Budapest as agreed but the Cup never appeared. Celtic made several applications for the trophy to the Budapest club and it was eventually discovered that when the war started it had been put up for a charity competition to raise funds for the Red Cross. So Celtic had to console themselves with the fact that it had gone to a good cause, the cause, in fact, for which the club had been founded.

Despite the wrangles over making the club a limited liability company, the early charter has never been forgotten and annually a goodly sum still goes to charity. Celtic in their earlier years backed many causes. When the Unemployment Rent Relief Fund was set up in 1921 Celtic gave £500.

The miners' strike also received a similar donation and right through the years Celtic have sent teams all over Britain and Ireland to play in the cause of charity. Always to their credit has been the fact that they are a cosmopolitan club. Some of the greatest Celts of all time were non-Catholics. Men like McNair, Hay, Lyon, Buchan, Cringan, the Thomsons and Paterson soon found out, even in those early days, that broadmindedness, the real stamp of a good Christian, existed to its fullest at Celtic Park, where a man has always been judged by his football alone. In more recent years players like Bertie Peacock, who came from a staunch Protestant Northern Ireland family, Jock Stein, the first non-Catholic manager, and Lisbon Lions like Ronnie Simpson, Tommy Gemmell, Willie Wallace and Bertie Auld all found the same and helped the club to great successes.

Perhaps an article from the *Glasgow Observer* dated 10 December 1904 sums up what Celtic are all about. From the outset the team had the benefit of a large and loyal following. Its foundations had been closely associated with Ireland and Catholicism. Its supporters were largely composed of first- and second-generation Irish immigrants who remained steadfast even after the club drifted towards being a limited liability company. The article was a weekly dialogue between Riley and Rogan, Celtic and Queen's Park followers respectively. With Rogan as first speaker, it reads:

I felt that the moment had arrived for the playing of my trump card. Whatever else we do at Hampden we are at least consistent. We admire and support our amateur team because it is really composed of amateurs. Now you Parkhead people drive out with green banners and shamrock emblems to cheer a supposedly Irish team which contains a majority of Scotch Protestants. One is said to be a Grand Master or past-Grand Master of an Orange Lodge.

RILEY: I have no means of knowing whether that statement is fact, but, even supposing it is true, there is nothing incongruous in the situation. Ten years ago it would have been a howling scandal. Nowadays it is merely a piece of smart business.

ROGAN: Then football has become a business has it? A mere mercenary, money-grabbing, dividend-forcing enterprise; no longer a game graced with the romance of tradition and the fine aroma of sentiment, but a sordid consideration of multiplied sixpences?

RILEY: Let us discuss the thing calmly and without any barbed invective that may rankle and remain. In the beginning the Celtic Club was started by Irish Catholics to assist local Catholic charities. Its players, the Maleys, Kelly, Coleman, Gallacher and Dunbar, and the others were certainly Catholic and at least supposedly of Irish extraction. This continued for some time hence there grew up around the team a purely Irish tradition.

ROGAN: Precisely, and now . . .

RILEY: Now they have changed all that. There came a day when the grand old brigade began to lag superfluous on the stage and had to make way for new blood. Unhappily, the available recruits, Irish, I mean, were not available. The management therefore had to look elsewhere and concurrently the limited liability company was formed.

ROGAN: Although they engage alien professionals they still call themselves Celts; still display the crownless harp on their flags and dress their players in jackets green.

RILEY: Sensible people realize that the patriotic idea died out when football became a money making speculation. The first function of a limited liability company is to create the largest possible dividend. In football this is done by drawing the biggest gates. For this purpose only the very best players must be engaged. For the biggest crowd will naturally go where the best players are to be seen. The Celtic directors must live up to their first princely dividend. *Ergo*, the Orange Grand Master.

ROGAN: Very good. That's all fair and square from a director's point of view; but what is to be said of the Celtic supporters who turn out in green panoply and make a party function of a Parkhead match?

RILEY: You hardly state the case correctly. What may be called 'the firm' remains Irish. At least five of the Celtic professionals are Catholics, and the majority of the five are Irishmen.

ROGAN: Quite so. But any one of the five is liable to lose his place if a cleverer player turns up, be he Anglo-Scot, New Zealander or Heathen Chinee.

RILEY: The fact is I cheer a Celtic player not because of his race or creed, nor yet because of his green shirt but because he is invariably clever. Why does an English crowd cheer Ranji when he hits up a century against Australia? Certainly not because of his name or race, but because of his superb prowess as a batsman. Our Celtic players are aliens and mercenaries, if you like; but they are in the service of an Irish firm, and they play football of a quality not found anywhere but Parkhead.

ROGAN: Of course, if you are satisfied, I have nothing more to say. But give me my lads in Black-and-White, who are what they appear to be; and keep your wearers of the Green who masquerade now in an emerald jersey and again in an Orangeman's regalia.

The season of 1907–08 saw Celtic clash three times with Rangers in the Glasgow Cup before winning by 2–1 and emerging with the trophy for the fourth successive year. It was another *annus mirabilis* for the team. To the Glasgow Cup they added the Scottish Cup, the Charity Cup and the League Championship – an achievement that had not been equalled before in Scottish football. In the 5–1 Scottish Cup win against St Mirren in the Final the team was: Adams, McNair, Weir, Young, Loney, Hay, Bennett, McMenemy, Quinn, Somers, Hamilton. A sportswriter commented: 'Celtic, in steadiness and headiness in all their lines were as near perfection as it is possible for football mortals to be.' And he added some advice to other clubs: 'The first thing to learn is the secret of Celtic's success, and that appears to lie in the fact that during their most victorious period there has been practically no change in team personnel. There has been no buying and selling of players, but there has been loyalty, obedience and good behaviour.'

1908–09 saw a most unusual switch with Alec Bennett leaving to go to Rangers while his place was taken by Willie Kivlichan who had a few years earlier been a Rangers player. But that was not the end of the shocks. The season is most remembered for what became known as the Hampden Riot. It came about because of a drawn Scottish Cup Final which in those days was always treated with great suspicion by the fans, many of whom thought there was a secret agreement between club treasurers for extra gate money – a suspicion one still hears in these modern times!

This particular season had an amazing run of drawn Cup ties. Celtic needed a replay before beating Rangers 2–1 in the semi-final of the Glasgow Cup on 3 October. In the Final of the same competition three games were required to separate Third Lanark and Celtic with Thirds winning 4–0. Two games had been necessary in the Scottish Cup before Celtic eliminated Clyde. So on 10 April 1909 Celtic lined up at Hampden against Rangers before 70000 spectators who wanted to see a duel to the death. The result was a 2–2 draw! A week later, after a replay, the teams were still locked together, the score on this occasion being 1–1. During that week, despite the SFA ruling, the idea that extra time would be played seemed to have spread among supporters.

The first signs of restlessness, which later developed into an orgy of destruction, came when the referee blew for time up and left the field with his linesmen. The shouts of 'play on' reached a crescendo and fans stayed on, encouraged by the fact that some players from both sides stayed on the field apparently willing to play on. The last player had barely left the field when the hooligans began vaulting the barriers. They were followed by scores of others and began uprooting the goalposts and pulling down the crossbars which were later used as battering rams. Part of the angry mob gathered outside the pavilion and shouted that the match had been a swindle. Mounted policemen who arrived and drove the mob in the direction of the north terracing soon found themselves facing a hail of stones and bottles and a threat from some carrying fragments of palings.

Others tore up barricades and set fire to them and to give an idea of the desperate lengths they were prepared to go they even poured their whisky on the flames! They wrecked pay boxes and added the wood to their fires, and as the flames and smoke ascended in the April air over Hampden the fire brigade was called out by worried officials taking shelter in the pavilion. But the firemen's arrival saw even more hooliganism. Spectators cut hoses with knives and unscrewed nozzles. The firemen, for their own protection, turned those hoses which were still working on the rioters and helped cool their ardour. The police seemed helpless because of the numbers of rioters who then proceeded to cremate a bundle of police capes and helmets. Some were cut up and passed about for souvenirs and many a penknife was at work for a piece of a goalpost or crossbar. Ninety-three policemen had been in attendance at the game but at the height of the riot their numbers swelled to 200. Yet only one man was arrested. Luckily only twenty-five people were injured and taken to hospital – most of them policemen – and only five were detained. It was, however, one of the most unsavoury incidents in the history of Scottish football and the authorities decided to withhold the Cup that year. Officialdom came in for a measure of criticism in the Press for failing to make the position crystal clear before the replay. The SFA gave Queen's Park £500 compensation and Celtic and Rangers handed over £150 each.

The decision to withhold the Cup robbed Celtic of another record – the chance of adding a trophy to the 1908–09 Championship as they had done every year since the start of their amazing run of consecutive Championships beginning in 1905. The 1909 League win was the fifth in succession. But the following year they managed to add the Glasgow Cup to their sixth consecutive Championship. The record over that six-year period was remarkable. They also won the Scottish Cup in 1907 and 1908, the Glasgow Cup in 1905, 1906, 1907 and 1909 and the Charity Cup in 1905 and 1908.

A sportswriter who had witnessed every important football occasion in the previous twenty-five years summed up the Championship run thus:

No better or stronger proof could be produced of the Celts' brilliant and sustained ability as a team than is supplied by these figures. If, however, we add to them their cup appearances and victories in the same years we have a joint record unsurpassed in British football. Those who ask for the secret can look at three major factors – good management, good players and harmony. All these have played their part in building this unique record. The 'No change' policy of the Parkhead management, allowing practically the same team to play season after season, went a long way to producing the records. [The article then went on to praise individual players.] There are few more earnest players in Scotland than the Celtic centre-forward Jimmy Quinn. He has been the potent force, the controlling pivot, in establishing this record. His escapement from injury has been phenomenal. His gritty, cast-iron and determined build have so persistently worked towards the objectives of the team. He is supported by McMenemy, a brainy, agile and methodical initiator of and combiner in, moves. He in turn is well supported by the genial Peter Somers, a great passer of the ball. Alec Bennett, before his departure to Ibrox, thrilled the Celtic crowds with his sparkling wing play. At half-back Young, Loney and Hay are without equal with McNair so versatile at the back. In Davie Adams Celtic have had a safe and at times brilliant guardian.

The teams for the six successive Championships were:
1905: Adams, Watson, Orr, McNair, Loney, Hay, Bennett, McMenemy, Quinn, Somers, Hamilton.
1906: Adams, Watson, McLeod, McNair, Loney, Hay, Bennett, McMenemy, Quinn, Somers, Hamilton.
1907: Adams, McNair, Orr, Young, Loney, Hay, Bennett, McMenemy, Quinn, Somers, Templeton.
1908: Adams, McNair, Weir, Young, Loney, Hay, Bennett, McMenemy, Quinn, Somers, Hamilton.
1909: Adams, McNair, Weir, Young, Loney, Hay, Kivlichan, McMenemy, Quinn, Somers, Hamilton.
1910: Adams (and Duncan), McNair, Weir, Young, Loney, Hay, Kivlichan, McMenemy, Quinn, Johnstone, Hamilton.

During the six seasons, out of 192 League matches played, Celtic lost only twenty-three games and out of a possible 384 points secured 305. In recognition of their feat in winning the League Championship six times in succession, a silver shield, with ornamental medals bearing the names of all the players who took part, was presented to Celtic by the other clubs at the twenty-first annual celebrations of the Scottish League. No apology is necessary for dwelling on this wonderful achievement, the magnitude of which was confirmed by the fact that it stood all the way until 1972 when the same Celtic

Football Club won the Championship for the seventh consecutive year and went on to record their nine-in-a-row which will surely never be equalled. The first of the six Championships had been a tie between Celtic and Rangers with Celtic winning the play-off.

The season of 1910–11 saw the club tour France, Germany, Austria and Switzerland, but it was on the home front that two very significant happenings occurred. From Mossend Hibs came outside-right Andy McAtee with the legs of a billiard table but the speed of a greyhound and a shot like a rocket. He was accompanied by the amazing Patsy Gallagher from Clydebank Juniors, a shrimp of a man who was to become the wonder of the football world and provide a name which would span all future decades of Celtic history. They arrived just in time because Somers had gone to Hamilton, Hay to Newcastle and Kivlichan to Bradford. Quinn, after so many injury-free years, was appearing only intermittently because of closer marking. But he returned to help his team win the Scottish Cup of 1911 when he scored one of the goals in the 2–0 defeat of Hamilton Accies. It was a campaign in which Celtic lost not a single goal. They came fifth in the League and went on a close-season tour of Dresden, Prague, Budapest, Vienna and Basle, returning in time to take in the Epsom Derby.

The season of 1911–12 saw Quinn reproduce some of his earlier form and he scaled the heights again in the New Year match with Rangers by scoring all three goals in the 3–0 victory. By this time McAtee and Gallagher were already making a name for themselves on the right flank. The team repeated their success of the previous season by again winning the Scottish Cup with goals by Gallagher and McMenemy, who had moved to inside-left, giving them a 2–0 win over Clyde. The winning team was: Mulrooney, McNair, Dodds, Young, Loney, Johnstone, McAtee, Gallagher, Quinn, McMenemy, Brown. They also beat Clyde to take the Charity Cup and improved their League position to second place. In the close season they played in Denmark and Norway. The nimble Gallagher was getting rave notices everywhere. He had elusive dribbling, artful passes and dangerous shooting, said one publication. The writer continued: 'He is a marvel. He has no stamina to make a song about, but he takes risks that many a bigger and heavier man would not think of, and the marvel is that he comes out of it scatheless.'

In the season of 1912–13 Celtic finished behind Rangers who won the Championship, but beat them in the Charity Cup Final, a match in which goalkeeper Charlie Shaw from Queen's Park Rangers made his Celtic début.

The last season before the war, 1913–14, was highly successful. After a weak start Celtic won the Championship which had a total of twenty-five teams! They played twenty-three consecutive matches without defeat, scoring fifty-two goals for the loss of only two. The Scottish Cup was won for the third time in four years with a 4–1 victory over Hibs after a drawn game and they also won the Charity Cup with a 6–0 win over Third Lanark. They then left on yet another tour of Europe.

It was in July 1914, referring to the assassination of the Archduke Ferdinand and his wife at Sarajevo, that a reporter who had accompanied Celtic on tour commented it was unlikely they would see Europe the following year.

How true his words were. With the outbreak of war it was to be several years before the opportunity would show itself again. In that climate there was naturally some uncertainty about the future of professional football.

There was a minor newspaper campaign to have the game stopped with the view that popular footballers seen joining up would be a tremendous lift to the nation. Another view was that if football stopped tens of thousands of young men would join up out of sheer boredom. The football grounds were also used to make appeals during half-time for volunteers. They were told that they should join up before they missed all the fun. The war was going to finish in 1915 and certainly by 1916! The Scottish and English football associations decided in that first war year to abandon international matches and the SFA, after consultation with the Secretary for War, also decided to scrap the Scottish Cup that year.

With a big increase in industry and more hands being required in the munitions factories professional footballers were obliged to take their place alongside the machines with everyone else. To ensure this the SFA ruled that players' wages be no more than £2 a week. No wages were paid during the close season and League matches were confined to Saturdays and holidays. There was a further ruling that no player would be allowed to take part in a game who had not devoted the rest of the week doing useful work – preferably government employment. In addition to the League Championship the Glasgow Cup and Glasgow Charity Cup survived.

Celtic's usual team in the season of 1914–15 was: Shaw, McNair,

Dodds, Young, Johnstone, McMaster, McAtee, Gallagher, McColl, McMenemy, Browning.

Although the dashing Quinn played only six times because of injury, Celtic took the Championship for the twelfth time in their twenty-five-year history – an amazing achievement. In thirty-eight games they won thirty, lost three, drew five and scored ninety-one goals for the loss of only twenty-five giving them a total of 65 points. They had gone through half the Championship without losing a single goal and dropped only one point in nineteen matches. They also won the Charity Cup, beating Rangers. In a game for the Belgian War Relief Fund in 1916 they beat an all-Scotland Select 1–0.

When the season of 1915–16 dawned the famous name of Jimmy Quinn was no longer there but the young Gallagher was coming along well. Though attendances were dropping because of the war-time conditions, the Old Firm could still bring out the crowds and this was demonstrated in the Glasgow Cup Final on 9 October 1915 when 90000 spectators turned up to see Celtic win by 2–1. The club added another milestone to their list that year. Celtic held the record – achieved in 1913–14 – for the lowest number of goals conceded by a League team – a total of fourteen.

On 1 April they beat Raith Rovers 6–0 giving them a total of 104 goals – one more than the record set by Falkirk in the season of 1907–08. But that was not the end of this remarkable achievement and remarkable day. Celtic had discovered that they had one game more than the number of remaining Saturdays of the season and because of the wartime regulations decided to play a second game later on in the day.

At 3.15 p.m. the following team lined up against Raith Rovers at Parkhead: Shaw, McNair, McGregor, Young, Dodds, McMaster, McAtee, Gallagher, O'Kane, McMenemy, Browning. At 6 p.m. the same team, with the exception of the injured O'Kane who was replaced by 'Trooper' Joe Cassidy, took the field at Motherwell and won 3–1. They played their last game the following Saturday and emerged Champions for the thirteenth time in the twenty-six years of the League and therefore held as many flags as were held by every other club combined. To complete a memorable year the Champions went on to play in their twenty-first Charity Cup Final and win it for the fourteenth time by beating Partick Thistle 2–0 at Hampden and making it five-in-a-row in that particular competition – a feat they had achieved in the years 1892–6. No other team in Scotland could live with their achievements.

1916–17 saw Celtic beat Rangers in the semi-final and Clyde in the Final of the Glasgow Cup to take the trophy for the eleventh time. They remained in rampant form and until the second-to-last League game of the season were unbeaten. But Kilmarnock ended a run of sixty-six matches without defeat which had stretched from 11 December 1915 until 14 April 1917 and ruined the team's chances of ending the season without a reverse. Despite that particular disappointment the Championship came to Paradise once more and for the fourth time in succession. To the Glasgow Cup and League Championship Celtic added the Charity Cup for the sixth year in succession and the fifteenth time in twenty-eight years.

It was in that Charity Cup competition that Willie Cringan made his début. He had been transferred from Sunderland, who had closed shop because of the war, for a then Celtic record fee of £600.

Celtic's chance of making it five championships in a row and a step nearer equalling that famous record of ten years earlier took a terrible knock when Johnstone, McMaster, Dodds, McAtee, McStay, Cassidy, Ribchester, Cringan, McCabe, Gilhooley and Jackson were called up to the Forces, and predictably they failed to win, coming second to Rangers by one point. But they did win the Charity Cup for a record-breaking seventh successive time. Although the City Fathers had failed to recognize the magnificent Charity Cup run with as much as a sociable cup of tea Rangers got a civic lunch when they won it the following season!

With the declaration of the Armistice on 11 November 1918 Celtic's players came home from war and by the spring of 1919 had again won the Championship. Had it not been for the heavy demand on Celtic players by their country that sixth successive championship would surely have come to pass.

Before passing on to the post-war era it is worth taking stock of Celtic's achievements. As a club they had made a phenomenal impact on Scottish football right from the outset. In all competitions they had created extraordinary records. The result was that no matter what they achieved they occasioned no surprise. Above all, however, they provided at all times for the spectator both as individuals and as a team a style of football that was unique and a delight to witness.

A disgruntled player once said that in any game in which Mc-

Menemy played there should be two balls – one for him and one for the rest of the players. McMenemy was the master of the deceptive movement. He could shake off a cloud of opponents by one simple turn. McNair was equally brilliant and had the science of achieving the maximum result with the minimum of effort. Then came the peerless Patsy Gallagher, reckoned by some to be the greatest Celt of all time. He had commentators of the time exhausting their repertory of metaphors. He was the mighty atom, the vital spark, the will o' the wisp and a dozen other extravagances. Jimmy Quinn had been a one-man army. These more than any made Celtic great. Obviously there were other fine players but the mention of these four indicates at least that brilliant football is not the monopoly of any particular period in the history of the game.

8 The Not So Roaring Twenties

Despite the First World War and its call on their playing resources, Celtic could muster a squad of twenty-four players in that first post-war season of 1919–20. They had: Shaw, McNair, Dodds, Livingstone, McStay, Cringan, Brown, Gilchrist, Price, McAvoy, McAtee, Gallagher, McColl, McMenemy, McLean, Cassidy, Craig, Pratt, Burns, Mitchell, McInally, McKay, Ribchester and Watson. Although high-scoring left-winger Browning left for Chelsea, Celtic had enough men to run a reserve side. The First Division had been expanded to twenty-two teams with the newcomers being Clydebank and the team which was to nurture Jock Stein a generation later – Albion Rovers. Celtic were unbeaten at home and lost only three League matches in the entire season yet only managed second place! They made up for that disappointment, however, by winning the Glasgow Cup, the Charity Cup and the War Memorial Benefit competition. With the great McMenemy reaching the end of his playing days young Joe Cassidy took his place and eighteen-year-old Tommy McInally began catching the eye. He scored thirty-nine goals and was hailed as the natural successor to Jimmy Quinn, although he was to develop into an entirely different type of player. The regulars of the day were: Shaw, McNair, Dodds (or McStay), Gilchrist, Cringan, Brown, McAtee, Gallagher, McInally, McMenemy (or Cassidy), McLean. These men played to big crowds eager for entertainment after four years of terrible war. Despite an increase in admittance charges from sixpence to one shilling gates rose and in that same season Celtic had an income of £45 600 – a record for Scotland.

The club had not forgotten about the great unemployment of the time and introduced what was commonly known as the 'Buroo Gate' for those who were on the dole. The end of that first post-war season saw the departure of McMenemy and Dodds who went to Partick Thistle and Cowdenbeath respectively. The great McMenemy had given eighteen years' service to Celtic and although he was past his best when he went to Thistle he was still good enough to help them to a Scottish Cup win in his second season. Dodds, after only a year with Cowdenbeath, returned to Parkhead.

The season of 1920–1 saw Celtic again with the Glasgow and Charity Cups and again finish second in the League. They spent a week in France at the end of the campaign during which they played at Lille and Paris.

The following season, 1921–2, saw Celtic reverse the trends of the previous two years. This time they won the League but no cups. It was their sixteenth Championship and they played twenty-three consecutive games in the tournament without losing a goal. In the forty-two games they emerged victors twenty-seven times, lost only two and drew thirteen with eighty-three goals for and twenty against. They lost only two points at home, one to Falkirk and one to Rangers, and only four of the twenty-one visiting teams were able to penetrate the Celtic defence – Queen's Park, Hibs, Ayr and Albion Rovers who each got one goal. The other seventeen were sent packing empty-handed with only Falkirk and Rangers preventing the Celts from scoring. The two defeats were by only one goal, with Kilmarnock winning 3–2 and Hibs winning by 2–1. With that majestic record to content them, they had the added bonus of winning the Reserve League.

The Continent called again with a close-season tour to Czechoslovakia. Celtic got a very rough passage from the local club Slavia, had eight players injured and had to postpone the following game. They moved on to Berlin and played in the new stadium which had been built for the abortive 1916 Olympic Games. Of the three tour games played the record was: won 0, lost 2, drawn 1.

That stormy petrel of Scottish football, Tommy McInally, had left under a cloud for Third Lanark and Dodds departed again – this time for good. Manager Willie Maley explained McInally's departure in the following words: 'He is not re-engaged due to the demands he made which were turned down by the Board.' But there were arrivals to offset the departures, among them Hughie Hilley from St Anthony's Juniors who went to left-back. John 'Jean' McFarlane, who had arrived from the Fife junior team Glencraig Celtic the previous year, got his chance in the forward position, and the new line-up read:

Shaw, McNair, Hilley, Gilchrist, Cringan, McStay, McAtee, Gallagher, Cassidy, McFarlane, McLean. From Glencraig also in 1922 came the clever Alec Thomson, one of the finest-ever Parkhead inside-forwards. But the really big signing of the year was a slip of a lad from St Roch's Juniors in Glasgow's rugged Garngad area – James Edward McGrory. At the time no one could have realized what an effect he would have on Celtic's history, promising as he was.

In a fabulous personal playing career spanning fifteen years he scored a world record 550 goals, goals which are still a British record to this day. He had the true Celtic spirit and the size of his heart made him a hero with the fans. Signed for a mere £10, he became the greatest menace to goalkeepers in the history of the game in these islands. He was top scorer every year from 1924 till 1936 with the exception of 1934, an amazing record of consistency. He scored eight goals in a League game against Dunfermline Athletic, still a British First Division record. He also scored three goals in three minutes against Motherwell. But it was to be the best part of a year before he would make his first-team début.

After winning the Championship of 1921–2 Celtic hit a bad patch of inconsistency. They lost in the first round of the Glasgow Cup to Queen's Park who had dropped into the Second Division. And as if that were not bad enough they had dropped twenty-five points by the middle of December.

Then, from 30 December 1922 when they beat Raith Rovers at Kirkcaldy, until they defeated St Mirren at Parkhead on 27 February 1923 they played eight League games without a victory. Despite the bad run they finished third. They won back favour with the fans by winning the Scottish Cup for the tenth time and equalling Queen's Park's record. The 1–0 win over Hibs in the Final saw the remarkable McNair, aged forty, stand head and shoulders above them all, giving the greatest performance of his life – knowing it was probably his last big chance. Another pleasing aspect of the season was the introduction of Paddy Connolly on the wing.

The season of 1923–4 saw the signing of Peter Wilson from Beith, a boy destined to become one of the great half-backs of all time. The Celtic captain, Willie Cringan, approached the Board on behalf of the players and asked for a £2 win bonus and £1 for a draw. But chairman Tom White, father of present chairman Desmond, would have none of it. He pointed out that Celtic players were being paid between £8 and £9, more than average, and that they got bonuses for important matches. An early exit in the Scottish Cup at the hands of Kilmarnock and a Glasgow Cup defeat by Rangers put paid to bonuses that year and to crown it all Partick Thistle beat Celts at Parkhead for the first time in twenty-five years of First Division football! In September Cringan left for Third Lanark and was replaced at centre-half by Willie McStay. Jimmy McGrory was recalled from Clydebank to whom he had been farmed out.

He played in a second-round Charity Cup tie against Queen's Park at Hampden and scored a characteristic goal within seconds of the start. Celtic went on to beat Rangers in the Final and lifted the Cup for the nineteenth time. Jimmy McGrory, at outside-left, gave a remarkable display. At the end of the season 1923–4 Cassidy left for Bolton and opened the door at centre-forward for McGrory, who began hitting the net with amazing regularity.

The young McGrory, with a Charity medal already in his possession, looked forward to a Scottish Cup medal at the start of the season 1924–5 and after a terrible run of injuries which had hit him, Gallagher and McLean, Celtic got off to a dream start in that competition by beating Third Lanark 5–1 in the opening round.

Next victims were Alloa and Solway Star and that set Celtic up for one of their most dramatic-ever confrontations in the Scottish Cup. The fourth round took them to Paisley to meet St Mirren and the game ended in a goalless draw. The replay ended 1–1 after extra time. So the scene was set for a thriller at Ibrox, venue for the second replay. McGrory put Celtic ahead and victory seemed certain as the game entered its final stages. But Gillies of Saints was tackled on the edge of the penalty box by McStay and the Paisley men claimed a penalty. Peter Craigmyle, a real character of a referee from Aberdeen, knelt down dramatically to examine the spot closely and awarded a free kick against Celtic. St Mirren would have none of it and they refused to touch the ball. Both teams stood facing each other and the tension was unbelievable. But the referee solved the problem by whistling for time up.

The semi-final attracted 100 000 to Hampden and the big question in the Press was: 'Can Rangers break the hoodoo?' Twenty-two years had elapsed since their last Scottish Cup Final victory but following the game they were still very much in the wilderness. Celtic hammered them 5–0 with McGrory (2), McLean (2) and Thomson (1) being the scorers. The Celtic team was: Shevlin, W. McStay, Hilley,

Wilson, J. McStay, McFarlane, Connolly, Gallagher, McGrory, Thomson, McLean. Although the Final itself attracted only 80000 it produced one of the great legendary tales of Scottish football and it was a combined, devastating move from the brains and feet of Patsy Gallagher.

Dundee had opened the scoring and with only seven minutes to go were stoutly defending their slender lead. When your author was writing *A Lifetime in Paradise*, the Jimmy McGrory story, Jimmy himself described in detail the goal which helped to bring him his first Scottish Cup medal at his first attempt. In that particular interview he said:

The Dundee goal came as a tremendous shock but it acted as a spur to bring about the greatest goal I have ever seen and aptly enough it came from the greatest player I have ever seen – Patsy Gallagher. He took a pass from Peter Wilson and with that peculiar, dragging motion of his he meandered past man after man. The Dundee left-back made a final desperate tackle to stop him and he crashed to the ground to the roar of 'penalty' from the Celtic crowd. But in falling he had craftily kept the ball lodged between his feet and as the keeper came out he somersaulted into the back of the net with the ball still firmly in the grip of his feet.

There was absolute pandemonium and the Dundee players were stunned. That move had beaten them and although it was only 1–1 they knew they were beaten. For me the greatest moment had still to come. In the closing minutes 'Jean' McFarlane took a long free kick and I kept my eye on it all the way. As it dropped I dived and headed it hard but I hit the ground so hard that I stunned myself. All I could hear was the roar and although I didn't see the ball go into the back of the net I knew it was a goal. I lay there and I remember saying to myself: 'This is the Cup.'

The young McGrory was handed the Cup by manager Willie Maley as the victorious team left Hampden and he was told to sit up front with the trophy. The end of that season saw Shaw, at forty, leave to become player-manager of a team in the United States. With him he took Andy McAtee and a few others. Alec McNair, at the age of forty-two, departed to become manager and secretary to Dundee after giving a magnificent twenty-one years of service to Celtic. To balance that, however, the wayward McInally came back and it could not have been at a more opportune moment because time and injuries were catching up with the magician himself, Patsy Gallagher. McInally had developed into a crafty tactician of the McMenemy type and he, McLean and McFarlane formed a highly polished trio. His main attribute was his ability to stop dead in his tracks with the ball and have the entire scene surveyed in a split second. On the other wing Thomson, with Wilson behind him, made the ideal partner for Connolly.

Meanwhile McGrory was improving with every game and developing that uncanny accuracy which was to bring him his record-scoring feats. Four of the five goals he scored in the New Year matches of 1925–6 were with his head.

A new official rule, which reduced from three to two the number of opponents required to place a player onside, and which was introduced to stop annoying defensive tactics, speeded up play and this suited Celtic who had a young and fast team. Wilson, Connolly, McGrory and Shevlin were mere youths and McLean, McInally, Thomson, McFarlane, Hilley and Jimmy McStay were still in young manhood. After an easy passage in the Scottish Cup they met St Mirren in the Final and flopped miserably by 2–0. But they won the League for the seventeenth time without losing a single home match. They lost the Glasgow Cup Final to Second Division Clyde, but won the Charity Cup for the twentieth time. McGrory scored a total of thirty-five goals and the club profit was more than £6000 – not altogether a bad year. The projected American tour, which had been a dream within the club from the earliest days, was again called off. The end of that year also saw the last of Patsy Gallagher in a Celtic jersey. He had all but vanished from the team in the previous months due to illness and injury. But when he was fit he could still summon to his aid, as he showed in the Scottish Cup ties, a superlative gift of artistry and an astonishing quality of endurance.

He was always outstanding on the field, but when his team faced the possibility of defeat then he became more than himself. He was one of the great characters of the game. Those who knew him would tell you that he would have been a star in any era. He was one of those naturally fit men. He did not have to train much and in his later years with the club, he would arrive and train alone in the afternoons, having obtained permission to look after his two pubs in the mornings. But he was the only player allowed such privileges. And only because of his genius and natural fitness. He could win games when other people were just thinking about it.

Off the field he had a touch of the Charlie Tully about him. He was a great practical joker. In the dressing-room he would always have a joke and a song for his mates before the most important of matches. Two of the best-known Celtic tales involve Patsy Gallagher. On one occasion he got hold of a young player who was out training and decided to take him down a peg or two because he was getting too big for his boots. He told him: 'Just you remember you are in the team because you have a bit of pace. Don't get any notions you are here for any other reason. When you get to the by-line I want you to get the ball across for Jimmy McGrory's head – and make sure the lace is away from his forehead.' The story goes that the young player, in awe, went off and practised. There was the other occasion when he dressed up as a woman to get out of an hotel at Dunbar where Celtic were on special training before a Cup tie. He borrowed clothes from a woman worker in the hotel and lowered his own clothes in a bundle out of the bedroom window onto the lawn. Manager Willie Maley was stationed down in the front hall that night to make sure there was no nonsense and everyone else was in bed. Then, bold as you like, Patsy came downstairs, a black veil over his face. Not content to slip by his boss, he could not resist giving a high-pitched 'Good night' to which he got a very courteous reply from Mr Maley. Off he went on the town after changing into his own clothes in a garden shed. But his plan did not work 100 per cent. Mr Maley found out the following day and gave him a real roasting. Jimmy McGrory asked him how the boss found out and Patsy's reply was: 'It's a secret.'

Patsy moved onto Falkirk from Celtic and did his old club a really good turn. He masterminded his team's victory over Rangers in the Scottish Cup. Rangers paid little heed to him as he was, in their opinion, well past it. So Patsy sent a perfect pass half the length of the field right onto a forward's boot and Rangers went out. Celtic went on to win the Cup that year.

Patsy's successor, Tommy McInally, himself a real character, had much of Patsy's cool craftiness. His imperturbable dribbling and placing of the ball came to the fore the following season, 1926–7, in which Celtic beat Rangers in the Final of the Glasgow Cup. Two weeks later, in a 6–2 win over Aberdeen, McGrory scored four with his head and one with a foot and evoked the comment from the Press: 'McGrory's head is now esteemed as Celtic's most priceless possession.'

Another priceless possession was added to the club's treasures that season – this time it was a pair of hands. They belonged to a young lad from the Fife club of Wellesley Juniors. His name was John Thomson. He was only eighteen when he made his début

E

against Dundee at Dens Park and the generation who saw him in action will agree that it would be hard for a chronicler to exaggerate his magical skill. This chronicler will not try. Instead I will reproduce, a little later, the entire chapter 'John' from *A Lifetime in Paradise*. It is in Jimmy McGrory's words and he was on the field of play the day John died. To my mind it is the finest account of John Thomson's life and death.

It was a season in which his great friend McGrory showed rampant form. On three occasions – against Aberdeen, Dundee United and Clyde – he scored five goals. In seven successive victories the team scored twenty-six goals and lost only two. They hit a bad patch however, in mid-season and it took McGrory to lift them out of the rut. On 26 February 1927 he beat the League record of forty-five goals in one season set by St Mirren's Duncan Walker some years earlier. When McGrory came onto the field that day at Parkhead – the opposition was aptly St Mirren – he had forty-three goals to his credit and by the end of the match he had scored another four and was carried shoulder high to the pavilion by players and fans.

A couple of broken ribs in a League match against Falkirk prevented McGrory adding to his impressive score. He raised it to forty-nine but his absence from the remaining games was the chief reason that Celtic failed to win the Championship. They reached their nineteenth Scottish Cup Final and won it for the twelfth time by beating East Fife 3–1 at Hampden on 16 April. John Thomson and John McMenemy, a son of the old player, won medals in their first season. McGrory, although he missed the Final, was presented with a Scottish Cup medal by the club in recognition of his achievements.

Hilley retired at the end of the season and his place at left-back was taken by William McGonagle, who, for some reason, became known as Peter. 1927–8 opened brightly for Celtic. John Thomson had taken over in goal from Peter Shevlin who had left on a free transfer to South Shields. Celts scored eighteen goals in the opening six League games and lost only one. Then at Hampden on 8 October in front of 90000 spectators they beat Rangers 2–1 in the Final of the Glasgow Cup. They again beat Rangers in the New Year game and then on 14 January 1928 McGrory created a world record by notching eight goals – not one with his head – against Dunfermline Athletic at Parkhead. The previous best had been six. There was just no stopping him and by January he had piled up a total of thirty-six League goals, including four against St Mirren and hat-tricks against St Johnstone, Queen's Park and Falkirk. By April he had scored forty-five League goals.

Celtic beat Motherwell in the fourth round of the Scottish Cup although they were without McInally who had been suspended for indiscipline – the second time that season. They beat Queen's Park in the semi-final and for the fourth year in succession lined up at Hampden Park in the Final. Their opponents were Rangers. Not since their victory over Hearts in 1903 had Rangers won the Cup. In the fifty years of their existence they had won it only four times. They were twenty-two years old before they won it at all. Celtic, more than ten years younger, had won it twelve times, and went into the game as favourites with the following team: J. Thomson, W. McStay, Donoghue, Wilson, J. McStay, McFarlane, Connolly, A. Thomson, McGrory, McInally, McLean.

Rangers sent out: T. Hamilton, Gray, R. Hamilton, Buchanan, Meiklejohn, Craig, Archibald, Cunningham, Fleming, McPhail, Morton. The turnstiles clicked 118115 times, a record for Scottish football, probably also a British record. Two higher claims from England had lacked the authenticity of a turnstile check. Rangers played against the wind in the first half and had keeper Hamilton to thank for leaving the field on level terms at half-time. He had defied McLean, Thomson and Connolly with brilliant saves. With the wind at their backs in the second half and a penalty award after McStay cleared with his hand, Rangers took control of a game that had threatened to go either way. Meiklejohn converted the kick and a short time later McPhail added a second. Archibald scored two more and Rangers ran out worthy winners and ended that twenty-five-year famine in style.

The 1928 Final was remembered not only for Rangers' four-goal victory but also for the admirable spirit in which Celtic players had taken the defeat. It was one of the cleanest-fought games ever played between the two great rivals. The Celtic players congratulated their conquerors at the end and the supporters of both teams stayed on in the ground to cheer and cheer. It was a good year for Rangers. They also won the League and the Charity Cup. After their fine start, all Celtic had to show was the Glasgow Cup and second place in the Championship. There was a bit of discord within the club at the end of the season and the strong man, manager Willie Maley, was not there to take control of matters due to illness which had kept him off for a considerable part of the season.

Again a proposed US tour was called off and McInally, who had those two blots on his copybook, was again on his travels – this time to Sunderland. His departure brought about anger from the support. He was the team's best brain and the sheep were now without a shepherd. McInally had been a natural footballer. He could think three moves ahead and he controlled play with ease. But, like most characters, he fell foul of the men at the top of the house. He was often a discontented player and irked the management. The time had come for a final separation. With him to Sunderland went the highly talented McLean, a man described by Jimmy McGrory as a far greater player than Alan Morton of Rangers, the Wee Blue Devil himself. McGrory certainly missed those accurate crosses after his departure. Sunderland and English football were lucky indeed to inherit such a left-sided partnership.

Besides advertising that McLean was for transfer, the management also circularized English and Scottish clubs that Connolly and Doyle were for sale. But the biggest shock of all came when they let Arsenal interview Jimmy McGrory. He had already signed for 1928-9 so the move was really a shock for the fans and, as it turned out, for the player himself. There was something far wrong at Parkhead when they were prepared to let go a player of McGrory's calibre and loyalty. A former Celtic player called the management of the time 'the Catholic Jews'. They bred players, he said, to sell them and make money. This was a charge that was strongly denied by the management.

The McGrory transfer story was incredible. He had already turned down an approach from Arsenal and thought the matter had ended. When he left on holiday with Willie Maley for Lourdes that summer he was shocked to find the famous Arsenal manager Herbert Chapman waiting to meet him in London. He again said he was not interested and he and Mr Maley continued on their journey to Lourdes. Tommy McInally was to have gone with them but his departure to Sunderland put an end to the holiday! Maley and McGrory did not discuss the transfer bid during their week-long holiday and headed back home. When they arrived in London Mr Chapman was again waiting for them. McGrory was furious but was talked into a meeting at a nearby hotel. Maley left the room and Chapman offered McGrory everything but the moon. He had also offered Celtic a British record fee of some £10000 – an absolute fortune in those days. Still McGrory would have none of it.

McGrory recalled some years later: 'He told me they would paint London to get me. I was very flattered but I had not the slightest intention of leaving Celtic. To put an end to the matter I asked Mr Chapman for £2000 knowing that it would do the trick. It did. He refused and I returned home with Mr Maley. It was an incident that upset me because although I was getting only £8 a week I wanted only to play for Celtic. Yet they had been prepared to sell me. But I got over it. McGrory of Arsenal would never have sounded as good as McGrory of Celtic.'

Jimmy McGrory continued to score goals for Celtic and he did not even get a rise, despite the fact that he could have become Britain's most expensive football property. Had he gone gates would surely have fallen. There was already a growing band of disgruntled supporters because Celtic had a healthy cash reserve yet they seemed hell-bent on killing the golden goose. The affair was smoothed over, however, with Connolly also staying on at Parkhead.

The new season opened with John McMenemy at inside-right and Alec Thomson moving to inside-left. Thomson assumed the position of McInally as playmaker and a newcomer called Peter Scarff arrived from Maryhill Hibs. The wounds of the previous season and close season seemed to have been cured and the team played traditional Celtic football. They beat Rangers in the first round of the Glasgow Cup and went on to beat a strong Queen's Park in the Final by 2–0 and won the trophy for the sixteenth time. John Thomson was turning in unbelievable performances and the crowds rolled in.

But as the season advanced, a bit of inconsistency crept in and injuries to McGrory meant a makeshift forward line for some time. They reached the semi-final of the Scottish Cup where they went down 1–0 to Kilmarnock who went on to win the trophy. From the end of March Celtic had to play all their home games at Shawfield because of a fire which destroyed the old pavilion on the 28th of that month. Most of the club records were destroyed but luckily trophies were housed elsewhere. The Grant Stand, mentioned earlier, was at that time in the process of demolition so there was nowhere to accommodate visiting teams.

The Glasgow Cup was the only trophy they had to show for that disappointing season and further sadness came to the club with the departures of Willie McStay and John 'Jean' McFarlane. McStay, who had signed from Netherburn Juniors in 1912, had given long service at half-back and full-back. He went to Hearts and his brother, Jimmy, took over as captain. McFarlane, a man with a long, raking stride and tremendous close control, went to Middlesbrough.

The covered terracing along the north side of the ground had been re-roofed and the new stand was ready for the start of the season 1929–30. Experienced players like Adam McLean had not been replaced and as a result the team struggled. There was much switching of players from position to position but it did little good. McGrory was again out with injuries. John Thomson broke his jawbone and fractured ribs against Airdrie and by the end of December Celtic were in the doldrums. They suffered four defeats in a row over the New Year period and worse was to follow. They were knocked out of the Scottish Cup 3–1 by St Mirren in the third round and in the Charity Cup such was their luck they could not even guess correctly in the tossing of a coin! When they lined up against Rangers on 10 May 1930 in the Charity Final the Ibrox side had already won the League, Scottish Cup and Glasgow Cup. Celtic already had the distinction of being the only team to win those three plus the Charity Cup. That had come in 1907–08. When the whistle blew for time up the teams were equal with two goals and four corners each. A coin was tossed and the Rangers skipper called correctly. So they too had won four honours although they can never claim to have won all of them outright!

So Celtic finished the season without a trophy. It had been a bad decade when compared with the brilliant days before the war. But they had still managed, despite the toll of that war, two Championships, three Scottish Cups, four Charity Cups and five Glasgow Cups. In John Thomson and McGrory they had two outstanding players and they had the memory of many fine players of the decade who had been worthy successors to the earlier players.

The end of the Twenties marked the end of the famous annual sports meeting at Celtic Park which had been such a regular feature since the early days of the club, the first being in 1890. Willie Maley, himself a keen amateur runner in his younger days, had been the mainstay of the meetings over the years and travelled far and wide to sign up every possible kind of attraction from a wide range of sports including, as earlier mentioned, cycling, motor-cycling and military displays. At its height it could attract crowds of around 25000. But the lean years after the war and the increase in unemployment saw a fall-off in the attendance figures. Several attempts were made to introduce new attractions but they failed. In 1926 it was held in midweek as opposed to the normal Saturday and when Scottish League commitments came earlier in August over the next few years it gave the club an excuse to abandon the event.

9 John Thomson

The regular Celtic line-up for the season of 1930–1 was: John Thomson, Cook, McGonagle, Wilson, McStay, Geatons, R. Thomson, A. Thomson, McGrory, Scarff, Napier. The two newcomers were Bert Thomson, a superbly skilful and swift winger, and Charlie Napier, later nicknamed 'Happy Feet' because of his zigzag runs. He also packed a powerful shot and could put in a hefty tackle when the occasion demanded. Jimmy McGrory was a late-comer to the action because of injury but could have picked no better occasion than the one he did to return. He lined up against Rangers at Celtic Park on 20 September and played his part in a 2–0 win. The following month Celtic played and beat Rangers again, this time by 2–1 in the Glasgow Cup Final at Hampden in front of 80000 spectators. It was their seventeenth victory in the competition.

But the big story of the season was not to take place until nearer the end. It was the Scottish Cup Final, Celtic's twenty-first appearance, and one of the most dramatic ever. Before reaching that particular pinnacle, however, Celtic had to beat East Fife 2–1 away, Dundee United 3–2 away, Morton 4–1 away, Aberdeen 4–0 at home and Kilmarnock 3–0 in the semi-final, far from an easy passage. Their opponents were Motherwell and 105000 people clicked through the Hampden turnstiles on 11 April. The longed-for tour of America was at last to take place in the close season and Celtic were particularly anxious to win the Cup to take over to the many thousands of exiles.

In the days leading up to the Final, most of Scotland's Press devoted large chunks of their columns to advising Motherwell how they could overcome Celtic. After eighty-two minutes of the game it looked as if all the coaching had paid off as Motherwell were leading 2–0. Celtic's team that day was: J. Thomson, Cook, McGonagle,

Wilson, McStay, Geatons, R. Thomson, A. Thomson, McGrory, Scarff, Napier. Motherwell fielded: McClory, Johnman, Hunter, Wales, Craig, Telfer, Murdoch, McMenemy, McFadyen, Stevenson, Ferrier.

Modern-day Celtic fans will be well aware of the tremendous glee which greets a Celtic reverse in other grounds in Scotland. At Parkhead Celtic fans cheer when Rangers are defeated but when Celtic lose the result is warmly greeted in most places. In more recent times one cannot help but recall Press reports in October 1971 when Partick Thistle defeated Celtic in a 4–1 League Cup Final win at Hampden. That day Rangers were playing at Ibrox and had been booed from the field at half-time. When they emerged for the second half they were greeted like heroes. There was uncontained jubilation on the terracings after the half-time announcement and Rangers went on to trounce the opposition.

So it was forty years earlier. Dr James E. Handley (Brother Clare), author of the early *Celtic Story*, was a spectator at Dens Park that day. He recalled in his book:

The writer remembers sitting that afternoon at the far end of the long, obtuse-angled stand at Dens Park when shortly after half-time a boy appeared in the distance and traversed the length of it with a board on his shoulder.

As he passed each section a mighty roar arose, which was taken up in turn until the whole stand was one stentorian paean and the game on the field had been forgotten. After the match was over the crowd tarried in pleasurable anticipation. In the distance the youth appeared again with the board on his shoulder but this time he made his way along in an atmosphere of graveyard stillness. Obviously something disastrous had happened – and obviously not to Celtic.

All those miles away at Hampden Celtic had been drawing on all their fighting tradition and launching attack after furious attack on the Motherwell defence which was conceding fouls by the second. McGrory's voice could be heard in the stand amidst the pandemonium from the crowd as he urged his mates to keep going. With six minutes to go Charlie Napier, who had been shooting on sight, changed tactics and lobbed the ball high over the Motherwell defence. The tireless McGrory launched himself at it and it ended up in the back of the net. The tension was unbelievable as the ball was quickly centred. Celtic got possession and surged forward again and again. Then, with only two minutes to go, it happened. Outside-right

Bertie Thomson crossed and McGrory came charging in for a header. Motherwell centre-half Alan Craig intercepted as from the corner of his eye he saw McGrory blur in. But – alas for Alan and brave Motherwell – he bulleted the ball past his own keeper as he tried to head clear for a corner. When the final whistle sounded seconds later, Craig was still lying face down beating the ground with his fists.

So late had come the equalizer that one Glasgow newspaper jumped the gun and released papers showing a result in Motherwell's favour and had then the frantic task of recalling them from shops and street corners!

As it turned out, that own goal was the launching pad for Celtic to win the Cup for the thirteenth time. The following Wednesday night 100000 turned up and saw Celtic win 4–2 with Bertie Thomson and Jimmy McGrory notching two goals apiece.

All eyes were now focused on the dream of Celtic generations – the first American tour. On 13 May, therefore, a party of around two dozen boarded the steamer *Caledonia* at Yorkhill Quay and were overwhelmed by the turnout of fans. The Scottish Cup was held aloft to 15000 cheers as the ship drew slowly away from the quayside. The party comprised directors T. Colgan, J. Kelly, J. McKillop and T. White; manager Willie Maley, and players J. Thomson, Cook, McGonagle, J. Morrison, Wilson, J. McStay, Geatons, R. Whitelaw, D. Currie, W. Hughes, R. Thomson, A. Thomson, J. McGrory, P. Scarff, C. Napier, J. McGhee, H. Smith, plus trainers. They landed in New York nine days later and the reception at that end matched the scenes they had left behind in Glasgow. But it was a reception which went on and on and was really no preparation for playing football, even if the games were termed friendlies. Jubilation and feasting became routine as exiles travelled hundreds of miles to catch a glimpse of their heroes and the Scottish Cup. To add to all the clamour Celtic players had also to contend with the humid heat of the Atlantic seaboard.

Despite all the distractions the team got off to a good start by beating Pennsylvania All Stars by 6–1. The following day the party returned to New York and Celtic beat the New York Giants 3–2. There was a six-day gap until the next game and the feasting and travelling began to take their toll. So it was no real surprise when the New York Yankees beat their famous Glasgow visitors by 4–3. The following day saw Celtic go down again, this time to the Fall River team by 1–0. That result was due largely to a stubborn goalkeeper called Joe Kennaway. Little did anyone know how soon they would be seeing him again.

Results picked up again despite the hard-baked narrow grounds which were more suitable for baseball than football and cramped Celtic's style indeed. They also found the American players with a win-at-all-costs attitude which made the games rather tough. Celts lost to Pawtucket Rangers 3–1 and added the scalps of Brooklyn (5–0) and Montreal Carsteel (7–0). The following game on 14 June against the Jewish side Hakoah was a real farce thanks to bad refereeing. McGrory had his jaw broken and was taken to hospital. And Celtic, like their opponents, had two men ordered off, namely Scarff and Napier. The game ended in a 1–1 draw. Celtic played five more games in quick succession and won them all, beating Chicago Bricklayers 6–3, Michigan All Stars 5–0, Ulster United at Toronto 3–1, New York Yankees 4–1 and Baltimore 4–1.

Of the thirteen games Celtic emerged with nine wins, three defeats and one draw. They scored forty-eight goals and lost eighteen. The highest attendance had been 40000 against New York Giants.

It was a tired group which boarded the liner *Transylvania* to return home although they had the deep contentment of knowing that they had given so much pleasure to so many exiles who had dreamed for years of such a visit. They arrived home laden with trophies and ornaments to enjoy the few weeks left before the hard slog of training for a new season. One famous name missing was Jimmy McGrory. He had left the boat off the north coast of Ireland and gone ashore by launch to get married in Moville.

The season of 1931–2 opened with more or less the same playing staff. One new name on the list was that of Bobby Hogg from Larkhall Royal Albert. He was only seventeen and the youngest professional footballer in the country. It was a season which began on a happy note. The American tour, it seemed, had not dulled the keenness of the players because one commentator described them after only a few weeks as 'the pure wine of soccer'.

But before long tragedy struck Celtic in a manner quite unknown before – or since. Those who were at Ibrox Park on 5 September 1931 will never forget it.

The following account of the life and death of John Thomson is taken from the chapter 'John' in the book on Jimmy McGrory, *A Lifetime in Paradise*. It was written by your author after many hours of interviews with Mr McGrory. He was a team-mate and personal friend of John Thomson and was on the field of play the day the Celtic goalkeeping legend died. Because of his intimate knowledge of the scene, Mr McGrory's account must be the finest of the many written. It reads:

If we turn the clock back a few years to 1927 with the likes of Peter Wilson and the McStays at their zenith with Celtic I can well remember a young goalkeeper in the reserves that every one of us admired. His name was John Thomson. He had been playing tremendously well and Willie Maley decided the time had come for him to make his first team début. The venue was Dens Park and the opposition for the League match was, of course, Dundee. Early in the first half their diminutive right-winger Willie Cook sent over a lobbed, speculative ball which our 17-year-old keeper fumbled and allowed to drop over his hands into the net. But he played soundly for the rest of the game which we won 2–1. I remember afterwards one of the directors, Tom Colgan, came into the dressing-room for a chat with the players, something he often did. Tom was a gem of a man and never spoke out of turn and all he said to John about that goal was: 'That was a bad one to lose, John.' And it was at this early stage of his career that we got the first hint of our keeper's confidence in his own ability – especially from a boy who was just breaking through and not even certain of a first team place the following game.

He replied immediately: 'Don't worry, sir. I've been taught never to make the same mistake twice. I'll be fine for next week.'

John Thomson, like other great athletes, always had belief in himself. It helped to make him in the five years which followed the greatest goalkeeper I have ever seen. Goalkeepers, like all last lines of defence, have it in common with wartime prime ministers that they must all have that belief in themselves. When all about them are crumbling, and they are the loneliest men on earth, it is all that remains to them. And sport does have its men of destiny. They are aware of their difference from other men. You get small glimpses now and again of that awareness. As when Alan Morton of Rangers was taking a corner kick at Dumbarton and the spectators were in a barracking mood. 'Come on then, Morton, let's see something now,' screamed one. Alan Morton paused in his move towards the ball, gave a hitch to the elastic on his shorts and turned towards the terracing saying: 'Is it a goal you want?' Turning he swerved the ball from the flag in a parabola that beat the backs and the keeper and ended in the back of the net for the footballer's hole in one.

Then there was Sammy Crooks, the Stanley Matthews of his time, on England's right-wing who scored a remarkable goal when England walloped Spain at Stamford Bridge. 'I was just cutting in,' he said, 'and had beaten the back and was just going to slip it across to the centre when I saw the goalkeeper's eyes shift. I then decided to go in and beat him myself.'

Saw the keeper's eyes shift! In the heat of the battle, the ball at his toes, the crowd roaring, the other back closing in – and he saw the keeper's eyes shift. There you have the heaven-born games player. They are the gifted of the Gods, blessed with a co-ordination of mind, eye and muscle that is a secret; and it would not matter what game they took up.

So it was with John. He was the son of a miner, went into the pits at fourteen but he played football every Saturday and rose to the heights of a place as goalkeeper in the local side, Wellesley Juniors. It was by sheer accident that he caught the senior eye. Steve Callaghan, the Celtic chief scout – who also signed me – went to Fife to watch a player in the Denbeath side but he could not take his eyes off the scrawny boy in the opposite goal. 'He could jump like a cat,' said Gallaghan later. Near the end of the game Denbeath were awarded a penalty and their burly centre-half took the kick. The boy in the Wellesley goal raised a lightning hand and the ball shot to safety. Callaghan spent the next two hours talking the persuasive age-old talk of football scouts and at last the boy said 'yes'. Callaghan produced a form from his pocket, held it against a telegraph pole for support, and John Thomson signed on as a Celt for £10.

Thomson, the first day he arrived for training at Celtic Park, was a comical looking figure. He wore a long, blue overcoat which could easily have belonged to his big brother. His doolichter cap was pulled down over one eye in the fashion that was no doubt all the rage at that time among the youth of Cardenden. He lived to become, as many of his contemporaries among players will tell you today, a classically moulded athlete.

It was his hands that fascinated those who studied them. They were no great double-octave spanning members like those of the legendary Frank Swift. They were an artist's hands, a surgeon's hands. Fine looking but terribly powerful. On training days he would give evidence of that power by grabbing the hardest of shots with ease. In a Glasgow Cup Final Andy Cunningham let go one of his famous pile drivers that sped for the corner of the net with all his weight behind it. Thomson dived and held the ball at the foot of the post with one hand above it and one below. But the great secret of Thomson's goalkeeping genius – for it was nothing less than that – was the way he could find extra muscular power to change course and find fresh drive in mid-air. It was a physical peculiarity equivalent to a hitch-kick like the one performed by Jesse Owens, the Negro, who gave one halfway through his long-jump at the Berlin Olympics, which enabled him to set up a world record.

The first time Thomson's ability to give himself additional thrust while his feet were off the ground, and so turn himself in another direction or gain him additional inches in his spring, was just a week after his first game at Dens Park. This agility was responsible for the save that his Celtic team-mates agreed was the best they had ever seen. It was at Park-head against Kilmarnock and the man who shot was the famous 'Peerie' Cunningham, a centre whose shots, taken on the pivot, left either foot with a velocity that was almost unique. Cunningham hit the ball in a manner that it seemed to go for the right-hand post and Thomson dived in that direction. But almost on the instant he divined his mistake. The ball was suddenly swerving towards the other post. Thomson twisted literally in mid-air, hurled himself across the goal and got the tips of his fingers to the ball to turn it round the post.

Then one day in 1928 at Birmingham, the Scottish League played the English League – a vastly superior English side – which nevertheless won only by the odd goal in three. Time and again John stood alone before the English raiders. From one save which brought him to his knees, the ball went clear to Ernie Hine, the fair-haired Leicester City inside right who stood alone and unmarked 20 yards out.

Hine's shot was one of those deliberate, tremendous, gather-pace-as-they-go majestic shots such as only great inside forwards seem capable of producing. Thomson was still on his knees as it raged towards him but he rose in a gymnast's leap, arms outstretched and body arched. Somehow he got the tips of his fingers to the ball and pushed it over the bar. The Villa Park grandstand echoed and trembled to a sustained burst of applause which went on for minute after minute. The clapping and cheering went on long after the ball-boy had retrieved the ball and placed it for the corner kick.

But after five breathtaking years and eight Scottish caps came a sultry, windless day at Ibrox. Those who attended that match of September 5th witnessed the greatest on-the-field tragedy in the history of the Scottish game. Celtic fielded John Thomson, Cook and McGonagle, Wilson, McStay and Geatons, R. Thomson, A. Thomson, McGrory, Scarff and Napier – the Cup winning team and the best team in which I ever played. Rangers sent out: Dawson, Gray and McAulay, Meiklejohn, Simpson and Brown, Fleming, Marshall, English, McPhail and Morton. A crowd of 75 000 turned up but they had little to enthuse over as both teams betrayed Old Firm symptoms – nervousness in every early move. As usual, throw-ins and free kicks were in abundance. The first half passed without the slightest touch of football craft although there were some great players on the field. Then came the fateful second half.

Rangers kicked off with a sudden slight breeze at their backs and within five minutes tragedy struck. Fleming of Rangers broke down the right wing after one of our attacks failed. His cross beat Jimmy McStay and left centre-forward Sam English racing in on goal. He seemed to push the ball a bit in front of him as if to tee it up for a good shot as John came off his line and threw himself at the ball. The two clashed and English's knee crashed against the keeper's head. The shot was diverted, but at a terrible price.

It happened at the traditional Rangers end of Ibrox – the Copland Road side – and the Rangers section began cheering madly just as some sections of our support have done under similar circumstances. Rangers skipper Davie Meiklejohn ran behind the goal and gestured at them to stop, which they eventually did. I had run back to see what had happened to John as he lay there quite still, pale and unconscious, surrounded by players, manager Willie Maley and the club doctor. Blood was spurting from his left temple just like a small fountain and I knew it was serious and it was at this moment, for the first time in my life, that I wanted to strangle a Rangers player. I overheard one saying: 'There's not much wrong with him.' But before I took the action going through my mind David Meiklejohn intervened and told his own team-mate to shut up. Now I was a rookie as far as medical science was concerned but it was obvious from the look of the injury that it must be bad.

I remember thinking to myself as John, his head swathed in bandages, was carried from the field: 'My God, what's to become of him and us.' Charlie Geatons took over in goal and there was no little relief when the referee signalled the end of a game played by two unwilling teams with the score at 0–0. In the dressing-room there was a hush. I asked Dr Willie Kivlichan – who had once been a Rangers player before coming to Celtic – how John was. 'Bad enough,' was the reply. The other players sat half-stunned not daring to mention it in case someone said he was dead and manager Willie Maley looked very distressed. Despite the gloom I never thought in a hundred years that he would die.

I can state here and now that not one Celtic player blamed Sam English for what happened. It was an accident. Shortly after we reached the dressing-room after the match Davie Meiklejohn came in to ask after John. I always admired the Rangers captain for his conduct that day yet he was a real bitter so-and-so when it came to playing against Celtic! Afterwards Jimmy McStay, being captain, left for the Victoria Infirmary with Mr Maley and director Tom Colgan. I was living in Ayr at the time and motored home. I can hardly remember driving I was in such a daze and when I got home I just didn't know where I was as I waited for news.

I was just married at the time and I sat with my wife all evening wondering if the phone would ever ring. Then I decided to phone the Victoria Infirmary myself but the switchboard was jammed with calls from anxious supporters. I eventually got through about 10 p.m. and asked for Jimmy McStay. He came to the phone and said: 'He died half an hour ago.' That's all he said and put the phone down obviously too choked to say anything more. I was dazed. I went through to the living room and said to my wife: 'He's dead,' and I remember her saying 'God rest his soul'. We just sat there in disbelief.

That was the only night in my entire career that I wanted to quit football. I was sickened. I was never afraid of physical contact or taking a knock but to experience a team-mate dying playing a game of football was just too much.

We reported back to Celtic Park on the Monday morning for training and the atmosphere was terrible. No one wanted to speak about it and we all felt hopeless in the situation. If John had been personal family we could have consoled someone but in this case we were strangers to his family and they lived over in Fife. The funeral came a few days later and we were all called to Celtic Park and left by coach and then train for Fife. Twenty thousand people gathered at Queen Street to see the mourners leave.

John wasn't a Catholic so there was no Mass. In fact, as far as I remember, there was no church service at all. We gathered at his parents' house in Bowhill and all had a brief word with his mother. Then we carried the coffin, four players at a time, to the graveyard a few miles away. Thirty thousand people lined the route, many weeping openly. I've heard it said that many walked from Glasgow to attend.

None of the players physically broke down that day but I had to fight back the tears as I helped lower John's coffin into the grave. He was just a boy of 22 and in my opinion he would have become the greatest goalkeeper of all time. Many, many honours would have come his way.

A million words were written about him after his death but Dr James E. Handley summed it up beautifully: 'A man who has not read Homer, wrote Bagehot, is like a man who has not seen the ocean. There is a great object of which he has no idea. In like manner, a generation which did not see John Thomson has missed a touch of greatness in sport, for he was a brilliant virtuoso, as Gigli was and Menuhin is. One artist employed the voice as his instrument, the other employs the violin or cello. For Thomson it was a handful of leather. We shall not look upon his like again.'

John was the type of player you dreamed about having in your team. You knew if you did your job and got a goal he wasn't going to let you down by losing a daft one at the other end. I only ever remember him having one bad game and that was against Hibs at Easter Road. He was in line for an international cap and perhaps pressure got the better of him. As it turned out my old friend Jack Harkness got the cap and John, like many Celtic players of the time, had to get used to the fact that caps were never thrown in your direction. We were always used to being overlooked on the international scene.

Despite his confidence on the park and the dressing-room he was quiet and unassuming away from Celtic Park. He lived with a great old lady at 618 Gallowgate who looked after all the young Celtic players from out of Glasgow. He and I used to go dancing along with Alec Thomson to the St Alphonsus Halls. He was also fairly quiet with the girls although he was going steady – I think in fact he was engaged – just before he was killed.

I have several other memories of his outstanding ability which I think are worth recording here. He once saved two penalties in a game against Queen's Park. The match was at Hampden Park and Queen's were in the First Division at the time. Their centre-half, Bob Gillespie, renowned for hitting them hard, took the first one and lived up to his reputation.

But John threw himself to the left and didn't just stop it – to the astonishment of the crowd he held it with both hands. When you consider the way Tommy Gemmell hit his penalties a few years ago it will give you an idea how Gillespie hit his and I hardly ever recall Big Tam missing one or a keeper managing to hold one. Anyway, when Queen's got their second award that day Gillespie lost his nerve and let one of his team-mates take it. Another powerful shot it was too but again John dived the right way and managed to push it round the post.

It may seem strange to say this about the best keeper I've seen, but

John wasn't built in the goalkeeping mould. He was not tall, but one of nature's athletes with the kind of co-ordination I mentioned earlier which meant that no matter which sport he tackled he was a natural. I first found this out at Seamill when we were on special training for a cup tie. We decided to go golfing in the afternoon and asked John to come along. He said he wouldn't bother because he had never played the game and didn't want to hold us up. But we eventually persuaded him.

He lined up on the first tee with one of my clubs and proceeded to hit one of the most colossal drives straight down the middle of the fairway – a shot that would have done credit to Arnold Palmer. On another visit there we were in the swimming pool and John was sitting on the edge with his feet in the water. 'Dive in, John,' shouted one of the players. 'I can't dive,' said John. But we all kept on at him and I got out and gave him a demonstration which wasn't exactly a model dive.

Next thing he took off in the most perfect leap I had ever seen leaving hardly a ripple in the water. That was John. He wasn't the type to have you on. If he said he hadn't done a thing before then he had not.

His death had a terrific effect on all of us for a very long time. It is strange that the accident happened in an Old Firm game which is already surrounded by and steeped in emotion and to one of our most famous sons. We have never seemed to fill his position since – apart from Ronnie Simpson who joined us very late in life and only had a few years at the top with us. It is strange that the only great we ever found ourselves was snatched away from us.

Poor Sam English. He was eventually driven out of the game by hostile crowds – even when he left the Scottish scene to try his luck in England. I never knew him but I was told by other players of that era that he was a nice fellow. No one would ever have deliberately injured an opponent like that. As far as I know it was his first big team outing for Rangers against Celtic. He was a very keen player and had been given his chance after scoring well in the reserves.

John's death was the one and only time I saw manager Willie Maley lose his composure. A journalist asked him as he left Ibrox that evening: 'Was it an accident?' He replied: 'I hope so.' He would never have said anything like that had he been his normal self and I know he never held the accident against Sam English.

The train which took mourners from Glasgow to Fife for the funeral also drew an open 44-foot-long wagon packed with wreaths from English clubs, schoolboys, from street supporters clubs and many other places. Players of the time and the past gathered to pay homage. In the cortège which tramped to the cemetery I noticed memorable sights like McNair and Dodds, the great Celtic full-back partnership of a decade before, marching silently side by side.

There are now memorials to John Thomson up and down the country in many football grounds. Every year schoolboys battle for trophies which bear his name. A life-sized portrait of him looks down on every visitor who walks in the main entrance of Celtic Park.

At the inquiry after the accident the sheriff told the jury to return the following verdict: 'That the deceased, while engaged in his employment as a professional footballer with Celtic Football Club, and acting as a goalkeeper in a football match with Rangers at Ibrox Park, Glasgow, in the course of the match sustained injuries to his head by coming into contact with the body of Samuel English, playing centre-forward for Rangers, in an attempt to save a goal by diving towards Samuel English while in the act of kicking the ball, and received a fracture of the skull from which he died in the Victoria Infirmary.'

While engaged in his employment . . . in an attempt to save a goal. That is possibly the epitaph my friend John would have liked best himself.

10   The Thirties

The death of John Thomson left a gap in the Celtic ranks which could never be adequately filled and the management were left with the dual tasks of trying to find a successor and restore heart to a team which had been left mentally shattered by the events at Ibrox Stadium on that September day. A stop-gap keeper, Johnny Falconer of Cowdenbeath, took over the following week but did not prove to be the answer and it was shortly after this that manager Willie Maley remembered a goalkeeper who had defied Celtic on their close season American tour – Joe Kennaway of the Fall River Club. Joe signed up and made his début on 31 October and although Celtic failed to win any honours in the season 1931–2 the fans took him to their hearts. For the second time in two years Celtic met Motherwell in the Scottish Cup, this time in the third round, and the Fir Park men gained revenge for the Final defeat the previous season by winning 2–0. Motherwell also went on to win the Championship and stopped Rangers equalling Celtic's record of six-in-a-row. But the following season – 1932–3 – Celtic were back at Hampden again for the Scottish Cup Final and the opposition were – yes, Motherwell. The team of Kennaway, Hogg, McGonagle, Wilson, J. McStay, Geatons, R. Thomson, A. Thomson, McGrory, Napier, O'Donnell proved too good on the day and a McGrory goal gave Celtic the Cup and the player his fourth Scottish Cup medal. The same month at the same ground brought another great memory for McGrory. He scored near the end to give Scotland a 2–1 victory over England and the bedlam from the 134170 spectators that day was christened the 'Hampden Roar'.

Although Celtic had won the Scottish Cup for the fourteenth time years were to elapse before they picked up another honour. Their disappointing play in 1932 and 1933 brought two blasts of criticism from within the club. The Celtic match programme for 3 December 1933 stated:

In the good old days it was a matter of pride with our players that they should always be at the top or in the immediate vicinity; nowadays one is tempted to think that players do not possess that pride nor appreciate their good fortune in being associated with a club which has such a glorious history. In short, we would like to see our players display more determination, more care, and if you like, more intelligence in their play. Of their ability we have no doubt but we hold that it ought to be exercised in a manner which brings success. In viewing many of the games recently we find ourselves wondering if this team-work, which means actual positional play and understanding, has become a lost art.

In the *Handbook* for the following season, 1933–4, manager Willie Maley wrote:

In reviewing the season that has gone I regret to have to put it down as the most disappointing one we have ever had. Since 1931 our lot has been one of trial and disappointment. We won the Cup in 1933 against all odds but we have since failed badly in the League race where our consistency used to tell its tale and where we wore down all opposition for years. That spirit seems to have been lost by our team. I agree that since 1931 our list of casualties has been an unprecedented one, but I hold that our fighting spirit of having 'aye a hert abune the 'a'' has not been so often on top as it should have been, whilst I also hold our greatest weakness has been the gross carelessness of our team.

At the beginning of the season 1933–4 Bert Thomson was transferred to Blackpool and at the end of it Jimmy McStay went to Hamilton Accies on a free transfer. By 1934 Alec Thomson and Peter Wilson were also on the transfer list. In their places were signed Divers from Renfrew Juniors and Delaney from Stoneyburn. Crum took over Bert Thomson's position. Despite the changes the results stayed pretty much the same. The opening game against newly promoted Queen of the South was watched at Dumfries by a record crowd of 11000 and the new boys beat Celtic 3–2. By October Celts were in the bottom half of the League with only ten points from the same number of matches. Two interesting Press reports from that stage of the season had the fans talking. The first came when an official of the SFA approached a Celtic official on behalf of the Irish Association before the Scotland–Ireland game on 16 September and asked that the Irish tricolour be removed for the duration of the match – significant in view of what was to come years later. The other interesting report followed a friendly match on 4 October between Celtic and a Chile–Peruvian team touring Britain. Football had been introduced only some forty years earlier in South America and although they lacked method it was reported that 'they showed dazzling footwork, could master the flight of the ball and pass it with remarkable swiftness'. A commentator remarked that he could never see such players winning much, a prediction which has been made to look a bit silly in the last two decades. It was also reported that when the forward Fernandez scored his side's goal in a 2–1 defeat he was 'hugged and kissed by his team-mates who thought nothing of embracing an opponent after fouling him. At the end of the game their goalkeeper shook hands with the referee.' Imagine such goings-on!

In the Scottish Cup Celtic went down 2–0 to St Mirren at Love Street in the fourth round and missed two penalties in the process. Towards the end of the season Alec Thomson and Wilson had disappeared from the regular team and age had robbed Celtic of two of the finest exponents of traditional Parkhead play. Over the years they had consistently served up the purest football and their artistry had always been a pleasure to watch. There was much chopping and changing in the side with Hughes, Buchan, Crum, Paterson, the brothers O'Donnell, McDonald and Divers coming in from time to time from the reserve team, then known as the Alliance team. McGrory broke an ankle in a League match against Clyde on 31 March and Napier also took an ankle knock which kept him out of the side for months ending with a cartilage operation. Celtic managed only third place in the Championship with a mere forty-seven points from thirty-eight matches. Rangers were top with sixty-six points and Motherwell second with sixty-two. While the top team was continuing to struggle the Alliance team was getting rave notices and the above-mentioned youngsters clinched the League. In the opening games of the season 1934–5, the management tried several combinations in their quest for a winning team, but again they failed. Only nine points were taken from the first ten games.

The Board became anxious about falling gates and decided on a whole new course of action. As Celtic were to do in the early Fifties in their approach to Jock Stein, they did in 1934 with an approach to their great former player Jimmy McMenemy. They knew they had the young players to do the job, but what they needed was experience behind them and McMenemy was appointed coach.

It did the trick. By mid-January the young players had been

introduced one by one and the team had thirty-eight points from twenty-eight games. Geatons, McDonald and Paterson formed a solid mid-line and up front Delaney, Buchan, Crum and Hugh O'Donnell proved a lively lot. Although it was another barren season they finished second in the League and the future looked a lot brighter. The season of 1935–6 began with a 3–1 defeat at the hands of Aberdeen, the Celtic team being: Kennaway, Hogg, McGonagle, Geatons, Lyon, Paterson, Delaney, Buchan, McGrory, McDonald, Crum. But in the next sixteen games they dropped only one point. It was to be McGrory's great year. A hat-trick against Dumfermline in a 5–3 win on 16 September gave him a Celtic and Scottish record of 351 goals – one below Steve Bloomer's world record of 352. McGrory failed to make the team the following week in which Celtic recorded with a 2–1 win their first victory over Rangers in the League at Ibrox since the season of 1920–1. But against Airdrie on 19 October McGrory scored two goals in a 4–0 victory to take the world record and was carried shoulder-high from the park by jubilant fans. The following week saw another milestone for the fast-improving Celts. They beat Motherwell at Fir Park for the first time in nine years. The performance of Murphy at outside-left that day finally buried the ghost of the great Adam McLean who had left the Celtic management with a tremendous headache in trying to fill the position following his transfer. Having beaten Bloomer's world record McGrory then discovered that a player called Hugh Ferguson had 326 goals to his credit but on 21 December a hat-trick against Aberdeen in a 5–3 victory gave McGrory a tally of 364. The title was now his beyond all doubt.

Although they went out of the Scottish Cup in an early tie against St Johnstone and had lost the New Year game 4–3 to Rangers, they went through the rest of the League programme undefeated and buried another bogey by beating Dundee at Dens Park for their first win there since 1928. McGrory's seventh hat-trick of the season against Ayr United was enough to clinch the Championship for the eighteenth time.

Ten years had elapsed since Celtic had last obtained the League – the longest spell in their history without a Championship. McGrory was the last surviving member of the 1925–6 League-winning team and had scored fifty goals in the Championship race. Injury denied him a place in the final game against Partick Thistle at Firhill which Celtic won 3–1. Had he played that day he might have added another record to his honours as McFadyen of Motherwell held the League scoring record of fifty-two goals. To add to the arguments it can be said that McFadyen missed only four games in his great season whereas McGrory missed six. McFadyen scored some of his goals from the penalty spot whereas McGrory did not. McFadyen's goals came the year Motherwell won the League, 1931-2 ending an Old Firm monopoly of twenty-seven years.

The Championship statistics for 1935-6 were: Played 38, Won 32, Lost 4, Drawn 2, Goals for 115, Against 33, Points 66. To the League they also added for the first time in ten years the Charity Cup, thanks to a 4-2 win over Rangers. It was their twenty-first success in the competition. For the second time in two years the Alliance team brought the Second Eleven Cup to Parkhead so everything looked good for the future as another season loomed. Despite McGrory's fabulous year the SFA again failed to choose him for Wembley, a ground this great player never graced. His treatment over the years by the SFA was disgraceful. Although he was Celtic's top scorer every year from 1924 until 1936 with the exception of 1934, he was given only seven full caps.

The season of 1936-7 opened without McGrory, missing through injury, and Crum took over at centre until the great man's return on 3 October. Early results were not great but by Christmas the team had slid into top gear with Kennaway safe in goal and well served by Hogg and Morrison at full-back. Delaney had developed into a dazzling winger and Buchan showed all the gracefulness of Peter Wilson. McGrory, although not as fast as before, still had enough zip to keep defences on their toes and it looked as if the Championship might once again be Celtic's until a black six-week period early in the New Year ended all hopes. But the Scottish Cup was under way and had always held a special magic for Celtic teams – especially struggling Celtic teams. Their game picked up again and they defeated Stenhousemuir, Albion Rovers, East Fife, Motherwell and Clyde. So for the twenty-second time they lined up at Hampden on Cup Final day and the opponents were Aberdeen. The game attracted a British club record crowd of 146 433 and outside were another 30 000 who had failed to gain admission. Reports of the time stated that Aberdeen carried two-thirds of the crowd but the Celtic team of: Kennaway, Hogg, Morrison, Geatons, Lyon, Paterson, Delaney, Buchan McGrory, Crum, Murphy were good enough to take the Cup by two goals to one. They again won the Charity Cup and the Alliance team won their Championship. To cap a good year the directors announced a healthy profit of £9172.

The following season, 1937–8, was a special one in the history of Celtic because on 6 November 1937 the club celebrated the golden jubilee of its existence. What a fabulous fifty years they had to contemplate. Their record was unsurpassed. Here are the bare statistics of their wins:

Scottish Cup: 1892, 1899, 1900, 1904, 1907, 1908, 1911, 1912, 1914, 1923, 1925, 1927, 1931, 1933, 1937.

Scottish League: 1893, 1894, 1896, 1898, 1905, 1906, 1907, 1908, 1909, 1910, 1914, 1915, 1916, 1917, 1919, 1922, 1926, 1936.

Glasgow Cup: 1890, 1891, 1894, 1895, 1904, 1905, 1906, 1907, 1909, 1915, 1916, 1919, 1920, 1926, 1927, 1928, 1930.

Charity Cup: 1892, 1893, 1894, 1895, 1896, 1899, 1903, 1905, 1908, 1912, 1913, 1914, 1915, 1916, 1917, 1918, 1920, 1921, 1924, 1926, 1936, 1937.

Their fifteen Scottish Cups were a record. They had won the League six years in a row, another record. They also won it five times in six seasons between 1914 and 1919. The Charity Cup they had won seven times in a row – also a record – and five times in a row. Their Glasgow Cup record too was consistency itself. In all they had done both on and off the field Celtic could justifiably call themselves the great pioneers of all that was best in Scottish football. Behind it all was the tall, commanding figure of Willie Maley who on 12 December that same year celebrated a fifty-year connection with the club as player, secretary and manager. A native of Newry in Northern Ireland, he was in his teens when the Maley family moved to Cathcart in Glasgow. At the Jubilee Dinner held on Wednesday 16 June 1938 at the Grosvenor Restaurant, Glasgow, Mr Maley was presented with a cheque by the Board for 2500 guineas – fifty guineas for each year of service.

William Maley had been invited with his brother Tom to help guide the fortunes of Celtic when Brother Walfrid was forming the club in late 1887. He played right-half in the first-ever Celtic team on 28 May 1888 in the 5–2 victory over Rangers. With Celtic he collected four League Championship medals, one Scottish Cup, four Glasgow Cup and five Charity Cup medals. He won three full caps and became match secretary in 1890. He gave up studying accountancy to devote all his energies to the club and by 1898 was manager. He lived for Celtic. He was much in the mould of Jock Stein, a strange mixture of soft heart and single-mindedness. He had a wonderful talent for spotting potential in young players and calmly experimented until he got a blend with no regard for what Press or public thought. It was due to his enterprise that the club pioneered so many things for Scottish football.

Jimmy McGrory summed him up with one amusing story. Mc-Grory approached him one Saturday just before the match and asked for two tickets for friends visiting from London. Maley handed them over, slapped Jimmy on the back and told him to ask any time. The following week Jimmy's friends were still in Glasgow and as luck would have it Celtic had another home game. Jimmy breezed into the boss's office confident after the previous week and asked again. Handing him the tickets Maley said: 'Don't your friends ever pay?' That was Willie Maley. A week after celebrating his golden jubilee Mr Maley deleted from his lists the name of Jimmy McGrory, probably his greatest ever signing. Jimmy was still a fine opportunist but injuries were forcing him out of the team more often.

Kilmarnock had made an approach to McGrory to take over as manager at Rugby Park and sadly he decided to hang up his boots and move on. Between 20 January 1923 when he played his first game for Celtic, and 16 October 1937 when he pulled on the famous green and white jersey for the last time he amassed 410 League goals and in other top-class matches took his grand aggregate to 550 – then a world record. Those goals still hold the British record today and are unlikely to be beaten. McGrory is mentioned twice in the *Guinness Book of Records*. The first is for his 550 goals. The second is for scoring eight goals in one League game against Dunfermline at Celtic Park on 14 January 1928 – a British First Division record. He was superb in and around the penalty area and it was said that he could kick the ball with his head, such was the force and direction with which he headed it. He was not tall – five feet six and a half inches – but he was sturdy and pushful. When the passes were not coming he could be a tireless forager. He scored the winner near the end in the famous Patsy Gallagher Final of 1925 and he created the first 'Hampden Roar' with his winner against England in 1933. With his departure the centre-forward position was filled by Crum. Buchan had left for Blackpool on a £10000 transfer and the usual forward line became: Delaney, McDonald, Crum, Divers and Murphy with

Kennaway in goal, Hogg and Morrison at full back and Geatons, Lyon and Paterson forming the steady half-back line. By 12 February 1938 they had played fifteen successive matches without defeat, losing only two points and scoring fifty-nine goals for the loss of eleven.

8·0/ Jimmy McGrory's first game as manager of Kilmarnock had come against Celtic at Parkhead and his men were thrashed 9–1. So it was the sensation of the season when he brought his team back for the third round of the Scottish Cup and beat Celtic 2–1 in front of the Parkhead faithful. They returned to Glasgow the following week and beat Rangers 2–1 in the League and then proceeded to knock the Ibrox men out of the Cup by 4–3 in the semi-final.

Jimmy McGrory's dream start, however, was not to be as East Fife beat Kilmarnock in the Final by 1–0 after a replay. Despite the Cup shock and a Glasgow Cup defeat by Rangers the players rallied and ended the Jubilee season by winning the Championship on 23 April, beating St Mirren at Paisley 3–1. They also won the Charity Cup for the twenty-third time by beating Rangers in the Final and had managed to escape defeat at home all season.

Celtic were the possessors of the Exhibition Cup of 1901 although they had not been the original winners. Rangers had put up the trophy in aid of the Ibrox Disaster Fund of 1902. Celtic had beaten Rangers in the Final after the Scots teams had accounted for Sunderland and Everton. Celtic were anxious, therefore, to add to it a new trophy which Glasgow officials were putting forward for the Empire Exhibition of 1938. Sunderland, Everton, Chelsea and Brentford were paired against Celtic, Rangers, Hearts and Aberdeen. All games were played at Ibrox with evening kick-offs and Celtic and Sunderland had the honour of playing the first match on 25 May.

Celtic, despite serious injuries to several key players, held on through extra time and won 3–1 the following evening in the replay. Everton beat Rangers in the opening round and Aberdeen beat Chelsea. Celtic took on Hearts who had beaten Brentford and moved into the Final thanks to a goal by Crum. The Final on 10 June between Celtic and Everton drew 80 000 spectators. Celtic's team of Kennaway, Hogg, Morrison, Geatons, Lyon, Paterson, Delaney, McDonald, Crum, Divers, Murphy had to go to extra time before winning by 1–0.

The Earl of Elgin presented the magnificent silver trophy which was a replica of the tower at Bellahouston Park, a constant landmark to the Empire Exhibition. The players each received a silver miniature.

Celtic's Jubilee year, therefore, had been one of the best in recent times both on the field and financially. The Jubilee team was hailed as one of the best in the club's history.

They lived up to their reputation at the beginning of 1938-9 by starting in rampant style. Two big scalps were Hearts who went down 5-1 and Rangers who were walloped 6-2. Their style of interchanging tactics brought victory in the Glasgow Cup by beating Clyde 3-0 in the Final on 15 October. But a form slump came at the turn of the year and matters were not helped by injuries to Paterson and McDonald which kept both out for long periods. Delaney broke his arm on 1 April against Arbroath and the season ended in disappointment. Motherwell knocked Celtic out of the Scottish Cup in the fourth round and Clyde dumped them out of the Charity Cup.

Manager Willie Maley, who had been missing for a good bit of the year through illness, commented that the season had been one of the most disappointing ever, especially when the supporters had been expecting so much of the men who had won the Empire Exhibition Trophy. He said in an article:

One does not know how to explain the form of our side with all its carelessness and weaknesses so apparent to everyone but themselves. In every game it is possible to have the breaks against you, but the law of averages counts in all sports and what is lost one day comes back another day. That, of course, does not apply to clearly indolent play backed by an imaginary superiority which is, like foolish pride in one's self, a major sin.

Few knew then, including Maley himself, that it was to be one of his last statements as manager of Celtic. With the war clouds rolling in once more the season of 1939-40 began in an atmosphere of uncertainty.

Celtic began with the same team, except for the injured Delaney, and had played only a handful of games when the dreaded announcement came. They defeated Clyde at Celtic Park on 2 September and the following day war was declared. On the Monday came the edict that professional football, along with other forms of mass entertainment, was to be abandoned. All players' contracts were suspended although the SFA ruled that their registration was still in force – they were still tied to their clubs. Government restrictions were lifted a short time later although ground capacities were greatly reduced.

Despite the lifting of restrictions the SFA and Scottish League knew that it would be impossible to carry on as in peacetime and regional divisions were drawn up keeping west and east clubs apart.

Players were paid £2 a week but no bonuses were paid. Those away from home because of war work were given permission to play for other clubs on a temporary basis. The new arrangement began on Saturday, 21 October, and Hamilton Accies came to Parkhead with three Anglo players guesting for them and beat Celtic 4–3. Willie Buchan, who had gone to Blackpool in 1937, played in the Celtic team under the same arrangement. The demands of wartime industry on fuel and transport meant very little movement of the population and therefore crowds at games were small. Players too were often very tired by the time match day came round. Several Celtic players, including captain Willie Lyon, had been called up and by the end of November Celtic were lying near the bottom of the Southern League table. The New Year game with Rangers should have been played at Celtic Park but bearing in mind that Ibrox had attracted 118 730 the previous year the Celtic management agreed to play there again as the larger capacity ground would be allowed a bigger crowd.

The game ended in a 1–1 draw in almost Arctic conditions and was a result which left Celtic at the bottom of the League with only eight points from twelve matches. But the big news of the winter for Celtic was neither their results nor the dreadful weather. On 1 February came the bombshell that Willie Maley had relinquished his post as manager at the age of seventy-two. His departure seems to have come as a surprise to him and to have been forced upon him. Despite his age he was still a reasonably fit man but it was true that the record of the team in his final eighteen months of stewardship had been extremely poor. Yet his departure did not bring about a change in Celtic's fortunes. Writing in a newspaper Mr Maley said:

In this my closing article for season 1939–40 my thoughts go back to August 1939 when we started off in what I imagined would be another successful season and which I did not think would be my last year in football management. Personally I can never forget the 1939–40 season. It has been to me the end of my football career and has robbed me of the very tang of life. Football has been my thoughts morning, noon and night for all the fifty-two years I have been in it, and it has been hard to fall out of my regular ways.

Following the 1938 Jubilee Dinner the directors had thought Willie Maley would retire. After all, he had been fifty years with the club and had been presented with 2500 guineas by Chairman Tom White. There were some who felt the Celtic Board could have handled his departure more tactfully, although present chairman

Desmond White explains the difficulties in his Foreword. Willie Maley went without a mention in the *Celtic Football Guide*, the official handbook, although other biographies appeared (perhaps the directors of the time felt it was better to say nothing rather than cause any further unpleasantness), and it took Willie Maley's death some twenty years later to repair the omission.

Former player and captain Jimmy McStay succeeded him as manager. He had gained some managerial experience with Alloa and a team in Dublin. He had taken Alloa into the First Division and although his contract still had a year to run the directors did not stand in his way when Celtic made their approach. Unfortunately Jimmy had no magic wand to wave and that really was what Celtic needed. Of thirty League games they won nine, lost fifteen, drew six, and had a total of twenty-four points. They scored fifty-five goals and had sixty-one against them.

Some clubs had to close their doors because of lack of finance and as League fixtures limped along it was decided early in 1940 to introduce a cup competition among the remaining thirty-one clubs in the two regional Leagues on a home and away basis. Celtic, in keeping with their form for the season, went out in the first round to Raith Rovers.

The Charity Cup was anything but charitable that year. Celtic and Rangers met in the semi-final before 21000 fans at Ibrox. Guilty parties on both sides began paying more attention to the man than the ball in the second half. The viciousness being perpetrated on the field soon spread to the terracing and things got out of hand. First, Ventners of Rangers was ordered off for disobeying the referee. Then, after a brush between Divers and Symon, the Celtic man got his marching orders. Caskie of Everton, playing for Rangers, had a fine match and was cleanly played by Hogg. He scored two and Rangers won 5–1. After the match the SFA summoned Ventners, Symon, McDonald, Divers and Lynch and suspended all for a month to take effect at the start of the new season.

The entire football set-up was proving so difficult to run that the Scottish League threw in the towel at their AGM in June 1940 and unanimously agreed to suspend the League competition until further notice. The ruling, however, did not preclude any group of clubs forming their own leagues and sixteen teams got together, promising a £50 guarantee to visiting clubs and £2 a week in wages for players. The clubs taking part were: Celtic, Airdrie, Albion Rovers, Clyde,

Dumbarton, Falkirk, Hamilton, Hearts, Hibs, Morton, Motherwell, Queen's Park, Partick Thistle, Rangers, St Mirren and Third Lanark. The new League opened on 10 August and Celtic drew 2–2 with Hamilton Accies at Celtic Park. The Celtic team was: Johnstone (Aberdeen), Hogg, Paterson, Geatons, Waddell (Aberdeen), Ferguson (Alloa), Kelly, Conway (Glencraig Celtic), Crum, Gillan (Alloa), Murphy. Despite the strange-looking line-ups attendances improved and Celtic and Rangers drew a crowd of 50 000 when they met on 7 September. The game ended in a goalless draw. Celtic beat Rangers in the Final of the Glasgow Cup in front of a similar crowd a few weeks later. On the League front, however, Celtic were having another rough season but they recovered by New Year and beat Rangers by 3–1. Delaney again missed many matches because his arm injury from the previous season was not responding to treatment.

A Scottish League Cup competition followed the League programme and the sixteen clubs were divided into four sections of four teams each. Celtic reached the semi-finals before going down 2–0 to Hearts in Edinburgh. Partick Thistle knocked them out of the semi-finals of the Charity Cup and Hibs ended their interest in the Summer Cup. Despite it all the club managed a profit of £2365. At the opening of the season of 1941–2 Celtic had the following players to choose from: Hunter (Kilmarnock), Hogg, Dornan (Kilmarnock), McLaughlin, Lynch, Waddell (Aberdeen), Corbett (Maryhill), Collier (Partick Thistle), Delaney, Riley (Perthshire), McDonald, Divers, Crum, McAuley (Douglas Hawthorn), Conway, Murphy and Nelson (Douglas Water).

Despite players going to the Forces Celtic had a good season compared with their more recent efforts. They finished third in the League. The season was marred for them, though, when they attempted to play their former player Fagan from Liverpool in the September League match with Rangers at Ibrox. He was unaccountably banned from playing by the League organizers. More than 50 000 fans turned up and saw a stormy game in which Delaney was thrown into the net. In the stramash which followed Murphy missed the resulting penalty. Both Delaney and Crum were stretchered from the field. A report in the *Evening Times* by Alan Breck read:

There was a scene at Ibrox Park following a penalty kick awarded to Celtic. A shower of bottles descended on the track and fights broke out. Celtic took a goal by Beattie which looked offside in good spirit. It was rather different when, after Gillick had scored a fine second for Rangers, Celtic were awarded a penalty for an offence on Delaney. Rangers' players clustered round the referee protesting while Delaney was carried behind the goal. This was the signal for the disturbance on the terracing.

Following the match, at which five spectators were arrested, the SFA (ignoring its own rule that a club is responsible for happenings within its ground) proceeded to order not the closure of Ibrox but of Celtic Park. The penalty, a mystifying decision, was for a month. For many years before there had been a desire within Scottish football officialdom to take such an action against Celtic and it was an action some would dearly liked to have seen even after the war. With players like Lyon, Milne, Corbett, Airlie, Paterson, Fisher, Duffy, Gallagher, Shields, Anderson, Watters, Rae and Paton in the Forces it was difficult to get a settled side and the season 1942–3 saw Celtic turning to inexperienced youth. In one match they fielded six lads who had been members of Boys' Guild teams the previous season. The loss of key men like Lyon, Waddell and Corbett made the situation practically impossible for manager McStay. He was not helped by a Board decision to stick to youth, turning down such distinguished players as Matt Busby who was in Scotland and eager to play in a green and white jersey.

Crum and Divers had moved on to Morton and took part with another ex-Celt, Kelly, in a 4–0 rout of Celtic at Greenock on 12 September. Rangers knocked Celtic out of the Glasgow Cup after a replay then in the New Year game things boiled over again. McDonald was sent off for arguing with the referee over a Rangers goal he claimed was offside. Then five minutes later Lynch joined him also for remarks made to the referee. The SFA swung into action and suspended McDonald until the following August, fining him £10. Lynch was suspended until 27 March and fined £5.

With Celtic's resources cut even more the season was yet another disappointing one although they did win the Charity Cup for the twenty-fourth time. The return of Divers for the season 1943–4 gave Celtic a boost and Delaney had also regained much of his zip. What was missing, however, was a resourceful centre-forward of McGrory's style to cash in on the chances made by these two. Celtic's play was better than it had been during the earlier war years and the supporters began turning out in greater numbers again.

In the Southern League Celtic finished second with forty-three points from thirty games. They won their League Cup section but lost in the semi-finals to Hibs. In the Charity Cup they reached the Final, only to lose 4–1 to Clyde. The landing of the Allied Forces in Europe cheered everyone and at long last it seemed that football would again have a future. Celtic kicked off the last of the war seasons, 1944–5, in front of 20000 spectators, the biggest crowd of the day. Hearts were the opposition at Parkhead and Celtic won by 4–1. The line-up was Miller, Hogg, P. McDonald, M. McDonald, McLaughlin, Paterson, Delaney, McPhail, Gallagher, McGinlay, McAuley.

The following week arrived one of the Celtic greats and he was drafted into the forward line – a position in which he was not to make his name. Bobby Evans came from St Anthony's and after taking a step back to the mid-line became a great anchorman to the club. His début against Albion Rovers was successful in that Celtic took the points. But Celtic's League form again took a dive and out of fourteen matches they lost nine. They lost 3–2 to Rangers in the Glasgow Cup Final after leading 2–0, Rangers getting the winner from the penalty spot.

Celtic's problems were highlighted by the fact that in one match they made nine positional changes from the previous week. The month of December saw fortunes swing again as they went seventeen games without defeat, including a victory over Rangers on New Year's day at Ibrox. No team in Scotland had changed less in personnel during the war than the Ibrox men, most of whose players managed to find jobs in the shipyards. Celtic's players had not been so fortunate for the kind of reasons that only the West of Scotland – and Northern Ireland – can produce.

The Celtic team of this era differed from the traditional Parkhead play in that it relied more on strength than skill with only McDonald and Delaney providing the kind of skill expected of Celtic players. But this type of situation had to be accepted in wartime. In the League they came second with forty-two points from thirty games. Bad performances against Partick Thistle and Falkirk cost them the Southern League Cup and neither the Charity Cup nor Summer Cup came their way. But in true Celtic style they won the hastily organized Victory in Europe Cup to mark the end of the war. It was up for keeps and they defeated Queen's Park on 9 May. Rangers had declined to take part. Celtic's winning margin was indeed narrow, being one goal and three corners to one goal and two corners.

The season ended with another managerial shock. This time Jimmy

McStay, who had never really had a chance to establish himself, resigned under pressure. Chairman Tom White, father of present chairman Desmond White, approached Jimmy McGrory and brought him back from Kilmarnock as manager. Like Maley, McStay was bitter at his treatment and said so in several outspoken newspaper interviews. But after a few months he seemed to have patched up his differences with the club and offered his services as scout to his old team-mate Jimmy McGrory. Despite what had happened both men remained close friends until Jimmy McStay's death a few years ago. Strange though to think that in their ninety-year history Celtic have had only four managers and two went within the space of five wartime years. It is also worth recording here that no contract has ever existed between Celtic and their managers.

F

11 Post-war Rebuilding

Although a 'Premier League' was not to happen for another thirty
years, the first concrete moves towards it came just after the Second
World War. Rearrangement of the Leagues had seen the First Division composed of the sixteen clubs with the biggest drawing power.
But some visionaries felt it was too big and unwieldy and pressed for
the winding up of the Scottish League and the introduction of a
'super league' of twelve clubs under the auspices of the SFA. It is
incredible that it took football until 1974 – when the Premier League
kicked off – to come to its senses. At the time of writing there is
debate going on in football's corridors of power about a possible
increase in the Premier League from ten to twelve teams which in
your writer's view would be a much better arrangement. It would
help take away the pattern of two or three teams in contention for
the title and the rest at each other's throats fighting off relegation and
thereby sacrificing entertaining football for survival.

The new post-war 'super league' was to consist of Celtic, Aberdeen,
Clyde, Dundee, Falkirk, Hearts, Hibs, Motherwell, Partick Thistle,
Queen's Park, Rangers and Third Lanark. The whole concept of the
new competition, in which there would be no relegation, was to
bring about more competitive play, better facilities for spectators
and higher wages for players in an effort to halt the drift to the richer
pastures of the south. There would be high cash prizes for the top
four teams and a special fund would be set up to pay out interest-free
loans for ground improvements. The home club's guarantee would
be raised from the pre-war £100 to £250. But the outsiders were
indignant, including Ayr United, Kilmarnock, Morton and St
Mirren, who had been told they could join, although it was commonly
appreciated that they could not bear the heavy financial responsibi-
lities involved.

After three weeks of agitation the smaller clubs successfully blocked the ambitions of their bigger neighbours, and eventually it was agreed all round to continue on the old lines. In that first post-war season of 1945–6, Celtic parted company with Divers, on a free transfer, Delaney, who went to Manchester United, and Malcolm McDonald who moved onto Kilmarnock. Seven years had passed since Celtic's last major success – the Scottish Cup of 1937–8 – and early form indicated that the barren years were far from over. In the twenty-one games which took them to the end of December they won only eight, drew nine and lost four, including a first-round Glasgow Cup defeat at the hands of Rangers. They finished the season in fourth place with only thirty-five points from thirty games.

There was no doubt that they could play fast, exciting football but the big problem was one of consistency. The story of the season surrounded the Victory Cup in which Celtic accounted for St John-stone, Queen of the South and Raith Rovers before meeting Rangers in the semi-finals in front of 90000 spectators on 1 June. It was a goalless draw and must have disappointed as only 45000 turned up for the replay the following Wednesday. The Celtic team was: Miller, Hogg, Mallan, Lynch, Corbett, McAuley, Sirrel, Kiernan, Gallagher, Paterson, Paton. The Rangers side was: Brown, Cox, Shaw, Watkins, Young, Symon, Waddell, Gillick, Thornton, Duncanson, Caskie.

Celtic faced a strong wind in the first half and were thankful to be only a goal down at the interval. Gallagher was injured and eventually had to go off and Sirrel, also injured, was a liability. Then, with twenty minutes to go, Rangers were awarded a penalty which caused an outcry from the Celtic players on the field and an outcry in the Press the following day. Paterson was sent off for protesting and Mallan joined him after kicking the ball away in disgust at the referee's decision.

When Young converted the penalty one fan ran onto the pitch to protest and the game was held up while he and three others were arrested. The *Celtic Football Guide* for the following season, 1946–7, described the incident as follows:

Referee M. C. Dale awarded two goals to Rangers which were debatable in the extreme. Two players, Paterson and Mallan, were sent off. Gallagher had earlier been carried off and Sirrel too was crippled and useless. Thus Celtic finished with seven fit men. The game from start to finish was a clean one and only the referee's peculiar interpretation of the laws of football reduced the contest to a farce. One cannot help recalling a parallel case in which M. C. Dale and the Rangers were involved six years ago. The following extract is taken from the *Daily Record* of September 23rd 1940 – 'We Must Not Have Such Refereeing'. Rangers 3, St Mirren 0. It was a good game wrecked by bad refereeing. In twenty years of sports reporting I have seen many bad decisions by referees, but I have never been an eye witness to such a glaringly bad verdict as I saw at Ibrox on Saturday.

The writer then went on to describe a St Mirren player being pulled down in the penalty area only for the referee to award a free kick just outside the box. 'For a moment,' said the writer, 'I thought either Dale or myself had gone crackers.' The writer also accused the referee of allowing an offside goal by Rangers to stand. Unfortunately Celtic could not be as outspoken as that writer because of SFA rules and the same SFA turned their big guns on Celtic by suspending Paterson and Mallan for three months from the beginning of the season with loss of wages. Celtic were fined £50 and ordered to post warning notices at their ground for a period of six months. A further shock came when Lynch was suspended for a month although he had not been ordered off. It took the player completely by surprise and even a signed letter from Duncanson of Rangers stating that Lynch had avoided trouble carried no weight with the SFA.

The beginning of the season 1946–7 saw the formation of the Celtic Supporters' Association, their aims being to cultivate sportsmanship among their members, help charitable causes and distribute tickets for matches. Celtic began the season without Paterson, Mallan and Lynch, who were serving their sentences from the Rangers game, and John McPhail, who was on the sick list. The omissions reflected in their play with the kind of start which had become commonplace for Celtic in that era. They took only four points from the first ten League games and went down to Clyde in the first round of the Glasgow Cup.

The newly formed Supporters' Association faced its first challenge before the opening League game against Rangers at Celtic Park. Celtic had decided to raise the stand admission charge to seven shillings and sixpence and the association sent a letter of protest. The Rangers Supporters' Association did likewise and threatened a boycott. In the event, only 30000 saw Rangers win 3–2, although the full effect of the boycott was never really known as the match had been played in dreadful weather.

Celtic's play became more jittery with each game. They went out of the Scottish Cup in the first round to Dundee at Dens Park by 2–1 and Rangers defeated them 1–0 in the Final of the Charity Cup. Before these reverses they had played Rangers in the New Year League game which had also come under the threat of boycott. The Rangers management had jumped on the Celtic bandwagon and upped their charges. Despite strong pleas from the Supporters' Associations not to attend, 85000 witnessed the 1–1 draw.

To compensate for their early Scottish Cup exit Celtic played some tour games in England and the Irish Republic and had to be content with seventh place in the League.

Celtic opened the season of 1947–8 without the driving force of Thomas White who had been a dynamic chairman for more than thirty years. His death a few months earlier could not have come at a worse time for the club because for the first season in their history they were to live with the spectre of relegation. Thomas White's death left only two men on the Board – the young Robert Kelly and the elderly Colonel Shaughnessy – and both wanted to be chairman. Desmond White, who had been secretary of the club for a number of years, was invited to succeed his father on the Board but at first declined in case it meant giving up the secretaryship – a job he enjoyed. He was allowed to hold the two posts. At his very first meeting he was put in the unenviable position of voting for the new chairman. Because it was only a three-man Board he, as junior director, found himself with what was the casting vote. He refused to give his decision despite pressure from both men and stated that he would be in a position to vote at the following meeting. Although Colonel Shaughnessy had been with the club a long time Desmond White decided to give his vote to Robert Kelly. His feeling was that the club needed a younger man to lead it back to the top.

The new League Cup competition had given a more competitive start to the season, the kind of edge one normally associated with the closing months. The qualifying section had thrown Celtic and Rangers together on the opening day and a shirt-sleeved crowd of 75000 watched the game at Ibrox. The Celtic team was: Miller, Hogg, Milne, McPhail, Corbett, McAuley, F. Quinn, McAloon, Rae, Sirrel, Paton. They lost 2–0 but gained revenge in the return match at Celtic Park. Injuries, however, to keeper Miller and McAuley in later games saw Celtic fall at the hands of Third Lanark and fail to reach the semi-finals.

By the beginning of January the injury position was very bad and two League defeats at the hands of Rangers had seen Celts in the same position as the previous year. Of the eighteen League matches played the record read: Won 6, Lost 9, Drawn 3. Further reverses saw them in the lower region with Hearts, Queen's Park, Airdrie, Queen of the South and Third Lanark. In a spell of games leading up to the end of February they scored only two goals and were not helped by the fact that the team was continually chopped and changed in a bid to halt the slide.

Despite home crowds in excess of 30000 the position was critical and the Celtic management decided to go into the transfer market. For £7000 they secured the services of Jock Weir, a forward with Blackburn Rovers who in his earlier days had been with Hibs. In view of what was to happen in the final weeks of the season the bright and breezy Weir was probably one of Celtic's most important-ever signings.

With their League position so perilous the thought of a Scottish Cup run was a daunting one. They reached the semi-finals before going down to Morton by 1–0. The month of April saw them in desperate plight. They had taken only twenty-three points from twenty-nine matches and faced the long trip to Dundee for their last match of the season in the knowledge that if they lost they would have to depend on others slipping. Queen's Park were already doomed and it was just a matter of whether Celtic, Airdrie, Morton or Queen of the South would go with them.

The atmosphere in Dundee was unbelievable and the newspapers had carried banner headlines on the matter for days. On the trip north on Saturday, 17 April, manager Jimmy McGrory knew that if Celtic went down he would have to quit. It would be a disaster for the club. So desperate was he that he decided to switch Willie Gallagher, Patsy's son, so that he would be in direct opposition to his brother Tommy who played wing-half for Dundee. His reasoning was that Willie would get a fair game. In the event Tommy nearly murdered him!

What Celtic did not know at the time was that the Dundee directors had offered their players the biggest bonus in the history of the club to beat Celtic. The fact that Dundee themselves could not win the Championship nor gain anything personally from defeating Celtic shows just what kind of men lurked in Scottish football in those days. There is no reason to believe that such men no longer lurk. Only Celtic's great successes of the last decade or so have kept them under their respective stones!

Dens Park was packed for the occasion with a crowd of 31000, many of whom were there to witness the funeral of a once great club. The only Celtic team ever charged with the responsibility of saving the club from relegation was: Miller, Hogg, Mallan, Evans, Corbett, McAuley, Weir, McPhail, Lavery, W. Gallagher, Paton. The Dundee side was: Brown, Follon, Irvine, T. Gallagher, Gray, Boyd, Gunn, Pattillo, Stewart, Ewen, MacKay. The referee, was Mr F. Scott of Paisley.

It certainly looked early on as if Celtic were to have no luck, McPhail twice having the ball in the net only to have the goals disallowed for infringements. Lavery scored a third and it was also chalked off. One is left to ponder how many times the average fan witnesses three disallowed goals in one match – especially a match of critical importance. But Celtic, playing for their very lives, got on with the job and Jock Weir put them one ahead after three shots had been cleared in quick succession by Dundee defenders. But the home side equalized before half-time and took the lead in the sixtieth minute. Even the stoutest Celtic heart could have been forgiven a seizure. Only thirty minutes from relegation, Celtic fought on and gained corner after corner. Then, towards the end, Weir squeezed home a second goal. With only two minutes to go the same man struck again for his hat-trick and Celtic were saved. He had been bought to give speed, thrust and power to the attack. On that one April afternoon he repaid his transfer fee a hundred times.

As Airdrie accompanied Queen's Park into the 'B' Division the Celtic Board were already in action to make sure that they would never again have such an experience. The former Burnley player Jimmy Hogan, who had been successful as a coach on the Continent, was signed up on a full-time basis and manager Jimmy McGrory crossed the sea to Ireland with £20000 to sign three promising players from Belfast Celtic. In the end he came back with £12000 and one of Celtic's greatest-ever captures – Charles Patrick Tully.

Some months earlier Celtic had tried to sign the great Wilf Mannion from Middlesbrough and failed. They tried a second time but still could not lure him to Scotland. They had better luck, however, with eighteen-year-old Bobby Collins of Pollok Juniors. He was to become another Celtic great although Celtic had to fight a famous off-the-field battle before securing his signature. The dispute involved

Celtic, Everton, the Scottish Junior Football Association, the Scottish League and the SFA. The late Sir Robert Kelly was to say some years later that he felt officialdom put as many obstacles as possible in Celtic's path over the Collins case.

On the very day that Celtic were in the bad books over an alleged offence in signing another junior player, Pat Buckley of Bo'ness, a complaint arrived from Everton addressed to the SFA. At a special meeting of both the Scottish League and SFA it was decided that Buckley was a St Johnstone player and Celtic were severely censured on the dating of the transfer forms and fined £50. Manager McGrory was fined £100. Celtic's case had been that Buckley had been signed by them on a provisional form and had been paid by Celtic although he was allowed to play on with Bo'ness. When he signed for St Johnstone he was regarded as a Celtic player and the player himself had been in breach of the rules. The same meeting upheld that Collins was an Everton player because of letters which had passed between Everton and Pollok Juniors. Everton had been in a position to offer Pollok £1000 for the player, but Celtic, being a Scottish club, were limited by rules to paying the club £100 and the player £20.

Celtic had to depend on Collins and his father to settle the issue. They described how they had travelled south only to find that there was no one there to meet them. They had signed no agreements and Collins later decided he would not to go England. He wanted, he said, to play for Celtic. Eventually Everton withdrew from the case although it was not to be the end of the story. The SFA, in one of those wise decisions designed to mystify the public, suspended Collins for six weeks without as much as giving him a reason. Collins tholed his assize and was free to join Celtic.

The fans who had been so loyal were obviously pleased with the signing activity during the close season as 55000 turned out on the opening day of the season 1948–9 for the match with Morton. By the end of August Celtic had played to more than 200000 spectators, an average of more than 40000 a match. The new forward line read: Weir, McPhail, Lavery, Tully and Paton and into the centre-half position came Boden from Duntocher St Mary's in place of Corbett who had moved to Preston North End. Hogg, in the twilight of a fine career, went to Alloa and Milne took over his position at right-back.

Despite the flurry of signings, performances continued to belie promise and the first three matches against Morton, Aberdeen and

Rangers failed to produce a victory. It was 28 August before they registered their first win against Hearts. But the 2–1 victory was marred by the ordering off of Jock Weir who had earlier dislocated an elbow.

It was the year of the great crowds. Despite their ups and downs Celtic played to 584000 spectators in only thirteen games. By the beginning of December the total had reached more than a million. Disgruntled they may not always have been, but to use the Wodehousian phrase, they were certainly far from being gruntled! They took thirty-one points from thirty games and could manage only joint sixth place in the League. The League Cup was also a flop with failure to qualify for the quarter-finals. The performances prompted chairman Bob Kelly to say: 'We have the players but it appears we haven't got a team. Our supporters are wonderful and we are determined to give them results.' The only trophy won that season was the Glasgow Cup.

In the determination to bring success Celtic offered two players and a cheque for £10000 in a last effort for Mannion but by this time Middlesbrough were talking in terms of £25000. Out of the disappointments many were taking comfort from the new boy Tully. He was something completely different. With his soft, Irish brogue he could charm everyone – and he did. On the field he was subtle, resourceful, impertinent, exquisitely clever and tricky. Against this he was petulant.

But the whole mixture turned him into an overnight box-office attraction and the sportswriters were delving into their memories for the descriptions used for Patsy Gallagher and Tommy McInally at their peak. One reporter wrote of a game at Hampden: 'Tully is without peer in the inside-left position. In the matter of sheer ball manipulation the Irishman was once again superb, and we can hardly blink the fact any longer that the boy from across the water is setting a standard in skill we used to monopolize.' In one of his first matches, against Rangers, he stopped the ball and invited challenges, he walked with it, he ambled with it, but he never bothered to run or break sweat and he was the best man on the field. He left the hapless Ranger Ian McColl in tatters.

Everyone connected with Celtic and football have stories about Charlie, who died very suddenly a few years ago, still in his forties. Jimmy McGrory remembers just a few weeks into a new season when the bold bhoy walked into his office asking for new boots. 'But, Charlie,' said the puzzled manager, 'you got new boots with the rest of the players at the start of the season.' Charlie insisted they were finished. McGrory said: 'Look here, I played for Celtic over sixteen years and went through only three pairs of boots.' Quick as a flash Charlie replied: 'Yes, boss, but you never used them.'

The gentlemen of the Press flocked around Charles Patrick because he always had a story to tell them and every newspaper of the day carried what became known as Tullyisms. He would go on about the time he visited Rome and the Vatican and everyone in St Peter's Square looked up at the balcony and asked: 'Who's the fella in the white suit with Charlie Tully?' Then there was the time he asked Jimmy McGrory to get him two pounds of sausages from the butcher on the way home. Jimmy was standing in the queue when in walked Scot Symon of Rangers. Scot asked: 'What are you doing in here?' Jimmy replied: 'I'm getting two pounds of sausages for Charlie Tully.' Scot said: 'That certainly seems like a good bargain.'

Charlie's wit as well as his skill made him a legend in his own lifetime. Your writer was speaking to him in the Estadio Nacional in Lisbon just minutes after Celtic had won the European Cup and he was overwhelmed not only by the result but by the fact that so many younger Celtic fans from a generation which had never seen him actually recognized him and came up to speak to him.

Celtic opened the season of 1949–50 with a victory, their first in the opening match for five years, and the fact Rangers were their victims made it all the sweeter. It was the day young Bobby Collins made his début and he was accompanied by another new boy, Haughney, from Newtongrange Star.

Collins played on the right wing against the famous 'Tiger' Shaw and Haughney played on the left flank. Both made a magnificent contribution towards the 3–2 victory with Haughney scoring the winner. But it was the return League Cup match at Ibrox which provided the big talking point. In front of 90000 spectators Charlie Tully took the ball for a walk towards the Rangers by-line only to be kicked in the pit of the stomach by Cox. The referee took no action as the Celtic player lay on the ground and this led to fighting on the terracing. Celtic's directors asked the SFA to hold an inquiry but that august body did a great balancing act instead in which they judged that two players, Cox and Tully, and an error of judgement by the referee had incited the crowd. Both clubs were ordered to post warning notices on the terracings and in the dressing-rooms and the players were severely reprimanded. No action was taken against the referee because of his 'previous good record'.

For once Charlie Tully was speechless. In an extraordinary piece of manoeuvring officialdom lumped the innocent Tully in with the man who had kicked him. Before the SFA meeting a sportswriter had remarked: 'Neutral members among Scottish football legislators should have no trouble in apportioning the responsibility for the trouble.' After the meeting he commented: 'The spectators saw Cox's action. If Tully provoked that action in a manner not apparent to the crowd, why have the Referee Committee not made public his share of the incident? Their findings imply that both players were equally to blame; that, so far as those who saw the incident can reason, was not the case.' He wound up his report by stating: 'If ever a committee had an opportunity to exercise its authority here it was, but their decisions to my mind, are a shirking of straightforward duty.'

The findings were not acceptable to the Celtic Board but again the SFA refused to conduct an inquiry. By 14 September Celtic and Rangers had already met three times since the opening of the season and in view of the tension which had developed the Celtic Board wrote to the Scottish League requesting postponement or cancellation of the match due between the clubs at Ibrox on 24 September.

Their application was turned down but the Celtic fans backed their Board with a boycott and the crowd was down by about 40000 on the previous gates. Practically the whole of the 'Celtic end' of Ibrox was deserted that day.

At their meeting on 28 September the SFA Council approved by twenty-five votes to five the minute of the Referee Committee finding in the Cox–Tully case. The chairman of the Referee Committee had stated that 'Tully simulated any slight injury he may have received and his actions may have been as blameworthy as an admitted indiscretion by Cox.'

The season finished with Celtic taking only fifth place in the League Championship but there was great satisfaction taken in the performance of the newcomers. Bobby Collins was described by one writer as 'one of the great inside-forwards of our time who demonstrates how a defence can be cut to ribbons without leaving any ghastly edges on the wounds'. The Scottish Cup had everyone thinking back to the famous 'snow final' of 1889 when Celtic and Third Lanark decided to play a friendly game after heavy snow fell just before the kick-off.

Sixty-one years later to the very month the same thing happened – this time it was the second round – and the opponents were the very same Third Lanark. With only half an hour to the kick-off a blizzard swept Cathkin Park and it was announced to the spectators already in the ground – about 20000 – that the match had been abandoned as a Cup tie but would be played as a friendly. When the actual tie was played Celtic won 4–1 after a 1–1 draw but Aberdeen ended their dreams of Hampden with a 1–0 victory.

The club's only consolation that season was the Charity Cup in which they beat Clyde and Third Lanark to contest the Final with Rangers. More than 80000 turned up with the added attraction of seeing the great American entertainer Danny Kaye who did a pre-match warm-up routine. Celtic's team of Bonnar, Haughney, Milne, Evans, McGrory, Baillie, Collins, Fernie, McPhail, Peacock, Tully went 3–0 up before Rangers managed a shot at goal. But the Ibrox men made a game of it by pulling back two goals and making Celtic fight to the final whistle.

The close season saw Celtic return to the European scene with a visit to Rome where they had been invited to take part in the fiftieth anniversary celebrations of the club Lazio – a team which was to create a reputation for violence in the European tournaments of the late 1960s. The journey was highly enjoyable for the players and management with short stops in London, Brussels, Lucerne and Milan en route. They played out a 0–0 draw in torrid heat on 30 May which was marred by the sending off of John McPhail and the Italian centre-half. The referee sent the Italian packing and turned to the Celtic players saying: 'And you go too, Mr McPhail, to appease the crowd.' Celtic were obviously annoyed at the ordering off and the referee made a unique offer at half-time when he said he would turn a blind eye if both players wished to go out for the second half!

But chairman Bob Kelly would have none of it. He told the referee: 'You put them off and it is off they will stay.' In the return game at Celtic Park in the September good old Scottish weather in the form of a downpour helped Celts to a 4–0 win and John McPhail had the last laugh on Lazio by scoring all four goals.

The season of 1950–1 saw two new regulars who had been blooded towards the end of the previous season – Willie Fernie from Kinglassie in Fife and Bertie Peacock from Coleraine in Northern Ireland – names which were to join the greats of Celtic Park. It was John Mc-Phail's great year. The centre-forward got the best out of his line as he ambled like a great St Bernard using his height and weight and a tremendous swerve which wrong-footed many an opponent. A total of 185000 spectators saw Celtic win their League Cup section although they succumbed to Motherwell, the eventual winners of the Cup, in the quarter- finals. They won the first game of the season against Rangers by 3–2 but before a ball was kicked more off-the-field controversy preceded the event.

During Celtic's Charity-Cup-winning run of the previous season an *Evening Times* writer had commented: 'I noticed at Hampden on Wednesday night that the Celtic players accepted every decision without showing the least complaint. The Celtic have long since insisted on that from their players.' A Mr A. Brown of Bellshill had been appointed to referee the Old Firm game mentioned but after a remark he made the Scottish League showed immense sensitivity. Mr Brown had said in an interview regarding an earlier Celtic match: 'I was delighted with the behaviour of the Celtic players against East Fife. They made my job easy. I feel they deserve a word of thanks. They accepted my decisions with consistent and pleasing assent.' Mr Brown's appointment was immediately cancelled!

Celtic went out of the Glasgow and Charity Cups but the season was to be a big breakthrough back into the trophy-winning business. Although the League Championship chances also vanished the Scottish Cup made it a year to remember. They beat East Fife in the first round after a scare and a replay at Parkhead and they accounted for Duns in the second. The following round against Hearts at Tynecastle was a memorable occasion not only because of a fine Celtic victory against the odds but because of a fabulous goalkeeping display which had every Celtic fan harking back to the days of John Thomson.

Regular keeper Willie Miller had moved on to Clyde and his place had been taken by nineteen-year-old George Hunter of Neilston Juniors. The crowd was so great that afternoon that police had to allow spectators to sit practically along the by-lines and yet it did not affect the nerve of the young Celtic goalkeeper who made save after fabulous save from the Hearts immortals of Conn, Bauld and Wardhaugh. Those who were there that day will remember his coolness when at one stage the game was stopped for a few minutes because of injury. Although he had been under great pressure just seconds earlier he sat on the ball next to his goal and stared into space as though he had not a care in the world.

But like many Celtic goalkeepers he was just another name within a year when a serious illness forced him out of the game. The quarter-finals with Aberdeen at Parkhead attracted 75000 and the gates had to be closed. A 3–0 victory took them into the last four to face Raith Rovers whom they defeated by 3–2. So the club entered its twenty-fourth Scottish Cup Final to face their famous rivals of 1931 and 1933 – Motherwell. As in 1931 the club was planning a tour of America and they were anxious once again to take the Scottish Cup with them as they had done on that first transatlantic crossing.

The Cup Final line-up was: Hunter, Fallon, Rollo, Evans, Boden, Baillie, Weir, Collins, McPhail, Peacock, Tully. A goal by McPhail in the first half was enough to capture the Cup for the sixteenth time and the Celtic fans in the 134000 crowd were delirious that a thirteen-year trophy famine had ended. Since their Scottish Cup win in 1937 – Jimmy McGrory's last year as a player – and their League Championship of 1938 they had won only three Glasgow Cups and two Charity Cups.

So on the evening of 8 May 1951 Celtic left Glasgow Central Station en route for the United States and the send-off was incredible, with Charlie Tully needing his very own police protection. The tour was a repetition of the previous one with receptions and feasting everywhere. Two novelties for the party were air conditioning in hotels and television appearances to promote their tour. Between 20 May and 20 June, with occasional rests at lakeside retreats and ranches, the Parkhead men played nine games, winning seven, drawing one and losing one. The results were: New York Stars (5–1), Fulham in New York (2–0), Eintracht in New York (3–1), Philadelphia All Stars (6–2), National League in Toronto (2–1), Chicago Polish Eagles in Detroit (4–0), Fulham in Toronto (1–1), Kearney Select in New Jersey (2–0), and Fulham in Montreal (2–3).

The match with Eintracht, which seemed to attract every German in the States, was the only trouble spot. Three penalties against Eintracht brought manager, coaches and other officials pouring onto the field. The referee was punched and so was manager McGrory although Jimmy Mallan exacted retribution from the offender for the attack on his boss. Even an exiled Scot, a Mr McGonagle, who had been leading a pipe band, came in for rough treatment. He had been a proud man as he piped the Celts onto the field but he was a pathetic sight and near to tears as he stood, his bagpipes in tatters. One laugh after that game came, however, when the players were introduced to a real Red Indian chief who claimed to be 120 years old. Charlie Tully turned to Jimmy McGrory and quipped in his usual fashion: 'Did he play against you, boss?'

Celtic came back home with the Scottish Cup and some additional trophies to more scenes of mass hysteria but it was the trophy they were about to play for which caused the big talking point of the year. The SFA and the Glasgow Corporation had got together to sponsor the St Mungo Cup as part of the Festival of Britain celebrations. All sixteen clubs in the First Division took part in it during the summer months and Celtic won all their rounds and the right to meet Aberdeen in the Final at Hampden on Wednesday, 1 August, before 80000 spectators. They sent out: Hunter, Fallon, Rollo, Evans, Mallan, Baillie, Collins, Walsh, Fallon, Peacock, Tully. The Aberdeen side was: Martin, Emery, Shaw, Harris, Thomson, Lowrie, Bogan, Yorston, Hamilton, Baird, Hather. The very fine referee of the time, Mr Jack Mowat, was in charge.

On three occasions during the competition Celtic had been two goals behind but rallied to win and the Final proved no exception when they turned a two-goal deficit into a 3–2 victory. Although they had been two down they had been the more skilful side throughout. Captain Bobby Evans, the best man afield, further enhanced his reputation when he took over in goal for ten minutes while Hunter received treatment for a head injury. Yorston and Bogan had Aberdeen 2–0 up after thirty-five minutes but the great Charles Patrick Tully got Celtic back into the game only two minutes from half-time with one of his immortal tricks. He took a throw-in off the back of an Aberdeen defender and won a corner. He took it himself and his cross gave Fallon a goal. Fallon also got Celtic's second five minutes into the second half and Tully scored the winner after a mazy run.

It was not until after the presentation of the trophy by the Lady Provost at the Kelvin Hall that all the uproar started. One of the Celtic officials, examining the heavily ornate silver confection, embellished with the Glasgow coat of arms, was shocked when a salmon, serving as one of the handles, broke off in his hand. He also discovered on further examination that the base was covered in verdigris and that the ornate decorations included a mermaid and lifebelt – hardly the kind of things one would expect to find on a football trophy. Then the big story broke in the Press. The Cup had been cast in 1894 as a yachting trophy. In 1912 it had been altered for a football competition between Provan Gasworks and a Glasgow police team.

During the arguments which followed Lord Provost Victor Warren was indignant. He was absolutely furious when Celtic asked for a new Cup. He said the trophy was worth £600 which turned out to be a bit of an exaggeration. It weighed 73 ounces and silver at that time was worth about £1 an ounce! The Celtic management then thought about buying a new trophy themselves but the whole issue blew over and it was decided that the winning of the competition was more important than the trophy itself. Certainly the St Mungo Cup, mermaids and all, sits proudly to this day with other trophies in the Celtic boardroom. It is a tangible memory of a Celtic team which, in keeping with tradition, had gone out to play for a permanent trophy and won it.

The season of 1951–2 was a poor one indeed with not a single trophy. It was particularly disappointing in view of the promise of the previous year. The one unenviable distinction was being knocked out in the first round of the Scottish Cup by Third Lanark in a replay – the first time in more than fifty years that Celtic had lost in a Scottish Cup replay.

There was however that season a happening of immense importance to the club with the unheralded arrival of a veteran player from the non-League club of Llanelli in Wales. He had played for Albion Rovers before going south and had been brought back by Celtic to coach their promising young players. His name was Jock Stein. In a short time he had broken into the first team because of injury and loss of form by other players. He showed a leadership which his team-mates admired yet no one at that early stage could have known just how significant his signing was going to be in the later pages of Celtic's history.

European Cup Final, Celtic *v*. Inter Milan, 1967. Goalkeeper Sarti beaten by Gemmell's shot for the equalizer. Gemmell is partly hidden by No. 9 Chalmers.

Stevie Chalmers beats Sarti of Inter Milan to score the goal which brought the European Champions' Cup to Britain for the first time.

Manager Jock Stein and Bobby Murdoch with the European Cup in the dressing room after beating Inter Milan 2–1.

Is this football? Riot police on the field in Montevideo as player trouble begins. Celtic players seek safety in numbers.

John Hughes — on the ground behind Leeds No. 2 Paul Madeley — has just scored at Hampden to put Celtic 2–1 ahead on aggregate in the European Cup semi-finals second leg, 15 April 1970. Jimmy Johnstone (No. 7) shows his joy.

Celtic players do a lap of honour at Hampden after defeating Leeds United in the European Cup semi-finals. *Left to right:* Tommy Gemmell, Bobby Murdoch, David Hay, George Connelly, Billy McNeill.

Milan 1970. Celtic players enjoy a laugh at their Varese training HQ. *Left to right:* Jimmy Johnstone, Bobby Lennox, Willie Wallace, Lou Macari. Their amusement is caused by the tennis style of Director James Farrell (*right*).

Like Francis Drake, Manager Jock Stein enjoys a game of bowls Italian-style before an important battle. But unlike Drake, he lost in the shock European Cup Final defeat to Feyenoord by 2–1.

Just before the penalty kicks drama with Inter Milan at Celtic Park, 19 April 1972. *Left to right:* George Connelly, Pat McCluskey, Lou Macari, Jim Craig, Billy McNeill and Evan Williams get drinks from trainer Neilly Mochan and Jock Stein. *Far right:* Jimmy Johnstone and Bobby Lennox get a sponge down from physiotherapist Bob Rooney.

Arrogance is still being shown to referee Babacan as he sends off one of Atletico Madrid's players in the European Cup semi-finals at Celtic Park on 10 April 1974. David Hay, standing over the ball, waits to take yet another free kick.

Celtic party at the Tinto Hotel near Symington, 1938. *Left to right, back row:* Manager Maley, John McKillop, Tom Colgan, Tom White, Colonel Shaughnessy (Directors), Tom Devlin and Desmond White (later to join the board), and Director Robert Kelly. *Front row:* Mary Colgan (Tom Colgan's daughter), Mrs Robert Kelly, Mrs Tom White, Mrs John McKillop and Adele White, daughter of Mr Tom White.

The Celtic Board of Directors and Management, 1977. *Left to right:* David McParland (Assistant to the Manager), Tom Devlin (Director), Desmond White (Chairman), James Farrell (Director), Jock Stein (Manager) and Kevin Kelly (Director).

Billy McNeill, a Celtic scarf around his neck, is carried shoulder high after the 1975 Scottish Cup Final win over Airdrie (3–1). The greatest Celtic captain of all time announced his retirement after the match. Manager Jock Stein, head bowed, walks from the field after congratulating McNeill. This was McNeill's seventh Scottish Cup medal and seventh win as captain — a record.

The record-makers, 10 February 1973. Bobby Murdoch who on this date scored Celtic's 6000th league goal, with, *left to right*, Adam McLean (2000th), Jimmy McGrory (3000th), Jimmy Delaney (4000th). Missing is Frank Brogan who scored the 5000th in the early sixties.

Easter Road, 16 April 1977. Celtic have just beaten Hibs 1–0 to win their first-ever Premier League. Skipper Kenny Dalglish, like the thousands in the background, holds aloft a Celtic scarf. The others left to right are : Andy Lynch, Pat Stanton, Johnny Doyle, Tommy Burns, Danny McGrain, Joe Craig, Roy Aitken and goalkeeper Peter Latchford.

Scottish Cup Final, 7 May 1977. The victorious Celtic team show off the Cup at Hampden – the first official lap of honour for twelve years. *Left to right:* Roddy McDonald, Johannes Edvaldsson, penalty-scorer Andy Lynch, Roy Aitken, Danny McGrain, Paul Wilson, Joe Craig, Alfie Conn, substitute Tommy Burns and Pat Stanton. Missing are skipper Kenny Dalglish and goalkeeper Peter Latchford who are searching for Dalglish's medal, lost during the lap of honour but later found.

12   The Fifties

When manager Jimmy McGrory was casually asked to find a new Irish tricolour to replace the rather tattered one flying above the old 'Jungle' in 1951 little could he imagine that his troubles – and Celtic's – were only beginning. He telephoned flagmakers all over Scotland and found that they either did not make Irish tricolours – or refused to make them! So he decided on bold action and wrote to no less a person than Eamon de Valera, the Prime Minister of the Irish Republic. He had been introduced to de Valera on an Irish tour some years earlier and explained his difficulties in writing. Within a few days a parcel containing the flag arrived at Celtic Park.

A tricolour of green, white and orange – the white signifying a band of peace between the green (Catholic) and orange (Protestant) communities – had been presented to the club during a tour by the new Free State government after partition in 1921. Before then the old Irish flag – all green with a gold harp – flew above Celtic Park as a tribute to the Irishmen who had founded Celtic. It is worth pointing out here that the Union Jack also flies at Parkhead. Thanks to many stitches in time the original tricolour had lasted. But by the early Fifties it was in tatters and finally irreparable. The new flag from Dublin was hoisted onto its pole at the beginning of the season of 1951–2 and on New Year's Day at the match with Rangers it suddenly took on a whole new meaning in the eyes of people not connected with Celtic or Ireland.

From their foundation Celtic had been closely associated with Ireland and Catholicism but never at any time had they been sectarian. The fact that most Celtic teams have been mainly Catholic has not been by design, as players have always been judged purely on merit, but because of those early club connections. Once, in the mid-1890s, a member of the rather large and unwieldy committee proposed that Protestants in the team should be limited to three. He put forward this motion in the mistaken belief that the Celtic support would not wish any more. But his motion was defeated by a counter-motion that the committee should have the right to sign as many Protestants as they wished. This decision was published in the minutes of the monthly meeting of the committee held in the old pavilion, later destroyed by fire, in March 1895.

Despite such a broad-minded attitude from those early days, there has always been a suspicion of Celtic motives in a Presbyterian country which harbours within its boundaries probably the biggest collection of bigots and religiously misinformed people in Western Europe. The fact also that Rangers have, over the years, had a policy not to play Catholic players, has not helped Celtic's cause. It has been said on more than one occasion that Rangers are not so much a Protestant club, more an anti-Catholic one, although hooliganism among their supporters has forced them in recent times to state that they will sign a Catholic. That remains to be seen. The fact that they have been totally Protestant has meant that every time Celtic have met Rangers the Parkhead team has been the 'Catholic' side no matter how many non-Catholics they have fielded.

It is a situation which has led to much violence over the years. Rangers, through their own fault, have attracted one of the worst sets of supporters in Europe. Celtic, to a much lesser extent, because of a tag they have been given, have also attracted a hooligan element under the disguise of a religious banner. So when Celtic and Rangers met at Parkhead on 1 January 1952 it provided the flashpoint for one of Celtic's greatest off-the-field battles. Eleven spectators were arrested after bottles had been thrown. Two were sent to prison and the rest were fined for incidents in and around Celtic Park. Glasgow's magistrates, after a meeting, decided to invite the SFA and Scottish League to consider the following four proposals.

1. That the Rangers and Celtic clubs should not again be paired on New Year's Day when, it was suggested, passions were likely to be inflamed by drink and when more bottles were likely to be carried than on any other day.

2. That on every occasion when these clubs met admission should be by ticket only, and the attendance limited to a number consistent with public safety, the number to be decided by the Chief Constable.

3. That in the interests of the safety of the public the Celtic Football Club number passageways in the terracing at each end of Celtic Park.

4. That the two clubs should avoid displaying flags which might incite feeling among the spectators.

The Referee Committee of the SFA considered the points but passed the buck on to Celtic saying that under Rule 114 of the Association the responsibility for the conduct of its supporters lay with Celtic. They came out against the proposal that Celtic and Rangers should no longer meet on New Year's Day. But the big shock to emerge from the meeting came in the form of a veiled order which was probably the most ridiculous ever given in football legislation. Apart from being warned that any further trouble would endanger the continuance of football at Celtic Park for a long time to come, Celtic were ordered to stop displaying at the ground any flag or emblem which had no association with Scotland or football. A further order was given, also applying to Rangers, that every step should be taken to prevent supporters from flaunting flags or banners which the committee felt were the root causes of sectarian bitterness. At no time was Rangers' attitude towards Catholics even hinted at. In the weeks which followed the storm clouds gathered over Celtic Park and the offices of Scottish football officialdom. When the SFA met to consider the committee's findings they voted twenty-six to seven in favour of the recommendations.

The battle was really on but Celtic were in confident mood. Everyone at Parkhead knew that they had the rules of the Association behind them yet when Celtic played a home game that weekend some newspapers printed in astonishment: 'They are still flying the Eire flag!' Chairman Bob Kelly and directors Desmond White and Tom Devlin were of the opinion that they might go as far as pulling Celtic out of the Scottish League. Mr Kelly told people within the club at the time: 'I would rather introduce Gaelic games here than completely close the club or give in to this order.' Mr Kelly's argument all along was that Celtic had broken no rule and at no time did anyone in the SFA chamber refute his argument that the order itself was in breach of the rules. During the battle Celtic found an ally in the form of Mr John F. Wilson, the Ibrox chairman, who supported Mr Kelly in his moves. Mr Kelly was highly appreciative of the gesture by the Ibrox chairman and was to say so many times over the next few years when people pointed to the poorer side of Old Firm relationships.

The Glasgow magistrates met again and expressed dissatisfaction that their recommendations had not been fully carried out but they endorsed the recommendations of the Referee Committee. Before doing this they had ordered the Celtic and Rangers chairmen from the room as both men had moved, on the grounds that the SFA had no powers to make such an order, that the part of the minutes relating to the flag should be removed.

The *Glasgow Herald* summed up the stormy meeting thus:

Not a member of the council or any of the office bearers, who in the course of a long and heated meeting had recourse to reading or studying the rules, confuted Mr Kelly's argument and by not doing so at least tacitly indicated that they realized a blunder had been made. The approval of the minute, therefore, brands the members who voted for it as individuals who approve a breach of their own rules. The position now appears to be that the SFA can have jurisdiction over a club or a member by adhering to the rules and have just as complete jurisdiction over them by breaking the rules.

Celtic continued to fly the flag and confidence grew each passing day. But in the SFA chambers phrases like 'anarchy against democratic government' were being bandied about by people with no great love of Celtic. At the next SFA meeting the Hibernian official Harry Swan, acting president, put forward a motion that Celtic should be given three days to comply with the order or suffer suspension. That motion even got a seconder although it was completely out of order. But there were enough men in the room who realized that such action would result in disruption of the League and financial loss to their own clubs through losing gate money in their matches against crowd-pulling Celtic. So by the narrow majority of sixteen votes to fifteen the Council decided to give Celtic some grace and extended the date from which suspension would begin until 30 April – the last day of the season.

The Celtic directors knew after the vote that they were within sight of victory. Again the *Glasgow Herald* commented:

The feelings of the Referee Committee, who met before the Council did, now are that in ordering Celtic to take down the flag they are not inflicting any penalty or punishment – they are simply trying something to stop hooliganism at football matches. More than once during yesterday's long discussion Mr Robert Kelly, chairman of Celtic, was asked to realize that. He was also asked to realize that the whole matter was no longer one of just taking down the flag; it was a matter of Celtic defying the instruction of the Council. He was told that if he would only make the gesture and take the flag down, even without prejudice to further discussion, everyone would be happy. At different stages several councillors made extravagant demonstrations of sympathy for Celtic even though they latterly voted for the shorter period of grace being given to the club. Not even Mr Kelly, I'm sure, appreciated that he had so many friends – up to a point, the point where finance joins forces with principles. 'You'll be the biggest man in football,' he was informed. 'You'll establish a reputation never possessed by anyone in football if you'll only take the flag down, even temporarily, and enable us as a Council to say that you accepted our decision.' That was the gist of many appeals for 'bigness'.

Perhaps Mr Kelly did not wish to be the biggest man in football, or perhaps he wishes to maintain or increase his present reputation for adhering to his principles. There could be no doubt that he struck his shrewdest blow when he said suspension could only follow a broken rule. No one had proved that Celtic had broken any rules.

Three weeks later, before the expiry date for the ultimatum, the SFA somersaulted on the matter. At the 7 April meeting they unanimously decided to cancel their order for the time being. This, they said, was to allow them and the Scottish League to reconsider the whole business. The astonishing thing concerning the SFA about-face was that their accompanying statement did not include a mention of the word Celtic or the word flag. Reference to suspension of a club was deemed sufficient. The flag came down at the end of the season as it always does – it flies only at first-team home games – and it reappeared the following season. It is still there today although it changes its flagpole occasionally. It vanished for a few weeks a couple of seasons ago but those who sought its removal in the Fifties must have been even more bitter in the Seventies. The reason was that Celtic had won their world-record ninth League flag in a row and because of a shortage of flagpoles the Eire flag had to take some time off to make way for all the Championship flags!

Some members of the SFA thought face had been saved when Celtic took down the flag after the last game of the season but some others wanted to keep the controversy going at the beginning of the season 1952–3 and tabled a newly worded motion for the flag's removal. Enough of the Council had learned from their folly of the previous season and the motion fell by eighteen votes to twelve. The flag of the Irish Republic flies with the flags of many other nations above Celtic Park. Those who take offence or think it causes offence can only be termed ignorant. It is a flag of peace and flies as a tribute to those Irishmen who founded the club. What a slight it would be if those early pioneers were ever forgotten. The Celtic Football Club are proud of their Irish origins and they are proud of being Scotland's most successful-ever club. Celtic are a Scottish club and by winning such trophies as the Coronation Cup and European Cup have brought more honour to their country than any other. They have no time for people who flaunt flags or banners of any type in a provocative manner.

Before moving on from the story of the Eire flag it is worth mentioning a rather amusing scene in the Easter Road boardroom at that time. Hibs chairman Harry Swan had been so involved in the controversy because of his position within the SFA that at one stage he attempted to get a free bit of legal aid. A certain top lawyer often attended matches at Easter Road, and knowing that Celtic were gradually winning their case, Swan asked the expert for some legal advice only to be shocked by the reply: 'I'm sorry I cannot discuss this matter with you as I am acting for the Celtic.' A week or so earlier Bob Kelly had asked co-director Tom Devlin to fix up a top legal expert in the east whom no one could say had a vested interest in what was happening in Glasgow.

It is difficult to know why Swan took such a hard line, especially as after it was all over he took a Celtic director aside and said: 'I never even noticed that flag and I couldn't care whether it stayed up or came down.' That statement would lend weight to the argument that he had been influenced by SFA secretary Sir George Graham. The secretary was very much anti-Celtic and down through the years had acquired a talent for leading the SFA from behind, ensuring he never got his fingers burned.

There was another significant happening around that time when the bulldozers moved into Easter Road and demolished a wall at the front gates. It was said by Swan that reconstruction work was being carried out yet a similar wall was rebuilt on the same spot. The title of Hibernian Football Club was also reinstated but the harp which had sat above it had mysteriously vanished!

At the first match involving Celtic and Rangers in the season of 1952–3 a moronic element proved that there was much more to hooliganism than a mere flag. During a one-minute silence (observed to mark the death of a young Celtic player, John Millsopp) howls of profanity about the Pope and blasphemous demands for the game to begin emanated from the Rangers end of the ground. A Union Jack also appeared over the terracing wall despite dire warnings from the Chief Constable.

It was a season which saw Celtic robbed of the services of Bobby Collins because of a broken arm from an Irish tour in the April of that year. It was to be December before he reappeared. His absence left the Celtic forward line without a steadying influence and much of their play in front of goal was rash. Only the Charity Cup came their way but there was one memorable part of Celtic folklore that season. In the third round of the Scottish Cup at Brockville an all-ticket crowd of 23000 witnessed not only a great Celtic fightback but an unrepeatable goal from unrepeatable Charlie Tully. Falkirk were leading 2–0 against the Celtic side of Bonnar, Haughney, Meechan, Evans, Stein, McPhail, Collins, Walsh, McGrory, Fernie, Tully.

Two minutes into the second half Falkirk missed an easy chance to go three up and from that point on Celtic never looked back. Tully took a corner kick which flew over Celtic forwards and Falkirk defenders and curled into the back of the net. But the joy of his team-mates and the fans on the terracing was silenced when referee Gerrard judged that the ball had not been placed inside the corner arc. So the bold Charles Patrick replaced it and amidst scenes of pandemonium placed the ball in exactly the same part of the net. It was unbelievable. To do it once was remarkable. Twice was surely impossible! Crush barriers gave way in the hysteria being generated amongst the Celtic faithful. They knew they had witnessed something very special. It is a goal which could not be scored today as the rules governing corner kicks have been changed. If the ball is judged to be outside the arc nowadays, a free kick is awarded to the opposition.

Willie Fernie and centre-forward McGrory scored the other two which gave Celtic victory and once again the crush barriers came down. Thirty people were injured and hundreds invaded the field to congratulate their heroes after the third goal. There was a danger at one stage that the referee would abandon the game but the Celtic players managed to persuade their followers to return to the terracing.

At the end of the season 1952–3 the Scottish and English football authorities got together in organizing the Coronation Cup for competition between Arsenal, Manchester United, Tottenham Hotspur and Newcastle United of England and Rangers, Hibernian,

Aberdeen and Celtic. Some people with a reputation of not being kind to Celtic suggested that they should really not have been invited to take part. And to an extent they had a point. The Celtic cupboard was bare whereas the other sides were at the top of their form. Arsenal had just won the English League Championship and Manchester United and Spurs had won it the previous two years. Newcastle had won the English Cup in 1951 and 1952 while at home Rangers were lifting honours and Aberdeen had won the Scottish Cup and Hibs the League. If Celtic had a right to enter it must have been that they have an unsurpassed record for winning new trophies, trophies they can keep.

Before they kicked a ball, however, there was a revolt behind the scenes over wages and for a time it seemed they would not take part at all. But chairman Bob Kelly interviewed the players individually and asked them one question: 'Are you prepared to play?' They were and took the field for the opening match against Arsenal at Hampden captained by Jock Stein. To everyone's astonishment they began playing the type of football which had been completely foreign to them.

Perhaps they were spurred on by remarks in the Press by some Arsenal officials who stated that they thought the game would be a formality. Although the score was only 1–0 it did not reflect the Celtic superiority. They accounted for Manchester United in the next round by 2–1 and were left to face Hibs – Famous Five and all – in the Final. That Hibs forward line of Smith, Johnstone, Reilly, Turnbull and Ormond was superb and could interchange like the earlier Celtic line of Crum, Divers, Delaney, McDonald and Murphy. They were deadly finishers and very much the favourites. So on Wednesday evening, 30 May, before 117000 spectators, Celtic sent out: Bonnar, Haughney, Rollo, Evans, Stein, McPhail, Collins, Walsh, Mochan, Peacock, Fernie. Tully was missing through injury from the previous round. The Hibs line-up was: Younger, Govan, Paterson, Buchan, Cowie, Combe, Smith, Johnstone, Reilly, Turnbull, Ormond. Celtic opened the scoring with a fabulous thirty-yard shot from Neilly Mochan after Bonnar had defied the Famous Five in perhaps his greatest game in a Celtic jersey. Walsh scored three minutes from time to put the final seal of approval on a great tournament.

The winning of the Coronation Cup must, in those days, have been the equivalent of winning the European Cup of today. It was to prove a springboard for further success. It was a tournament in which Celtic had found themselves once again. Stein had been so wily in enticing the dangerous Reilly into his favourite left-foot tackle and Evans had been supreme, showing that he was one of the greatest half-backs of all time. It was he who began the move leading to Walsh's vital goal. And so, to the array of permanent trophies won over half a century – the Exhibition Trophy of 1901–02, the League Shield to mark six consecutive Championships, the Empire Exhibition Trophy of 1938, the Victory in Europe Cup of 1945 and the St Mungo Cup of 1951 – they added the Coronation Cup.

Despite the marvellous boost they began the season of 1953–4 in poor fashion. They collected only three points from their League Cup section and failed to reach the quarter-finals. They lost a Glasgow Cup semi-final replay to Rangers and just when things were looking gloomy a positional switch in the team brought about transformation. Mochan moved to the left wing and scored twenty-six goals as the entire team hit brilliant form and went on to take the League Championship with forty-three points from thirty games – five ahead of their nearest rivals, Hearts. The Scottish Cup gave them a bye in the first round and then away matches with Falkirk, Stirling Albion and Hamilton Accies – all of whom they beat.

Motherwell were the opponents in the semi-finals and fought out a 2–2 draw in front of 102000 spectators at Hampden before going down 3–1 in the replay which was watched by 93000. Celtic sent out Bonnar, Haughney, Meechan, Evans, Stein, Peacock, Higgins, Fernie, Fallon, Tully, Mochan against Aberdeen in the Final in front of 130000 spectators and a 2–1 victory gave them the much coveted 'double' of League and Cup, a feat they had achieved only three times previously in 1906–07, 1907–08 and 1913–14. It had been Celtic's finest year for decades and as a reward the directors took the playing staff to Switzerland for the 1954 World Cup Finals. It was a journey which widened the football horizons of Jock Stein who the previous year had paid his own way to Wembley to watch the great Hungarians in action. Stein was injured the following year while touring Ireland with the club, an injury which has left him with a limp to this day. It led to his giving up the playing side of the game and he was appointed coach to the reserve side.

Celtic returned from Switzerland in confident mood for the season 1954–5 but within weeks their inconsistent form had the fans baffled. They reached the Scottish Cup Final again only to lose 1–0 to Clyde in a replay. The winner was scored by Tommy Ring, the famous Clyde player who came from a Celtic-daft family. The story has it that when he visited his parents' home the following night his mother put down a plate of piping hot soup in front of him only for one of his brothers to whip it away. It was some time before the rest of the family spoke to him again!

Celtic had as fine a team as they could wish yet their effectiveness was not commensurate with their skill. They were not helped in the season 1955–6 when the First Division was expanded to eighteen teams, making opposition much tougher and the climb to the top more strenuous. Bonnar, Haughney and Stein had dropped out of the team and there was a rebuilding job on hand. They managed to win the Glasgow Cup with a 5–3 victory over Rangers and reached the Scottish Cup Final for the third consecutive year only to go down 3–1 to Hearts. The following season, 1956–7, they won for the first time the League Cup. They topped their section which included Aberdeen, East Fife and Rangers, defeated Dunfermline in the quarter-finals, Clyde in the semi-finals and Partick Thistle by 3–0 in the replayed final.

But the following year brought the big League Cup story. Celtic again reached the Final and their opponents were the hot favourites Rangers. They lined up on 19 October 1957 at Hampden after accounting for Airdrie, East Fife and Hibs in their section, Third Lanark in the quarter-finals and Clyde in the semis. Celtic's team was: Beattie, Donnelly, Fallon, Fernie, Evans, Peacock, Tully, Collins, McPhail, Wilson, Mochan. Against them were: Niven, Shearer, Caldow, McColl, Valentine, Davis, Scott, Simpson, Murray, Baird, Hubbard. The referee was Jack Mowat.

From the very start Rangers were overrun and the Celtic attacks did not cease until the final whistle. They had recaptured, it seemed, for those ninety minutes the great play of their Coronation Cup days. Billy McPhail, a younger, slimmer version of his brother John, toyed with the opposition while Fernie, Evans and Peacock coped easily with what Rangers had to offer in the way of attacks. Mochan streaked through the right flank of the Rangers defence like a hot knife through butter and for the first twenty minutes Rangers were lucky to keep their goal intact. Celtic were two goals up at half-time, thanks to Wilson and Mochan, while Collins and Tully both hit woodwork. Rangers had the wind and sun behind them in the second half but neither the elements nor their hastily rearranged attack made any difference to the pattern of play. The procession continued and further goals from Mochan, McPhail who got a hat-trick and Fernie from a penalty had the Rangers defenders panic-stricken and praying for the final whistle. It had seemed that day that a goal would come just about every ten minutes and it all became too much for a section of the Rangers supporters who invaded the field. It was the biggest hammering the Ibrox team had ever taken in a Cup Final and it stands to this day as a record score for a national Cup Final in Scotland. It was a tremendous occasion which will never be forgotten by those who witnessed it – at both ends of Hampden!

But little did the delirious Celtic fans know that day that they would have to wait almost another eight years before seeing a national trophy held aloft by a green-and-white-clad arm. It marked the beginning of the end of the fine sides of the 1950s and over the next few seasons players like Tully, Evans, Mochan, Fernie and Fallon either bowed out or moved on to pastures new.

In the ranks of the reserves a revolution was taking place. Jock Stein had a couple of years' coaching experience behind him and the Celtic reserve team was winning things for the first time in nearly twenty years. In a way his success was causing a bit of embarrassment because the first team could win nothing. He had introduced training methods unheard of in Scottish football and introduced football tactics.

Players dropping out of the first team into the reserves suddenly found themselves facing a hard, uncompromising and ruthless Stein who was hell-bent on success. In those days lapping the track around Celtic Park was very much a part of the training routine and before Stein's arrival it was not unknown for players to jump down into the 'Jungle' for a rest or even a quick draw on a cigarette! But Stein was always on the trackside, not just content to watch from a distance. He monitored every lap, counted the players and even timed them. Reputations did not matter to Stein. If Charlie Tully had dropped into the reserves for a week or two he had to toe the line – or else.

During this period a very valuable partnership sprung up. A young player called Billy McNeill had signed on from Blantyre Victoria in 1958 and showed from the start that he had remarkable ability in the air. He travelled by bus from Lanarkshire to Celtic Park for midweek training and had for company Jock Stein, also a Lanarkshire man. Often making up the team was Kevin Kelly, now on the Board of directors. All three spent their travelling time talking football and listening to each other's points of view although obviously McNeill and Kelly did most of the listening!

The season of 1958–9 saw the winning of the Charity Cup for the twenty-seventh time but in the League Celtic managed only thirty-six points from thirty-four games and lost the semi-final of the Scottish Cup to St Mirren by 4–0. The following season – 1959–60 – brought even less cheer. They went out of the Charity Cup to Rangers on the toss of a coin and also fell at the hands of the Ibrox men in the Glasgow and Scottish Cups. A new decade had dawned but seemed to hold little promise. The club had embarked on a youth policy with Bob Kelly stating that the future of Celtic lay in the hands of youth.

Meanwhile Jock Stein had left to take up the Dunfermline manager-ship and in the last half-dozen or so games saved them from what had seemed certain relegation. The Press began writing stories of how he actually went to spy on other clubs who were about to meet his team. He was doing all kinds of things which had been unheard of in Scottish football and in next to no time had welded Dunfermline into a club to be reckoned with. He got a good mixture of youth and experience together and within a year was to give due notice to Celtic that they had made a big mistake in letting him go.

The knowledge of why Bob Kelly never appointed Stein as manager before allowing him to go to Dunfermline died with him. Perhaps he still wished to keep the tight control he had over team matters. He was to prove once more just how much that control was when he pushed through the transfer of young Bertie Auld to Birmingham City in 1961. Manager Jimmy McGrory was to say years later that he had 'one hell of a job' keeping Auld in the team. Often Kelly would say he wanted Auld dropped and eventually he got his way.

Bertie Auld, who of course came back to become a Celtic immortal in the Lisbon team of 1967, recalls now with a smile those days in the late Fifties. He concedes that he was not the most disciplined of players at that time yet he had a respect – and fear – of Kelly as most players did. Bertie recalled one day:

Bob Kelly always seemed to be around Celtic Park night and day. He would be there in the morning watching the full-time players and back in the evening watching the part-timers. He would look right through you with those steely eyes of his and I used to always just nod, say 'Good evening, Mr Kelly' and keep moving. He was an imposing character. One night I was walking up the tunnel from the pitch with a young boy who had just joined us and there as usual was Mr Kelly standing in the main hall looking at us. Before I could say anything the young lad said 'Good evening, Bob' and I thought the legs had gone from under me as I tried to get to the dressing-room door.

13   Advent of Europe

Such was the success of the European Cup by the beginning of the 1960s that the Fairs Cities Cup (now UEFA Cup) had also established itself and in turn was followed by the European Cup Winners' Cup. The epic Real Madrid–Eintracht Frankfurt European Cup Final at Hampden in 1960 had opened the eyes of the Scottish public who until then had been quite content with the domestic scene. But after that sunny evening when a whole new concept of football was witnessed the public clamoured for more. The Celtic support had seen only a few visiting foreign teams in friendly matches and had been deprived of the real thing because of the team's lack of success in the national competitions. Yet Celtic had been the Scottish pioneers in playing Continental opposition. They had blazed trails across Europe from their earliest days. Now the Sixties were about to bring a renewal of their foreign travels.

On 14 May 1960 Dutch champions Sparta Rotterdam had come to Glasgow to play Celtic in a friendly and were soundly beaten 5–1 by the Parkhead youngsters. Apart from the scoreline, the evening is remembered as the one in which Celtic players wore numbers for the first time. Celtic had for years opposed the use of numbers on their famous green and white hooped jerseys because it was felt they ruined the appearance. Those who remember Kilmarnock and Morton playing in hooped jerseys will agree that the numbering system looked clumsy. Celtic had found a way round the problem by having large numbers printed on both the front and back of the players' shorts. Unfortunately for Celtic, UEFA sent out a directive in 1975 that numbers must be shown on jerseys and for European competitions Celtic are now faced with the choice of playing in an alternative strip or defacing the sacred hoops.

The season of 1960–1 showed little hope for the future although the team reached three Cup Finals.

The Charity Cup was shared with Clyde after a 1–1 draw. The Glasgow Cup, in which Celtic had beaten Rangers 4–2, was lost to Partick Thistle by 2–0 and in the Scottish Cup Dunfermline, under new manager Jock Stein, won by 2–0 in a replay. On the League front Celtic had improved their position to fourth place with thirty-nine points from thirty-four games and the reserve and third teams won their respective Championships. It was the third successive year the reserves had won their League and the first time it had been achieved by the club.

Celtic by this juncture were very much a club of youth with Bobby Evans having departed to Chelsea and Charlie Tully having returned across the sea to Ireland. They had been the heart and intelligence of the team. At the beginning of the season 1960–1 only Fernie, Peacock and Mochan were left from the great side of the Fifties. But youth got a boost after a well-built seventeen-year-old called John Hughes had made a sensational first-team début against Rangers in the League Cup and overran their defence in a 3–1 victory. On the way to the Scottish Cup Final Celtic had beaten Hibs in a replay at Easter Road and a newspaper report of the game referred to the Hibs keeper Ronnie Simpson as a veteran. Little was that writer to know that Simpson's greatest hour was still some seven years away!

The feats of the reserve and third teams moved chairman Bob Kelly to state in the club's *Handbook*:

Though failure to win any major honours has disappointed the management and supporters alike, I am sure that all of us are in agreement that the promise of our many young players is almost at the stage of fulfilment. In one respect, the season just gone past was just as successful as any in our long history because the reserves won a very important consolation prize.

Some of the finest Celtic teams of the past have been reared and coached at Celtic Park and it should delight all who have Celtic's interests at heart, that unless there are unforeseen circumstances we shall be fielding in the forthcoming season in top-class football in Scotland a team composed entirely of players who have joined us from no higher a grade than juniors. Our policy of creating a team of players imbued with the Celtic spirit and tradition will continue, but that does not mean to say that we shall not engage more seasoned men if the necessity arises. And despite what some may choose to think we shall continue to bring to Celtic Park players of any creed or colour so long as they are prepared to do their best for Celtic.

Mr Kelly went on to point out that among the League-winning

Celtic reserves of 1934 were players like Buchan, Crum, Divers, Morrison, Paterson and the O'Donnell brothers.

The youth policy had to take another sudden spring forward when at the end of 1960–1 Bertie Peacock, Celtic's longest-serving player, suddenly decided to quit and return home to Ireland. The Board, management and supporters were sorry to see him go but he parted on the best of terms and went into football management in Northern Ireland.

It had been a season which had seen Celtic take faltering steps into Europe when they were one of four Scottish teams invited to take part in the Friendship Cup. They were beaten 3–0 by their French opponents Sedan Torchy and in the return at Celtic Park could only manage a 3–3 draw. In the Scottish Cup they had beaten Falkirk 3–1 at Brockville, Montrose 6–0 at Parkhead, Raith Rovers 4–1 at Stark's Park, Hibs 1–0 at Easter Road and Airdrie 4–0 in the semi-finals at Hampden.

The Final against Dunfermline saw the fast-rising Jock Stein pit his wits against his old club. He had saved the Fife club from relegation the previous season with an amazing string of victories. Now in his first full season with the club he had taken them to a new frontier. The *Glasgow Herald* reported just a couple of days before the match on Stein's novel approach to training sessions: 'Dunfermline players are wondering what their manager has thought up for their practice match. Before the previous ties he had the pitch reduced in size to match the grounds of Second Division opponents. Then he had his second team play against his first in the manner of Aberdeen, their next opponents.'

The first game in front of 113000 provided plenty of thrills and fine play but no goals, thanks mainly to the Dunfermline goalkeeper Eddie Connaghan who brought off a miraculous save when John Hughes diverted a shot from Crerand. It was to be only one of many such saves from him. Crerand showed in this match that he was developing into one of the best passers of the long ball in British football. Despite an injury to their centre-half who had to play the last quarter of an hour on the wing, Dunfermline never lost their ability to play coolly out of defence and through midfield.

For the replay in front of 87000 spectators Celtic were without left-back Jim Kennedy who on the day of the match was rushed to hospital with appendicitis. He was replaced by Willie O'Neill who was making his début and some critics maintained that Peacock should have been played instead. The teams which lined up under leaden skies and in drizzling rain were: Celtic – Haffey, McKay, O'Neill, Crerand, McNeill, Clark, Gallagher, Fernie, Hughes, Chalmers, Byrne; Dunfermline – Connaghan, Fraser, Cunningham, Mailer, Miller, Sweeney, Peebles, Smith, Thomson, Dickson, Melrose.

It was a game which was to become known as Connaghan's Final. Hampden has surely never seen such inspired goalkeeping. On the kind of night goalkeepers normally make mistakes he clutched balls firmly and eventually broke the hearts of the Celtic forwards. Very much against the run of play Peebles broke clear in the sixty-eighth minute to beat Haffey, and another goal near the end took the Cup to Dunfermline. The Celtic players were later praised for the manner in which they congratulated the Fifers at the final whistle. This was followed up in the *Celtic Football Guide* for the following season in which manager Jimmy McGrory wrote: 'I know that every Celtic supporter will join me in congratulating Jock Stein on his club's fine performance during his first full season as manager.'

Chairman Bob Kelly was heard to say after the Final: 'A friend's gain is no loss.'

On the international scene that season goalkeeper Frank Haffey and centre-half Billy McNeill had gone to Wembley with Scotland and suffered a 9–3 humiliation at the hands of England. It marked the end of Haffey's international career but happily for Billy McNeill, whose début it was, he was to represent his country many times after that day. The two full-backs in that match were Shearer and Caldow of Rangers. Many years later Shearer managed to smile about it all and said: 'The trouble that day was that they used an orange-coloured ball. Caldow and I were afraid to kick it and McNeill was afraid to touch it!' The story also goes that after the match a group of the players, including McNeill, were sitting in a rather depressed state and drowning their sorrows. With a refreshment or two under their belts they got talking about the next match – a World Cup qualifying game against Czechoslovakia the following week.

One player reckoned that after their Wembley defeat none of them would ever play again and suggested that they should all tear up their visas and set them alight in an ashtray. They agreed and he led the way. But the others burst into howls of laughter and put their visas back in their pockets. Needless to say there was only one player missing from the Wembley party when they travelled out to Czecho-slovakia!

G

During the close season Frank Brogan of St Roch's and John Cushley of Blantyre Celtic joined the club. Both had runs in the first team from time to time although they never fully established themselves. Frank, however, got himself into the record books as the man who scored Celtic's 5000th League goal in a match against Partick Thistle at Firhill. With them came Bobby Murdoch from Cambuslang Rangers. He was described as a very promising inside-forward and equally promising on the wing.

The season of 1961-2 was again to prove an exasperating one with the fans having to wait until the last game of the season to see a trophy won – the Glasgow Cup – in which Celtic defeated Third Lanark 3-2 in a replay. The Championship saw them have their best results since their 1953-4 victory with forty-six points from thirty-four games which put them in third place behind winners Dundee (54 points) and runners-up Rangers (51). Celtic had kept themselves in with a chance of the League after defeating Dundee at Celtic Park on the run-in. But that victory also enhanced Rangers' chances of the title. However, a 1-1 draw between Celtic and Rangers saw Dundee once again take the initiative and both the Parkhead and Ibrox challenges fizzled out in the remaining games.

The Scottish Cup had started earlier than usual with a December game against Cowdenbeath at Celtic Park which finished in a comfortable 5-1 victory. Morton, who were setting all kinds of new records in the Second Division, were defeated at Cappielow in the following round. In the third round Celtic beat Hearts 4-3 at Tynecastle, thanks to a controversial re-taken penalty kick by Pat Crerand. Third Lanark were the opposition in the quarter-finals and succumbed 4-0 after a 4-4 draw at Parkhead.

So Celtic faced up confidently to St Mirren in the semi-finals at Ibrox. Most clubs were behind in their fixtures due to bad weather and Celtic had travelled to Paisley in the League the previous Monday night. A comfortable 5-0 win with goals from Divers (2), Chalmers (2) and Carroll was the worst thing that could have happened to Celtic. They lined up on 31 March against a St Mirren team which included ex-Celt Willie Fernie. Celtic went down 3-1 and the afternoon brought disgraceful scenes from some Celtic followers who invaded the pitch in the hope of having the match abandoned. In the labyrinths of their twisted minds they had thought they could bring about a replay.

What they did not realize was that the Celtic directors had conceded the match within minutes of them invading the field. It was a sorry scene but happily one which has not haunted Celtic over the years as it has done with Rangers whose fans are wryly said to be undefeated throughout Europe. This point must be made as from time to time sections of the media tend to lump Celtic fans in with those who cause trouble abroad.

In the November of 1961 Jock Stein was attracting more attention – this time from Hibernian. They made it known that they wanted him as manager and there was talk of them paying a £30000 transfer for him which would have been a novel way of getting a manager. Stein was interested but the Dunfermline directors knew that he was worth more to their club than money and held him to his contract.

Towards the end of the season 1961–2 three new and very significant names joined the club from the junior ranks. They were Tommy Gemmell, described as 'a very speedy full-back', from Coltness United, outside-right Jimmy Johnstone from Blantyre Celtic, and Bobby Lennox, an inside-forward from Ardeer Recreation. Lennox in fact played in the last game of that season and won himself a Glasgow Cup medal. Meanwhile players like Pat Crerand, Billy McNeill and John Hughes were establishing themselves on the international front, as were full-backs Duncan McKay and Jim Kennedy. McKay was years ahead of his time and one of the first full-backs to indulge in overlapping. But at that time such things were frowned upon. Full-backs were defenders and not really supposed to cross the half-way line! Nine players were freed and the management looked to the season of 1962–3 hoping for the long-awaited breakthrough.

But it was to be another barren year. In the League Cup a 0–0 draw at Tannadice prevented Celtic reaching the quarter-finals and in the Championship they dropped back from third to fourth place. Because of that third place the previous season Celtic had qualified for the Fairs Cities Cup but made an early exit at the hands of Spanish club Valencia in the first round, the results being 4–2 in Spain and 2–2 at Celtic Park.

Before those ties, however, Celtic had staged a very memorable European-flavoured night in a challenge match at Parkhead for charity. Real Madrid were reckoned to be past their peak but with men like Di Stefano, Puskas and Gento still playing they could still match the best and defeated the young Celtic by 3–1. Once again the club had to depend on the reserves to bring some prizes. The Reserve League was won by fifteen points taking sixty-four out of a possible sixty-eight. That achievement must have come as a bit of a blow to the sportswriter who, at the beginning of the season, had written that Rangers should field their reserve team in the First Division and keep their top team for European matches! Rangers Reserves had managed only third place on goal average and just to rub it in the third team won the Combined Reserve League for the third year running.

The club had signed Bobby Craig from Sheffield Wednesday during the season in a bid to add punch to the attack which was suffering from that old failing of missed chances in front of goal. His arrival coincided with a purple patch which saw Celtic beat Airdrie 6–1 and St Mirren 7–0 in successive weeks. Just when it seemed they were finding some consistency one of the worst winters in decades struck and little football was played between December and March. Craig never really settled and in the end moved on.

In the Scottish Cup Final Celtic had played well in the 1–1 draw with Rangers. But for the replay they dropped Jimmy Johnstone despite the fact that he had shown so much promise in that first game. It was a night of humiliation for Celtic who went down 3–0 without even a fight. Long before the end large gaps had appeared at the Celtic end of the ground as supporters trooped away unable to watch Rangers toy with their team.

The Glasgow Cup had also been a big disappointment, especially after beating Rangers in a first round replay. Celtic went on to dispose of Partick Thistle in the semi-finals but lost the Final to Third Lanark 2–1.

Perhaps the greatest disappointment of the season for many Celtic people had come a couple of months earlier. Pat Crerand had been transferred to Manchester United in February of 1963 for around £60000. Crerand had been a strong-headed character and chairman Bob Kelly felt he showed a lack of discipline. There had been a few upsets behind the scenes involving Crerand which culminated in a row with Sean Fallon following a 4–0 defeat at the hands of Rangers in the New Year game. Crerand was an ambitious player and like some of his team-mates who were breaking through at international level he was frustrated and disillusioned at Celtic's lack of success and the fact that the set-up at Parkhead provided little hope for the future. Players such as Billy McNeill were a bit more patient although

McNeill would certainly have left Celtic but for the return of Jock Stein as manager in 1965.

Crerand's transfer was handled by the chairman and manager Jimmy McGrory was called in only at the last moment to rubber-stamp the transfer papers. Just seconds after the formalities were over Manchester United manager Matt Busby left the room leaving Crerand with Jimmy McGrory and Bob Kelly. The player burst into tears and said to McGrory: 'I don't want to leave the Celtic.' Bob Kelly got up and left the room. As he had done two years earlier in the transfer of Bertie Auld to Birmingham City, he showed once again that he was very much the man in charge at Parkhead. In the event, Auld was to return to Celtic and share their greatest triumph in Lisbon in 1967 and just a year later in 1968 Crerand was also to win a European Cup medal with Manchester United.

The only good thing to come out of the 1963 Scottish Cup Final against Rangers was the fact that it qualified Celtic for the European Cup Winners' Cup as Rangers had also won the Championship and would be playing in the European Cup.

So the season of 1963–4 saw Celtic make their first real mark in Europe by reaching the semi-finals at their very first attempt in that competition. It was a quite outstanding achievement and with a bit more professionalism behind the scenes at Celtic Park they might have gone on to win the trophy. The fact that they were 3–0 up against MTK Budapest of Hungary after the first leg of the semi-finals and lost 4–3 on aggregate proves the point. Although it is worth pointing out that at the after-match banquet the referee sat at the top table flanked by the MTK President and a beautiful blonde, while the Celtic party sat at a side table.

In the earlier rounds Celtic had beaten Basle 5–1 in Switzerland and 5–0 at Celtic Park. In the second round they had beaten Dynamo Zagreb of Yugoslavia 3–0 at Parkhead before going down 2–1 in the return. They drew a real tough nut in the quarter-finals in the shape of Slovan Bratislava of Czechoslovakia. The young Celts won 1–0 at home and it was generally believed that their more experienced opponents would prove too much for them in the return leg. But Celtic confounded everyone by not just holding their slender lead but by winning 1–0 again. It was a tremendous result and showed that the team was maturing. They had come a long way since that Scottish Cup Final defeat the previous season. MTK Budapest came to Glasgow on a sunny April evening in 1964 and were overwhelmed by a team growing in confidence with each passing game. Chalmers got two goals and Johnstone the other in the 3–0 rout which should have seen Celtic with a bigger lead at the end of ninety minutes. The 4–0 defeat in Budapest would never have happened had a shrewd tactician like Jock Stein been in charge.

It was a case then at Celtic Park, as it had been for so many years before, that the chairman had too much control over team matters. That very same month Hibs had at last managed to get Jock Stein to Easter Road and within a very short space of time he had them the best team in the land. He invited Real Madrid to Easter Road, packed the ground to bursting point and managed the first Scottish team ever to beat the great Spanish masters. That very season he had travelled to Italy to study the training methods of Helenio Herrera of Inter Milan, the world's highest-paid football coach. Stein had obviously learned and used that knowledge to add to his already wonderful ability.

Despite their fine performances in the Cup Winners' Cup, the domestic scene at Parkhead in the season of 1963–4 had been yet another disappointment with the shadow of Rangers constantly over the young Celts. In five outings against the Ibrox men they had been beaten on every occasion. They finished third in the Championship, eight points behind Rangers and two behind Kilmarnock, thereby qualifying for the 1964–5 Fairs Cities Cup. They managed to win the Glasgow Cup with a 2–0 win over Clyde in the Final.

In their League Cup section earlier in the season Celtic had lost the opening game to Rangers, dropped a point to Kilmarnock in the second and in the following match on 17 August dropped another point to Queen of the South at Parkhead. That result prompted a demonstration outside the main door after the match. The angry crowd, which had to be dispersed by police, chanted for the resignation of chairman Bob Kelly. But Mr Kelly, unknown to the demonstrators, had travelled with the reserve team to Dumfries. The season ended with fifteen players being freed.

The most amusing story of the season of 1963–4 had come in Zagreb in the European Cup Winners' Cup. After the first leg Celtic had laid on a wonderful night's entertainment for their guests which included haggis, bagpipes and tartan souvenirs. So overwhelmed were the Zagreb officials that they promised Celtic a day to remember in Yugoslavia. They lived up to their word and part of the hospitality included a cable-car trip into the hills with a lavish lunch at the top.

and everyone in the party seemed to be enjoying the occasion. Everyone, that is, except John Hughes. He was terrified of heights. He had plucked up enough courage to make the ascent of several thousands of feet. But having survived that he quietly decided to make his own way back down on foot, not realizing that it would be a journey of several hours.

The Celtic party finished lunch and made their way back in the cable-car enjoying the scenery and being told by their pretty guide that the tree-covered hills were famous for their wild bears. Back at the cable-car base director Desmond White did the routine head-count as the party boarded the team bus and to his horror realized not everyone was there. The alarm went out and Zagreb football officials organized helicopter patrols and ranger jeeps to begin a search. By this time Big John was nearly half-way down the hill and as he was crossing a pathway from one wooded area into another cluster of trees he was luckily spotted by one of the patrols and picked up. When he got back to the main party and heard about the dangers he changed colour. As everyone howled with laughter one of the players christened him Yogi Bear after the cartoon character and it was a name that stuck to him for the rest of his career and was to ring out over many a stadium in the years ahead.

It was around that time that Neilly Mochan returned to Parkhead as assistant trainer.

After so many years in the wilderness and early season hopes dashed, the season of 1964–5 saw Celtic qualify for the later stages of the League Cup for the first time since the season of 1958–9. After managing only a 0–0 draw with Partick Thistle in the opening match at Celtic Park, they scored three against Hearts, four against Thistle and six against Hearts in consecutive matches. In the final sectional game at Rugby Park, Celts went down 2–0 to Kilmarnock mainly due to a broken ankle sustained by centre-half and captain Billy McNeill which kept him out of the side for several months. But with eighteen goals for the loss of only five and nine points out of twelve they had qualified for the quarter finals where they defeated East Fife 6–2 on aggregate after losing the first match by 2–0 in Methil.

Centre-forward Stevie Chalmers scored five of the six goals and was nicknamed 'Di Steviano' by a newspaper the following day which pointed out that Celtic should not be too upset at having failed to lure Alfredo Di Stefano to Parkhead just after he had retired from

Real Madrid. It had been a bold move by the club to bring a big personality to Celtic Park. The newspaper report went on to state that with a man like Chalmers performing in such a manner Celtic had no need to look further. Chalmers was to score another five at the same stage of the competition four years later in a 10–0 rout of Hamilton Accies at Celtic Park, Bobby Lennox getting the other five. Stevie was a wonderful servant to Celtic. Few players ever gave the effort he gave. He played every ball until it went out of play or into the net. On more than one occasion he chased seemingly hopeless balls to see them come back off a corner flag and give him possession. And despite most of his success coming towards the end of his career he remained the same likeable man he had been during the barren years. It was fitting that the winning goal in the European Cup Final in Lisbon fell to him.

If ever the Celtic youth policy provided a player imbued with Celtic spirit then that player was Stevie Chalmers. By the time he had left Celtic at the beginning of the Seventies he had become the club's second greatest goal-scorer to Jimmy McGrory although within a couple of years he was overtaken by his old team-mate Bobby Lennox, a man very much in the Chalmers mould.

In the semi-finals of the 1964–5 League Cup Celtic marched on by beating Morton 2–0 to face Rangers in the Final. Alas, Celtic still could not break the Ibrox jinx over them in Cup Finals and despite a brave fight and a ball which appeared to cross the Rangers goal-line but was ignored by the referee, Celtic went down 2–1. Billy McNeill was still missing through injury for that Final and the team was captained by Jim Kennedy.

Before the disappointment of the League Cup Final Celtic had again been involved in European football. In the first round of the Fairs Cities Cup they defeated the highly temperamental Portuguese team Leixoes 3–0 at Celtic Park, having gained a 1–1 draw in Portugal. But the star-studded Barcelona team put an end to Celtic's hopes with a 0–0 draw at Celtic Park after a 3–1 victory in Spain.

In the Championship things had begun promisingly with 3–1 wins over Motherwell and Rangers and twelve points were taken out of the first sixteen. But inconsistency had crept in again and by the turn of the year Celtic were out of things with Hearts and Kilmarnock carrying the battle.

Saturday, 6 February 1965, saw Celtic go to Paisley and win 3–0 in the first round of the Scottish Cup. Just a week earlier Jock Stein had been appointed manager although he was not to take over until the following month. Bertie Auld, signed in the January, was already showing great maturity and his influence rubbed off on the rest of the team.

In the second round they struggled a bit to beat Queen's Park 1–0 at Hampden then defeated Kilmarnock 3–2 in an excellent game at Celtic Park. The semi-final match with Motherwell at Hampden saw Celtic depend on an Auld penalty to get a 2–2 draw. The Fir Park team's goals had been scored by centre-forward Joe McBride who was to sign for Celtic just a couple of months later. In the replay Celtic ran out easy winners by 3–0 with goals from Chalmers, Hughes and Lennox.

A few weeks later on 24 April 1965 they lined up against Dunfermline in the Scottish Cup Final for the second time in five seasons. It was a remarkable game and a remarkable day. As in the semi-finals Celtic twice fell behind and twice fought back. The first equalizer followed a spectacular thirty-yard shot by Charlie Gallagher which hit the crossbar and crazily spun high into the air. Bertie Auld never took his eyes from the ball as he began his run and outjumped the Dunfermline defence to head it into the net – a net from which he had to be disentangled by his ecstatic team-mates. It was Auld who also scored the second equalizer after Celtic had gone in at half-time 2–1 down.

Then came the climax which had old Celtic men weeping and young supporters unable to believe it had actually happened. There were ten minutes left when Celtic, with Dunfermline under constant siege, won yet another corner-kick. Gallagher crossed from the left at the Mount Florida end of the ground and there sprinting towards the edge of the penalty area was centre-half Billy McNeill. He rose away above everyone including goalkeeper Herriot and hammered the ball into the roof of the net with his head. A few seconds seemed to pass before it sunk in that the goal had been scored and an almighty roar erupted from the packed Hampden bowl. It was not just a Cup Final roar or a roar for a winning goal, special as they are. It was a roar which had built up for eight long years and suddenly been released in one go.

Those old Celtic men had thought they would never hear it again and the young had despaired of ever hearing it at all. On the field the players leapt on top of Billy McNeill. It was so apt that their captain should have scored the winner and they all showed the emotions

which a first medal brings. There were 108 800 people in the ground
and every one of them seemed to be holding aloft a green scarf or
banner giving a sort of umbrella effect to the stadium. The scenes as
the team bus made its way from Hampden into Glasgow were
incredible and reached fever pitch in the old Gorbals which was, of
course, a Celtic stronghold. Fans actually threw themselves in front
of the bus to slow its progress and give themselves a better view of
the Scottish Cup. Then they crossed over the Clyde bridges in their
thousands to stand and cheer outside the Central Hotel where the
team celebrated. They refused to go home without saluting their
heroes and the Cup and Billy McNeill and his men had to walk
through the hotel kitchen and risk life and limb balanced on a narrow
window ledge overlooking Hope Street.

If 25 May 1967 was the most significant day in ninety years of
Celtic then 24 April 1965 was not far behind it. The lean years were
over at last. Jock Stein was there, the players needed were there and
the hunger for success was there. That wonderful afternoon was the
launching pad for all the fabulous honours which were to follow
in the club's greatest era – an era which was to stretch for many
years with only one blot, that European Cup Final night against
Feyenoord on 6 May 1970 in Milan's San Siro Stadium which was
examined in Chapter 5.

Its aftermath brought Celtic some of their unhappiest days and
much to contend with in the following the season of 1970–1.

14 Heading for Nine in a Row

Only forty-eight hours after returning from the chaos of Milan's Malpensa Airport and the numbing defeat at the hands of Feyenoord, the Celtic players had gathered at Prestwick to leave on a tour of Canada, America and Bermuda. The *Celtic Football Guide* for the following season was to state: 'If it's true what the old proverb says – "All's well that ends well" – then there can be no question of the success of Celtic's 1970 tour.' The author of that report could not have been further out with his assessment because the tour, organized earlier in the year, had turned out to be the most unfortunate and badly timed in Celtic's history.

In view of the nature of the defeat in Milan few of the players felt like travelling or facing more football. The sixteen-hour flight to Toronto was exhausting and a burst tyre on landing for a fuel stop at Montreal did not help the nervy, unhappy party. Some of the players were still angry at manager Stein's summing up of the Dutch opposition, while that very morning he had expressed in his weekly *Sunday Mirror* newspaper column a disappointment in the players' financial talks before and after the game.

That atmosphere coupled to the jet lag was not the best build-up for the opening game against Manchester United the following day. A cup competition had been prepared by the organizers but in such a complicated manner that Celtic had to win their opening match to stay in the tournament! In the event they lost 2–0 and any competitive spirit they had managed to muster just vanished. Two days later, in the humidity of Randall's Island, New York, Celtic ran up against what one journalist described as a brick wall called Bari. The Italians showed a complete disregard for the rules of the game and at the end of the day Celtic had to depend on a penalty equalizer from Harry Hood to give them a 1–1 draw.

The following Sunday, 17 May, Celtic lined up for the third game of the tour in the Canadian National Exhibition Stadium, Toronto, and the opposition once more was Bari. The match had been postponed from the previous day because of bad weather and considering what was to follow would better have been forgotten altogether. With the score at 2–2 five minutes from the end, the Italians walked from the pitch in protest against a penalty award to Celtic and the match was abandoned. Two of their number – including the goalkeeper – had already been sent off and Celtic's forebodings about a second meeting with them had been very much confirmed.

It was immediately after the match that the tour shocks began and they were an obvious spin-off from the shattering disappointment of Milan. Within hours of the final whistle Jock Stein, without consultation with anyone in the Celtic party, had disappeared and was on a plane back to Scotland. He refused to speak to waiting pressmen at Prestwick Airport but in a brief statement before his departure from Toronto he had said he was going home for a hospital check-up on his ankle and to deal with an ultimatum from Jimmy Johnstone. The little winger, who had been allowed to stay at home because of an arduous season and his fear of flying, had stated that he would not sign a new contract unless he got more money. The manager's unheralded departure caught everyone on the hop and senior director Desmond White, who had not gone on the tour because of business reasons, had to make arrangements to fly out and take charge of the party. Chairman Sir Robert Kelly who had been ill for many months had insisted on going to Milan but after the gruelling delays on the way home he had been unfit to travel on the tour.

Shock number two came before Desmond White's arrival when Tommy Gemmell and Bertie Auld were sent home by acting manager Sean Fallon for breaches of club discipline. The players were to admit later that it had all been caused by the drop in morale after Milan plus general frustration at a singularly unsuccessful and meaningless tour.

It was generally felt that had manager Stein still been with the party the situation would never have escalated to the extent it did.

Gemmell had in fact stated in a newspaper immediately after the Milan game that he wanted to leave the club. He had already asked for a transfer the previous October after being dropped from the League Cup Final team on a disciplinary matter. Gemmell's newspaper statement had brought the following reply from Stein: 'His situation has not altered since he asked for a transfer. Not a single offer was received for him. He stayed in the team last season simply because it would have been unfair to the fans and his team-mates to upset a team that had started the season and was doing well.'

With those unhappy echoes still ringing in their ears, the Celtic team got on with the job of playing football and in the final match of the North American part of the tour met West Germans Eintracht Frankfurt. The team, now badly depleted because of injuries and the loss of Gemmell and Auld, not surprisingly went down 3–1.

On a happier note the paradise island of Bermuda beckoned and at last the Celtic party had a chance to relax and forget the pressures of the European campaign and the other upsets. In between sun-bathing, deep-sea fishing, golf and swimming Celtic beat the Bermu-dan national side 7–1 and local club Somerset 4–1. It was on that sunny island that the talent of youngsters like Kenny Dalglish and Victor Davidson got a chance to shine and it was obvious from their displays that they were not far away from knocking on the first-team door. Celtic's previous visit to Bermuda had been in 1966 prior to the build-up for Lisbon and their all-conquering season. This time it had not been so happy and it was obvious that the season ahead would pose certain problems for the club.

That month was a mixed one for Jock Stein. In the Honours List he was awarded the CBE, the penultimate stage before knighthood, and had a £10 fine slapped on him by the SFA for verbally attacking referee Bobby Davidson after the Celtic–Aberdeen Scottish Cup Final, one of the many clashes he had with Davidson over the years.

Angered by Davidson's award of a penalty to Aberdeen and two other shattering decisions against Celtic, Stein had emerged from Hampden to say: 'I wonder if there will be an inquiry into the refer-eeing of this match as in other important matches this season.' Behind that comment was a reference to the fact that Glasgow referee Jim Callaghan had been suspended following a complaint by Rangers over his handling of a match which they had lost to Celtic. It was the first time a referee had been suspended in such a manner.

Before the new season of 1970–1 dawned the great Ronnie Simpson had decided to retire. His shoulder injury was not responding to treatment and with his fortieth year not far away he knew that time had at last caught up with him. Ronnie had been goalkeeper with Queen's Park from his early teens when most of his Lisbon team-mates were in their cradles. In 1948 he played for the British team in the Olympic Games and his other clubs had been Third Lanark, Newcastle United and Hibernian. He won two English Cup medals with Newcastle in the 1950s. In 1964, after a spell with Hibs, it was generally felt that he was drifting out of the game. Then Celtic stepped in and bought him for less than £3000. The man who sold him to Parkhead was none other than Hibs manager Jock Stein! In no time Simpson had broken into the first team and in his few seasons with the club he won every honour in the game including international caps.

It was apt that his last act as a Celtic player was to stop a goal. With one of those famous reflex actions he threw himself to his right and with one hand stopped the ball dead in its tracks. In doing so he dislocated his shoulder for the second time in a few months and had to be helped from the field by trainer Neilly Mochan and physiotherapist Bob Rooney. The match was a League Cup semi-final tie against Ayr United at Hampden – the ground where he had started his wonderful career some twenty-five years earlier.

Ronnie, although only with Celtic a few years, was the most successful and consistent goalkeeper since John Thomson more than thirty years earlier. Known to his team-mates as 'Faither', he had vast experience and always remained cool. He would lose the odd daft goal but it never affected his game.

In the club's *Handbook* for 1970–1 manager Jock Stein stated in a message to the supporters: 'I would like to hope that, in our respective roles, we go forward to a new season confident that there will be much to be proud of waiting ahead of us in the long stretch to April.' But those respective roles were very nearly to go their separate ways in the months ahead. As the team advanced in the League Cup and the Championship rumours began that Jock Stein was leaving for Manchester United. The rumours became fact and Manchester United made an approach to the Celtic manager which came to him through a New York source.

Negotiations had reached a very advanced stage and it looked 100 per cent certain that Celtic would lose their manager. Stein must have been tempted by United's offer. In fairness to the club and the Celtic support, chairman Desmond White and his Board took a firm stand and told Stein he must clear the air. The manager travelled to Manchester, looked over the set-up, and the following day telephoned White to say he wished to stay with Celtic. Just when it seemed he was about to go, he had changed his mind. There is no doubt that a combination of a safe job at Celtic Park and family pressures to stay in Scotland weighed against having to prove himself all over again in a strange environment.

The season of 1970–1 also witnessed the greatest disaster ever to hit football in these islands. On 2 January 1971 sixty-six Rangers fans were crushed to death just minutes after the final whistle of the Old Firm match at Ibrox Stadium. Celtic had scored near the end through Jimmy Johnstone. With some Ibrox fans already leaving, Colin Stein equalized for Rangers in the very last seconds following a free kick.

It was not an unusual ending to an Old Firm match but on that fateful day it brought some Rangers fans running back up stairway 13 when they heard the roar. They collided with others leaving and a terrible tangle of bodies rolled downwards twisting metal barriers on the way. It was quite some time before the full extent of the disaster was known. Bodies were carried back up that stairway, across the terracing, and gently laid in rows along the pitch. Dr John Fitzsimmons, the Celtic club doctor, worked marvels that evening in the mist-shrouded stadium using all his skill and experience in the battle to save life. Some of those still alive were carried to the dressing-rooms for oxygen treatment. Among the many stretcher bearers were managers Jock Stein of Celtic and Willie Waddell of Rangers. Ambulances lapped the track around the stadium ferrying people to hospital as nurses, their white caps beacons in the mist, did what they could to comfort the injured and dying.

Your writer had witnessed the first hint of trouble after the match when about a dozen police and ambulance men began running diagonally across the sanded, cast-iron pitch which gave off a copper glow under the floodlights. Another fight, everyone thought, but this time it was much more than that as they ran to the top of stairway 13.

In the days ahead the terrible tragedy brought the people of Glasgow and Scotland together in a way seldom seen. Celtic immediately gave Rangers a cheque for £10 000 and offered any other assistance in the Ibrox club's most trying hours. A Requiem Mass was held at St Andrew's Cathedral, Glasgow, by Archbishop Scanlan and the Catholic hierarchy which was attended by the entire Rangers and Celtic clubs who a few days later also attended a service held in Glasgow Cathedral.

In a season which had more off-the-field talking points than actual football, Rangers had beaten Celtic 1–0 in the League Cup Final the previous October. It had been a fine match with both sides playing excellent football and Rangers just deserving their win. In three years as Rangers' manager, it was Willie Waddell's only victory over Celtic.

It was Rangers' first trophy since 1966 and it was to be their last for another three seasons in the Ibrox club's blackest era. That defeat ended Celtic's record-breaking run of five League Cups in a row between 1965 and 1969. On the Championship front Aberdeen challenged all the way until a crunch game with Celtic at Pittodrie on 17 April with just three League matches to go. Celtic scored through Harry Hood and although Aberdeen equalized it meant that the title was virtually assured for Celtic.

With typical Stein timing, the manager had announced just twenty-four hours before that game that he would be staying with Celtic. The months of uncertainty and the approaches by Manchester United were all in the past and the roar which greeted him from the huge Celtic following at Pittodrie just before the match showed that the wounds of Milan were healing.

In the Scottish Cup Celtic had beaten Queen of the South 5–1, Dunfermline 1–0, Raith Rovers 7–1 and Airdrie 2–0 in the semi-finals at Hampden after a 3–3 draw. Rangers had reached the Final, accounting for Falkirk, St Mirren, Aberdeen and Hibs.

Only two years had passed since the last Old Firm Scottish Cup Final and that had been the spectacular 4–0 win for Celtic. They had met only eight times before the 1971 Final with the score standing at 4–3 for Rangers, the 1909 Cup having been withheld after the infamous Hampden riot.

On Saturday, 8 May, Celtic sent out Williams, Craig, Brogan, Connelly, McNeill, Hay, Johnstone, Lennox, Wallace, Callaghan, Hood with Macari substitute. Rangers' team was: McCloy, Miller, Mathieson, Greig, McKinnon, Jackson, Henderson, Penman, Stein, McDonald, Johnston, with Derek Johnstone as substitute. The referee was Mr Tom 'Tiny' Wharton.

It was the first meeting of the two clubs since the Ibrox disaster and it was hoped that the fans would not make a mockery of the relationship which had been forged in tragedy those few months earlier. Since Stein's arrival as manager Celtic had won the Cup every second year – 1965, 1967, and 1969. So it was a good omen for 1971 and things looked rosy when Bobby Lennox gave Celtic a 1–0 lead before half-time. It was a lead which should have been increased but in the dying minutes Derek Johnstone headed the equalizer for Rangers after a mix-up between keeper Williams and his defence.

Four days later, on Wednesday, 12 May, the teams faced each other in the replay. Celtic had brought in the young Lou Macari for Willie Wallace and Rangers brought in an unknown youngster called Jim Denny at right-back in place of the injured Miller. Willie Waddell, the Rangers manager, said he had no fears for the boy but Rangers fans thought differently. In the event it was a major blunder by Waddell to have the boy make his first-team début in such a match. Stein, of course, took full advantage and sent everything down the left wing against the obvious weak link. Tommy Callaghan, the former Dunfermline player, ran riot on that flank. But the man of the match was little Jimmy Johnstone who must have reached the heights of his Red Star performance of a couple of years earlier. He teased and tormented the Rangers defence, beating men at will. It is a game remembered as the Jimmy Johnstone Final.

The match ended in a 2–1 victory for Celtic but it was a much easier victory than the scoreline suggested. Lou Macari scored Celtic's first goal following a corner kick and Harry Hood put the game beyond doubt with a penalty kick before half-time. Rangers' goal was scored by Johnstone near the end. Stein had brought in the nippy Macari to pull Rangers centre-half McKinnon out of position. The tactic used that night was to become Macari's trademark in the years ahead. The midfield men were instructed to play the ball short so that Macari could move away from the Rangers goal and back-head the ball over his marker. The victory gave Celtic their twenty-first Scottish Cup and denied Rangers the chance of catching up in that competition.

It also gave Celtic their third League and Cup double in five seasons and more than made up for a disappointing European Cup campaign. They had beaten the amateurs Kokkola of Finland 9–0 in the first round at Celtic Park – their biggest-ever win in the competition – and followed that up with a 5–0 canter on a village green just 150 miles from the Arctic Circle two weeks later in the northernmost match ever played in the European Cup.

Waterford of Eire were the opponents in the second round and were beaten 10–2 on aggregate. The club had been disappointed at not drawing a bigger name but were even more disappointed at trouble caused by Northern Ireland fans in Dublin during the first match, which ended 7–0.

Celtic got their big name wish for the quarter-finals when they drew Ajax Amsterdam, arch-rivals of Feyenoord and the first leg was held in Amsterdam on 10 March 1971. Celts played well in the opening thirty minutes but squandered two good chances. Ajax punished those misses by hitting three brilliant goals in the last half-hour. The result meant that for the first time in the tournament Celtic faced the problem of having to wipe out a three-goal deficit.

The best they could do two weeks later was a 1–0 win from a goal in the twenty-eighth minute by Jimmy Johnstone. The match was played at Hampden because of reconstruction work at Celtic Park. Ajax played well within themselves and never looked in any real danger. For the second time in two seasons Celtic had learnt that Dutch football was something special.

With the 1971 Championship clinched against Ayr United at Hampden the following month and equalling Celtic's earlier record of six consecutive championships between 1904–05 and 1909–10, Jock Stein pulled another of his master-strokes. Celtic had one outstanding fixture to play in the League against Clyde and the match was fixed for Parkhead despite the fact that the old stand was in the process of demolition. Instead of a meagre end-of-the-season crowd, the ground was packed out. Stein had announced the previous week that he would field for the last time the Lisbon Lions.

It was a day of great nostalgia. Ronnie Simpson could only take part in the pre-match warm-up because he had officially retired. In the end Celtic won 6–1 and Bertie Auld, whose last game it was for the club, was carried shoulder-high from the field by his team-mates. The Lisbon Lions had roared for the last time and in a manner befitting Scotland's greatest ever club side. Auld moved on to Hibs and in a period of great change over the next few months the club saw the departure of Gemmell to Nottingham Forest, Hughes and Wallace to Crystal Palace and Chalmers and Clark to Morton. Those departures meant that only five of the Lisbon team remained at Celtic Park. Charlie Gallagher, who had played such a vital part in Celtic's run to Lisbon, had gone the previous year to Dumbarton.

In a fine gesture the Celtic Board under their new chairman, Desmond White, a former Hampden goalkeeper, gave £10 000 to Queen's Park to help defray the costs of ground maintenance and repair in the sincere hope that the SFA, the League and possibly

Rangers would contribute, and that an approach could then be made to the government for additional finance on behalf of our semi-national stadium. Even in those days Hampden was beginning to fall down, a situation which today has become acute. Sir Robert Kelly, whose health was failing, had handed over to Mr White and was made President of the club.

During the summer months word reached Celtic Park one morning that the great Charles Patrick Tully had died suddenly in Ireland at the age of forty-seven. It came as a terrible shock to everyone connected with Celtic. Charlie had joined Celtic in 1948 from Belfast Celtic for £8000 and given the club a great lift with his personality in those difficult years just after the war. He was a great showman for the fans although some of his field conduct at times annoyed the management and directorate to a great degree.

The season of 1971–2 began with a history-making run by Celtic against Rangers. Both League Cup sectional games had to be played at Ibrox because of major alterations to Celtic's new stand. Chairman Desmond White, in the interests of safety, had informed the Scottish League many weeks earlier that Celtic Park was not capable of housing major matches. Mr White had also asked the League to avoid scheduling any major fixtures for Celtic Park at the beginning of the season. Yet almost immediately the club found itself drawn to play Rangers in the opening match at Parkhead. Mr White then insisted that the game could not go ahead but got no sympathy from the League. At a meeting Rangers chairman John Lawrence eventually agreed that both games could go on at Ibrox. Mr White was then asked to leave the room and recalled a few minutes later when to his amazement he was informed that the League were censuring him for his persistence on the matter. Mr White, an authority on football ground safety and a pioneer of the inverted 'V' system which prevents crushing at stadium exits, felt angry and very much let down. He could not fathom how a club chairman, or anyone else for that matter, could be censured for taking safety measures, his action coming only eight months after the Ibrox disaster.

He and his fellow directors had hoped that following the gesture of their £10000 gift to Rangers after the disaster a new spirit of goodwill would permeate Scottish football. Another shock was in store when he went to Ibrox accompanied by James Farrell to iron out arrangements with Rangers manager Willie Waddell and found he got cold comfort there also. Waddell gruffly told the Celtic delegation that both matches would be regarded as home games for Rangers and that Celtic season tickets would not be valid.

Certainly his attitude did nothing to help Old Firm relations. Mr White and his directors knew that following the engineer's report they would have been criminally liable for neglect in the event of any spectator being injured. In the event, the repair job cost Celtic £250000. The motion of censure on Desmond White was nothing short of a scandal and showed once more a lack of foresight at the top in Scottish football.

Following the unpleasantnesses off the field the Celtic directorate, management and fans must have taken great satisfaction from what happened on the field over the next month. On the opening day of the season – 14 August – Celtic beat Rangers 2–0 with goals from Jimmy Johnstone and Kenny Dalglish from the penalty spot. Dalglish, Macari and Connelly were all getting well established in the team and Dalglish in particular was showing signs of the great player he was to become in the seasons ahead. Carelessness in a sectional match against Morton at Celtic Park saw both points gained at Ibrox slip away in a shock 1–0 defeat which meant that Rangers were very much back in business for the second Ibrox match on 28 August. However, Celtic recaptured top form and won 3–0 with goals from Dalglish, Callaghan and Lennox in what was a positive rout. Having qualified for the quarter-finals, Celtic returned to Ibrox two weeks later for a third encounter – this time in the Championship. Down 2–1 at the interval, Celtic fought back and little Jimmy Johnstone outjumped the Ibrox defence in the very last minute to give Celtic a 3–2 win and a unique hat-trick at Ibrox.

In that same month Celtic suffered a great loss. On 21 September Sir Robert Kelly died. He was just a few weeks short of his sixty-ninth birthday.

Perhaps the finest tribute to him came from his successor as chairman, Desmond White, who said:

Sir Robert was the game's outstanding legislator of his time. His talents as an administrator were recognized by his appointment as president, first of the Scottish League and subsequently of the Scottish Football Association. In both these high offices his qualities of leadership and his awareness of the need for constructive and positive policies earned him universal approbation and respect. But, understandably, we at Celtic Park remember him best for his quite unique contribution to the successes at home and overseas of our own club which was always so dear to his heart. For him Celtic was a way of life and his fondest wish was to see the team triumphant not only in domestic tournaments but in the much more testing and competitive fields of Europe.

Lesser men might not have worried overmuch about how these ambitions were to be realized. To win could well have been enough. But for Sir Robert it was not the success that counted as the manner of its accomplishment. He held firmly to the conviction that skill and technical competence must have their outlets in attractive, entertaining football that stimulated players and spectators alike. And there was one other vital proviso. Victory was for him an empty, hollow thing if it was gained at the expense of Celtic's good name. Bad sportsmanship on or off the field, the shady tactic, the underhand deal, all these things he shunned. Against this personal background it was all the more satisfying that the club's finest hour in Lisbon in 1967 should have been achieved by enterprising, adventurous, attacking football unsullied by any demeaning action. Sir Robert's high ideals and integrity never wavered, whether at the high noon of success or in time of shadow. These qualities continue to influence the thinking and the policies of those who now direct the club's affairs.

Knowing him as I did, I am satisfied that he would have sought no other assurance for the future of his beloved Celtic.

In the quarter-finals of the League Cup Celtic beat Clydebank 11–2 on aggregate and dismissed St Mirren in the semi-finals on 6 October by 3–0. But the Final on 23 October was a terrible anti-climax to a fine campaign. They lined up against Partick Thistle without injured skipper Billy McNeill and played a double centre-half with Connelly and Brogan. It was a partnership which never really struck up an understanding and Thistle cashed in with four goals in an amazing first half. Celtic lost Jimmy Johnstone just after the start following a bad tackle by Thistle's Ronnie Glavin, a man who was to join Celtic some years later. The game ended 4–1 in Thistle's favour and gave their manager Davie McParland – another man who was later to go to Parkhead – his first trophy as boss.

The European Cup campaign had started in Copenhagen against Bold Klub and after a little complacency and the shock of a 2–1 defeat, Celtic recovered to win 3–0 at Celtic Park. The second round saw them drawn against Sliema Wanderers of Malta which brought a 5–0 victory at Parkhead in the first leg.

That farcical match had come just three days before the League Cup Final and was probably the worst thing that could have happened to Celtic. Sliema had every man in their penalty area from start to finish and in ninety minutes had not one shot at goal. It was such a stroll for Celtic that it could have been partly responsible for them being caught cold against the much more competitive Thistle.

In the Championship Celtic showed wonderful consistency and faced Rangers once more in the New Year game at Celtic Park. Could they make it four in a row against their great foes in one season?

Johnstone gave Celtic the lead before half-time but with only ten minutes to go Colin Stein equalized for Rangers as he had done that fateful day a year earlier. Then, just on time up, Hood hooked a high ball over his head into the Rangers goalmouth. It looked a lost cause to everyone except Jim Brogan who gamely chased after it and did not so much head it as 'nose' it into goal for a sensational winner. It gave Celtic their first League double over Rangers since 1912.

They continued to move confidently in the Championship and the Scottish Cup and John 'Dixie' Deans, newly signed from Motherwell, was forming an excellent scoring partnership with Dalglish. Deans had joined Celtic the previous November and it was a typical Stein signing. The player had a bad disciplinary record with Motherwell. He was under a six-week suspension and the wily Stein waited until around the third week when everyone had forgotten the name of Deans and got the player for a modest sum of £20000. It was a timely signing because Celtic lost Macari's services for quite some time because of a bad injury. Both Deans and Dalglish were to finish the season as the club's top scorers.

Goalkeeper Denis Connaghan of St Mirren was another signing for that season. He had always excelled against Celtic.

Next loomed the European Cup quarter-finals against the Hungarians Ujpest Dozsa, known as a highly talented team. A draw in the first leg would have been a good result but the young Celts went one better and returned home with a fabulous 2–1 victory. Horvath of Ujpest put Celtic ahead with an own goal and the same player equalized for his club in the second half. But near the end after some Celtic pressure Macari lobbed the winning goal.

On top of that great result the 130 fans who had travelled on a charter flight to Budapest were entertained by film stars Elizabeth Taylor and Richard Burton who were staying at the same hotel – the luxury Duna Intercontinental on the banks of the Danube. That night is now part of Celtic folklore and provided your writer with a great 'scoop' for his newspaper. After I had offered the famous couple two tickets for the match, Burton sent his black Rolls-Royce which whisked me to the film studios on the fringe of the city where

Burton was making a film with such names as Raquel Welch and Virna Lisi. It was there that he decided he would throw a party for the Scots fans and later in the hotel's magnificent ballroom he declared: 'The till rings up £5000 before the party ends.' The scenes were unbelievable. Imagine ordinary football punters from Glasgow mixing with the world's highest-paid movie stars! Liz and Richard accepted Celtic hats and scarfs as souvenirs and spent over an hour chatting to the mesmerized group. Just a week earlier Burton had thrown another party in the very same ballroom for his wife's fortieth birthday. That had cost £40000 and was attended by people like Princess Grace of Monaco and film celebrities from all over the world. The players and officials missed out on the occasion as they had returned to Glasgow immediately after the match.

The result in Budapest was one of Celtic's best-ever in the European Cup and two weeks later came the evidence when Ujpest scored within five minutes of the kick-off at Parkhead. It took a Macari goal in the sixty-fifth minute to put the tie beyond doubt and Celtic looked forward to a semi-final against their great rivals Inter Milan, the team they had last met in Lisbon. In the first leg at San Siro Celtic played brilliantly despite a crop of injuries to their recognized full-backs.

Danny McGrain, who had emerged promisingly, fractured his skull at Falkirk, David Hay had been badly injured at Tynecastle and Jimmy Quinn was also injured. Jim Brogan was not fully fit but managed to play part of the match before being replaced by young Pat McCluskey who used his European début to show he could play like a veteran. The match ended 0–0 and hopes were high of Celtic reaching a third European Cup Final. Getting such a result at San Siro helped players and fans forget about the previous visit there against Feyenoord.

Just four days before the return game with Inter at Celtic Park, Celtic created a new Scottish record when they clinched the Championship for the seventh successive year, beating their own record of six which had stood for more than sixty years. The 3–0 victory over East Fife at Methil saw Celts extend their unbeaten League run to twenty-seven games. Once more they had shown remarkable consistency, losing only eight points out of sixty-eight. They won the Championship by ten points from second-place Aberdeen, the record reading: Played 34, Won 28, Lost 2, Drawn 4, Goals for 96, Against 28.

On the night of 19 April 1972 Inter Milan came to Parkhead and in true Italian fashion put up the shutters. After half an hour of extra time the score was still 0–0 and the tie went to a penalty-kicks decider. All week Celtic had practised penalties at Seamill just in case it came to that particular crunch.

The man who kept hitting the net in training was Dixie Deans who came on as substitute for Dalglish in the second half. It was Dixie's European début and because of his success at training he took the first kick. He moved forward, seemed to hesitate for a split second, and scooped the ball over the bar to groans from the packed terracing.

That was the fatal slip after three and a half hours of football and although the four other Celtic kickers scored, Inter Milan hit five out of five. Celtic had gone out at the penultimate stage in a most unsatisfactory manner and it prompted Jock Stein to say wistfully later: 'We came within a whisker of reaching the European Cup Final for the third time. We may have a better team in the seasons ahead – but who can say we will ever have a better chance of winning the supreme European club trophy?' Certainly, Celtic would have loved a tilt at Ajax in the Final in Rotterdam which was virtually a home tie for the Dutch.

As had happened two years earlier when AC Milan knocked them out of Europe, Celtic still had the Scottish Cup Final to look forward to and as in 1969 reserved their best attacking football of the season for the occasion. They lined up against Hibs on 6 May for a Final which captured the imagination of the public. Both teams were loaded with talent and the Press duly dubbed the match 'Battle of the Greens'. The 'battle' was only a minute old when Billy McNeill, as he had done so often in the past, put Celtic ahead not with one of his famous headers but with a shot from close in. Hibs equalized but Celtic had restored their one-goal lead before half-time through a Deans header. The second half saw a complete transformation in the match with the kind of display by Celtic which no team in Europe could have withstood and it was all over when Deans scored his own second and Celtic's third. It was hailed as the goal of the century and had old timers drawing comparisons with Patsy Gallagher's incredible goal in the 1925 Final when he somersaulted into the back of the net with the ball firmly gripped between his feet.

Dixie chased a ball which had glanced off the head of a Hibs defender out to the left wing. He beat full-back Brownlie, then another man, only to find Brownlie recovered and waiting for him again.

Then he spurted for the by-line only to be blocked by keeper Herriot. When it seemed the ball must go out of play he staggered forward past the keeper and as another Hibs man closed in for a tackle Dixie slammed the ball into the net. It was unbelievable stuff and Hampden rose to the chunky striker who had been so unfortunate against Inter. He completed his hat-trick and Macari added another for a 6–1 win.

It had been a majestic display, perhaps the greatest in a Scottish Cup Final this century, with not a weakness in the team. Murdoch had recaptured the form which made him the best in Britain and Johnstone was a maestro in vintage form. There was just one sad tinge to the day. Jim Craig announced afterwards that he was retiring from Scottish football and going to South Africa. Near the end of the game he had gone on the kind of overlapping run which had brought the equalizer in Lisbon and laid on one of Macari's goals. It was a fitting end to a great career and his departure meant that only four of the Lisbon Lions were left in the den. It could be said of Jim Craig that some flaws in his defensive game were more than adequately compensated by his attacking flair. He had the ability to use the ball to full advantage after a run took him to the by-line.

So another season was over. Such were the high standards Celtic had set themselves it would be remembered mainly for the European Cup disappointment. Yet ponder the record for 1971–2. League Champions, Scottish Cup Winners, League Cup Finalists, European Cup semi-finalists. It had been all the more remarkable in view of the transition which had been taking place in the team.

In addition to lifting their fourth League and Cup double in the space of six seasons – the eighth in their entire history – they created four other milestones of great statistical interest. Their seventh consecutive Championship had broken their own Scottish record of six in a row established between 1904–05 and 1909–10. They had recorded their first League double over Rangers since 1912 and won the Scottish Cup in successive years for the first time since 1911 and 1912. The Scottish Cup Final victory over Hibs equalled the scoring record set in the 1888 Final when Renton beat Cambuslang 6–1.

As a reward for their efforts the club took the playing staff to Bermuda for a holiday. Only two games were played and both against local opposition. Celtic beat Somerset 2–0 and a few days later ran up an 8–1 victory against Pembroke. The match was marred by the sending off of captain Billy McNeill. The referee, a character named

Carlisle Crockwell, seemed to enjoy a bit of controversy because a few years earlier he had been responsible for Tommy Docherty, manager of Chelsea, being suspended. McNeill was sent off, said the referee, because of a remark he had made. Bearing in mind that by that stage Lennox had scored four goals and Macari two it would appear that the only person taking things seriously was Mr Crockwell.

Rangers, who had just won the European Cup Winners' Cup in Barcelona amidst great controversy – their fans on three occasions invaded the pitch – had failed miserably once more at home. They reached neither the League Cup nor Scottish Cup Finals and were a staggering sixteen points behind Celtic in the Championship. Such statistics tend to prove that the gulf between the European Champions' Cup and the others is wide indeed.

The Ibrox club were banned from Europe for two years, later reduced to a year, because of the infamous riot by their fans which caused terrible damage to the Barcelona Stadium and put many policemen in hospital with serious injuries. It was without doubt European football's blackest night. Rangers, who had gained entry to the European Cup Winners' Cup because Celtic had won both the League and the Cup, were allowed to keep the trophy although players from Moscow Dynamo, their opponents, claimed they had been intimidated by the Rangers fans who invaded the field.

The season of 1972–3 began in unexciting fashion with a new-style League Cup section which saw Celtic drawn with East Fife, Arbroath and Stirling Albion. Before it had reached the half-way stage the fans let the organizers know that they did not like seeding and wanted to see the top teams in opposition. It was around this time that terracing hooliganism among youngsters seemed to be reaching a new peak throughout Scotland and at the match in Stirling manager Stein vaulted the barriers and went into the crowd to give chanting fans a piece of his mind.

Celtic went on to beat Stranraer, Dundee and Aberdeen on their way to the Final which they lost 2–1 to Hibs. With the new stand at Parkhead requiring further repairs Celtic moved once again to Hampden where they recorded League victories over Kilmarnock (6-2) and Rangers (3–1). The Old Firm game is remembered not only for its noon kick-off but for being so one-sided. Celtic cruised to a three-goal lead and when Ibrox skipper John Greig scored near the end he did so to some ironic cheers from the Celtic end. The kick-off had been brought forward in the hope of cutting down drinking among fans before the match.

By the half-way stage of the Championship Celtic had lost only one game – a defeat by Dundee at Dens Park – and had established a seven-point lead.

There had been, however, disappointments in an early exit from the European Cup. Celts made heavy weather of beating Norwegians Rosenborg 2–1 at Hampden but played better in the return, winning by 3–1. The second round saw them drawn against Ujpest Dozsa of Hungary for the second time in a few months and this time the Hungarians came out on top. Celtic won 2–1 at Celtic Park but went down 3–0 in Budapest. In seven attempts at the European Cup, it was only the second time Celtic had failed to reach the quarter-finals, and it took much excitement out of the season.

On the domestic front there was further disappointment after a flu epidemic hit Celtic Park and knocked the club out of action between 23 December and 6 January. Celtic had undertaken a midweek match in Jersey which was played in torrential rain and this no doubt contributed to lowering the players' resistance. Jock Stein was the main victim and was taken to Glasgow's Victoria Infirmary. At first it was thought he was suffering from a heart attack. He was still missing when Celtic played Rangers at Ibrox on 6 January and lost 2–1. It was just after this that Lou Macari departed for Manchester United on a £200000 transfer. The player signed for Tommy Docherty who just before that had been manager of the Scottish team in which Macari was a regular player. There was just no way Celtic could hold on to Macari. His mind was made up that he was going. He was a loss to Celtic because he played so well alongside Dalglish and had a knack of scoring goals in tight situations which made him a valuable player in European games. In the weeks which followed Celtic lost silly points to Airdrie, East Fife, Partick Thistle and Dundee United which opened the door for Rangers once more.

Goalkeeper Ally Hunter, who had been bought from Kilmarnock, began to command a first-team place and in the last seven games of the Championship conceded only one goal. There was one upset, however, and it involved referee Bobby Davidson yet again. In the Scottish Cup quarter-final match with Aberdeen at Celtic Park on 17 March he disallowed a Jimmy Johnstone goal in the first minute and then ordered the same player off for an alleged incident which he later admitted he had not seen. Johnstone was later exonerated and justice done although the little winger had to be left out of the team the following week because he was so upset at the ordering off.

The Championship ended on a high note and a day of great emotion at Easter Road on 28 April. Dixie Deans, so often the scourge of Hibs, scored two goals and Dalglish got a third to give Celtic a 3–0 win and their eighth successive Championship. About 40000 Celtic fans had travelled to Edinburgh and they made the scenes unforgettable. Eight Championships in a row; it seemed no one could stop Celtic. With that excellent victory behind them they faced Rangers the following Saturday in the Scottish Cup Final at Hampden. It was Rangers' centenary year and they had won nothing.

Royalty was in attendance and not for the first time a campaign had begun on Rangers' behalf in certain circles of the Press. Celtic ruined the script by taking the lead through Dalglish but Rangers took a 2–1 lead right at the start of the second half. Celtic equalized through a Connelly penalty and Jimmy Johnstone scored what looked like a good goal after rounding the goalkeeper. A linesman gave offside, although television pictures later showed that decision to be wrong, and Celtic never recovered from the blow. Rangers scored a third and winning goal and for the first time since Jock Stein's first full season in charge Celtic had failed to take at least two honours. Yet considering the team was still in a transitional state, had lost the manager at a vital stage of the season and had their progress halted through a flu epidemic, that eighth League win ranked with the best of them.

Towards the end of the season Celtic had bought Aberdeen midfield player Steve Murray for a club record fee of £50000 and he made his début in a fine testimonial game at Leeds for that club's retiring centre-half Jack Charlton. Celtic won the match by 4–3. Murray's arrival saw Bobby Murdoch's departure. One of Celtic's greatest-ever players, Bobby went to England where he helped Middlesbrough to gain promotion to the First Division. Now only McNeill, Johnstone and Lennox were left of the 1967 side. Murray in fact lasted only a couple of years, being forced to quit football because of injury.

The season of 1973–4 saw Celtic suffer their fourth consecutive League Cup Final defeat, this time at the hands of Dundee. In the qualifying section the rules had been changed which meant that the top two teams went forward to the quarter-finals and both Celtic and Rangers, who had been paired in the same section as Arbroath and Falkirk, qualified, having scored a victory over each other. They met up again in the semi-finals at Hampden where Celtic gave Rangers a real hiding thanks to a hat-trick by Harry Hood in a 3–1 victory.

The Final, not played until 15 December, was an absolute farce. New offside rules had been introduced to the competition and the match went on in heavy sleet and snow. It also had to have an early kick-off because of a government ban on the use of floodlighting. As a result the terracings were bare and there was a truly ghostly atmosphere. Celtic never really got going and were beaten 1–0 by a Dundee side – including Tommy Gemmell – which mastered the conditions much better. Manager Stein was very angry with his players afterwards as their record in the Final was becoming an embarrassment to the club after the very fine efforts of the 1960s. Moving the date from October to December was a real blunder by the Scottish League and after a couple of seasons they reversed their decision.

Despite a bad injury to young Brian McLaughlin, a player of great promise, which put him out for the season, the League campaign went well. Up to the turn of the year Celtic had lost only one game and dropped only four points out of thirty-two. The highlight of a high-scoring run had come on 17 November at Celtic Park when Dixie Deans scored six goals against Partick Thistle in a 7–0 victory, a post-war record for a League match. One man sweating a bit that memorable day was Jimmy McGrory. Seated in the directors' box he thought he would see his all-time British First Division record of eight goals beaten. Just four weeks later Deans scored another four in a League match and ended the season as the club's top scorer with thirty-three goals – twenty-four of which were scored in the Championship. Celtic won the New Year game against Rangers at Parkhead by 1–0 and, having won the earlier game at Ibrox by the same score, completed their second double over Rangers in three seasons.

Just before the turn of the year George Connelly went missing from training and this was to be the first in a long line of such instances of unfortunate disturbances which eventually led to him walking out on the club and giving up football. Connelly had been voted Scotland's player of the year just months earlier and played well for Scotland against England at Wembley. His departure from the game was a tragedy for both club and individual. Players of such talent do not grow on trees. He joined Celtic at the age of 15 and came to prominence when, still as a teenager, he entertained a big crowd before a European match at Celtic Park with his incredible ability in playing 'keepie uppie'. In his first Scottish Cup Final in 1969 at barely 20 years of age he scored an unforgettable goal which killed Rangers' challenge even before half-time. The player of the year award coming on top of club and international honours saw him with the world at his feet. He was world-class material but his true potential was never to be realized.

In the European Cup Celtic had beaten Turku of Finland 9–1 on aggregate and narrowly scraped through against Vejle of Denmark by 1–0 after a 0–0 draw at Celtic Park. Two rousing quarter-final ties with Basle of Switzerland ended with a 3–2 defeat in Basle, a 4–2 win in Glasgow and a place in the semi-finals. It was Celtic's fourth semi-final appearance in eight seasons – a wonderful record. But it was to become a nightmare for the club through no fault of their own. The draw paired Celtic with Atletico Madrid of Spain who had recruited some of their players from the Argentine.

The first game at Celtic Park on 10 April 1974 must rank as one of the worst nights in the history of the European Cup. Atletico sent out a collection of thugs in football jerseys, including a defender named Diaz who had played for the Racing Club against Celtic in 1967. Before the game was many minutes old he had tackled Johnstone waist-high and made clear his intentions. The Turkish referee, Mr Babacan, had little chance to keep order as Atletico booted their way through a game which was eventually reduced to a farce. Three of their players were sent off and seven booked. Those who remained on the field packed their goalmouth and leapt around with uncontrolled joy when the final whistle sounded with the score still at 0–0.

It is to the credit of the huge Celtic support that night that they did not lose their heads. The provocation by the callous, arrogant visitors could have led to a riot. At time up there was an incident in the tunnel leading to the dressing-rooms when Jimmy Johnstone, who had shown so much courage, was kicked in the stomach. It was not until the following day that Press reports began to filter back from Madrid in which Atletico players claimed they had been beaten up by Glasgow policemen as they headed for the dressing-rooms. That outrageous allegation was only the forerunner of many more and the most amazing hate campaign possible was stirred up against Celtic in Spain. From being sinned against, Celtic suddenly, in the eyes of Spain, found themselves to be the sinners. Yet the Parkhead game had been shown live in Madrid.

Even if Mr Babacan had ordered off a player in the first half it would probably have made little difference. Atletico, coached by the notorious Argentinian Juan Lorenzo, a former manager of Lazio of Rome who had been banned from European competition, had actually dropped skilful forwards for the first leg and introduced their heavy team. They had come to Glasgow with the clear intention of not being beaten. Mr Babacan, who was visited in his dressing-room at half-time by the UEFA observer, was not slow to show his red card in the second half. But he could only have administered proper justice by abandoning the match and awarding the tie to Celtic. Such action would have forced UEFA to take a stronger line than they eventually did.

In the days after the match every decent football follower called for the disqualification of Atletico from the tournament. Celtic held an emergency Board meeting and the club were so sickened by Atletico's approach at such a high level of competition that they would gladly have opted out of playing a second match. But a responsible decision had to be taken and Celtic waited to see what UEFA would do. They in fact suspended five of the Spanish players and left Celtic to travel. The situation was now tailor-made for Atletico. The five they had lost, with the exception of the talented Ayala, were dispensable and they were in a position to reintroduce the skilful players they had left out in Glasgow. With a home match to come in front of their own partisan crowd they had really got what they wanted.

As in the debate before playing the third game against Racing in Montevideo, the Celtic directors were again in a quandary. They had to take into account the safety of the players and any fans who might travel. They did not wish to be called cowards by anyone, although such a charge would have been unfair in the extreme, and they did not wish to incur a possible suspension from UEFA for refusing to play. The decision taken was to go although travel agents were asked by the directorate to cancel charter flights for hundreds of fans who had been planning to fly to Madrid and this was done.

Your writer flew to Spain with the Celtic party in late April, two days before the match, and the first hint of upset came just after take-off. The pilot was informed by Spanish air-traffic control that as the party was travelling by Aer Lingus jet they would have to fly to Dublin, land and take off from there for Madrid. To people like Jimmy Johnstone and your writer, who share an intense dislike of aeroplanes, the thought of an extra landing and take-off was anathema. While Jimmy, as a professional footballer, had to calm himself with neat orange juice your writer, in the rear seat of the plane, fortified himself with something a little stronger.

On landing at Madrid Airport the real trauma began. A Land Rover full of grey-uniformed armed guards escorted the team to the terminal building where Atletico chairman Vicente Calderon and his colleagues greeted the Celtic directors like long-lost brothers. Jock Stein, trailing a little behind, muttered: 'How can these people act like this?' The armed guard escorted the team bus to the hotel on the outskirts of the city and throughout the three-day stay rifle-carrying soldiers stationed on the perimeter of the grounds were a constant reminder of the troubles ahead. It was an unbearable atmosphere for what was after all supposed to be the build-up to a game of football. The players could not leave the hotel grounds and on one occasion when the directors went out walking they were jeered at. The armed unit followed the Celtic group to training sessions and stationed themselves along the top tier of the vast Calderon Stadium.

The worst moment of all came on the second night when Jimmy Johnstone got a call to his room late on and the voice said: 'Johnstone you are dead.' Rumours in the Press then spread that a sniper would await the little winger on the way to the match or at the stadium itself. Although it sounded far-fetched Johnstone was worried and had every right to be in such a situation. Jock Stein told the player he could call off if he wished but Johnstone said he would play. On the high-speed journey to the stadium on the evening of 24 April police lights flashed and sirens wailed.

The Celtic party were shepherded through an angry mob outside the main entrance and when the team took the field they got the most hostile reception ever known at a European football match. The booing and jeering continued through half-time and the Celtic substitutes who had been loosening up had to leave the field. It was an atmosphere of terror. The Atletico fans had been whipped up into a frenzy by the Spanish Press and the night had been turned into a Spain versus the World confrontation. The future King, Juan Carlos, was there as a guest of the club and one got the distinct feeling that Atletico were playing on nationalist feelings.

Before the kick-off a Press conference was called by Vicente Calderon and his directors. Writers and photographers had the offer of limitless champagne and food as Señor Calderon said his club could not understand what had happened in Glasgow. But that was all in the past, he said with typical Latin flourish, and he wanted the occasion in the stadium named after him to be a footballing feast. How they must have been laughing up their sleeves.

In the end Atletico won by 2–0, both goals coming late in the second half, and they had the victory which had been so important to them. Jimmy Johnstone ran from the field sporting two ugly-looking black eyes which had been presented to him via the elbows of his opponents – behind the referee's back, of course. The Celtic players showered quickly, boarded their coach and were driven straight to the airport. Within four hours of the final whistle they were safely back in Glasgow. Jock Stein summed it up on the flight home as his players slept around him: 'The frustrating thing is that we'll never know if we were good enough to win the European Cup for we were never given a chance in the semi-finals.'

Atletico contested the Final with Bayern Munich of West Germany and were within a minute of winning the trophy when the Germans equalized. In the replay they were slaughtered 4–0 and many Celtic people must have felt a little peace of mind as they watched it on their television sets.

At a time when UEFA could have done so much to stamp out brutal play they pussy-footed around the issue. Atletico were there to be used as an example to all, yet they were allowed to play in the Final of the world's greatest club tournament after debasing it.

Just three days after Madrid Celtic went to Brockville, where a 1–1 draw with Falkirk clinched their ninth consecutive League Championship and equalled a world record set up by CSKA Sofia of Bulgaria between 1952 and 1964. That feat is now firmly established in the *Guinness Book of Records* where Celtic have more mentions than any other football club. Apart from their nine Championships it is pointed out that they were the first British team to win the European Cup and the first team to sweep the domestic boards in the same season as winning in Europe.

Under 'Crowds' the publication states that Celtic hold the European Cup attendance record for the semi-final match with Leeds at Hampden on 15 May 1970. The official attendance of 136505 was swelled considerably when fans charged a huge gate and gained entry. Against Aberdeen in the Scottish Cup Final of 24 April 1937 Celtic played in front of a British club record crowd of 146433 with an estimated 30000 locked outside. Against Rangers at Ibrox on

H

2 January 1939 Celtic played in front of a British record League crowd of 118567.

Under 'Goalscorers' the book states that James Edward McGrory of Glasgow Celtic holds the British First Division record of eight goals in one match against Dunfermline Athletic on 14 January 1928 and that the same player scored the greatest number of goals in British first-class football – 550 (410 in League matches). The book also records that Celtic hold a record of twenty-five Scottish Cups.

Celtic, of course, hold so many other records that they could fill a book of their own. But to have so many mentions in a publication which records great feats from all over the world is certainly another measure of Celtic's fantastic success. To have won the League Championship nine consecutive times in a modern, highly competitive era is a wonderful achievement and will surely stand for all time.

A couple of weeks after clinching that Championship Celtic defeated Dundee United on 4 May in the Final of the Scottish Cup at Hampden. Goals by Hood, Murray and Deans gave Celtic a 3–0 victory and their fifth League and Cup double under Jock Stein's management. They had accounted for Clydebank (h 6–1); Stirling Albion (h 6–1); Motherwell (h 2–2; a 1–0) and in the semi-finals beaten Dundee 1–0.

The season was brilliantly rounded off when Celtic went to Liverpool to provide the opposition in the Ron Yeats Testimonial Match, paraded the Scottish Cup and beat Liverpool 4–1. As David Hay, Jimmy Johnstone, Danny McGrain and Kenny Dalglish went off to West Germany to represent Scotland in the World Cup Finals it seemed that Celtic had much to look forward to in the seasons ahead.

15 Ninety Years On

28 May 1978 marks a very special date for the Celtic Football Club. On that day it is exactly ninety years since they played their first game which was held at the original Celtic Park beside Gallowgate. The facts that Rangers were the opponents and the new Celts defeated their established visitors 5–2 made it a sweet beginning indeed.

Although Celtic are some fifteen years younger than the Ibrox club and many others in the land their record is unsurpassed. They have won the League Championship thirty times, creating records in winning it four, six and in recent times nine years in succession. They have won the Scottish Cup a record twenty-five times and the League Cup eight times. In the latter competition they have established a run of thirteen consecutive Finals between 1964 and 1976 and a run of five successive victories between 1965–6 and 1969–70 – both records. The Glasgow Cup, although not now holding the place of prominence it once did, still has a proud niche in the club's history and has been won twenty-seven times and shared once with Rangers. The Charity Cup, abandoned at the end of the season 1960–1, was won twenty-seven times and shared between Celtic and Clyde after a drawn game in its final year. Celtic won it five years running between 1891 and 1896 and then for seven consecutive years from 1911 to 1918, the latter being a record for the competition.

The club holds on a permanent basis the Glasgow Exhibition Trophy of 1901–2, the Empire Exhibition Trophy of 1938, the Victory in Europe Cup of 1945, the St Mungo Cup of 1951 and the Coronation Cup of 1953. These highly prestigious trophies were won outright from the élite in the game and no other club in Britain can match the collection. The greatest Cup of all came, of course, on that sunny evening in Lisbon – the European Champions' Cup, the first time it had been won by a British team. A replica of that magnificent trophy sits in the Celtic boardroom.

In twelve years under the managership of Jock Stein one-third of the club's entire Championships and Scottish Cups have been won – statistics of daunting proportions for his successors in the years ahead and those who follow the players who have achieved these records on the field.

The last lustrum, although not living up to the late Sixties and early Seventies, has seen its share of successes – but at a price. After a shake-up behind the scenes the club went on a spate of player-buying never before known at Celtic Park. Following the first blank season for ten years the directorate were galvanized into action and in June 1976 appointed Davie McParland, the former Partick Thistle player and manager, as assistant to Jock Stein, and reorganized a scouting system which was no longer producing the goods. The Board's action came while Jock Stein was still recovering from a car accident which, the previous summer, had almost cost him his life. In the early Seventies, with honours still pouring the club's way, all had seemed well. But too heavy a reliance had been put on the Celtic Boys' Club to produce quality players.

With almost professional backing it was thought that the Boys' Club would provide practically a custom-built team for the future. As a result the scouting net was not cast as wide as it had been. The policy of farming out players also seemed to have had its day and several promising youngsters who could have developed later on were allowed to go for modest fees. Andy Ritchie, who left for Morton, was one player many fans thought should have been retained or farmed out.

The loss of the Championship in 1975, followed by the manager's crash and then a blank season, hit the club hard and the directors had to make their move. With no guarantee that Jock Stein would fully regain his health or be fit enough to carry out managerial duties they moved for McParland, a man they had admired for a number of years, and appointed ex-Celtic players to a new scouting set-up under the leadership of Sean Fallon who had been in charge of the team during the difficult and unsuccessful 1975–6 season which saw Rangers win the League Cup, Championship and Scottish Cup. Even if Jock Stein had been at the helm that season it would still have been a difficult one.

The club had by then lost some integral parts of the team which they thought would see them through the mid-Seventies. Apart from the obvious wear and tear on veterans like Johnstone and McNeill, Lou Macari had departed to Manchester United, David Hay had gone to Chelsea and a short time later, after many upsets, George Connelly finally walked out on the club for all time. Victor Davidson, a player of great promise, had not satisfied the management and went to Motherwell while Paul Wilson was still struggling to produce the wonderful talent he showed in training. Hay, Connelly and Macari were potentially world-class players and could not easily be replaced.

The transfer of David Hay in the summer of 1974 was the greatest disappointment of all. He was a real dyed-in-the-wool Celt but became soured after a bad injury received in a Scottish Cup tie at Tynecastle. Because of the Celtic payment structure he lost a lot of money. Although the basic wage is much lower than with most top English clubs, the bonus system brings annual payments up to the English level. He became involved in a long-drawn-out financial battle with the manager and directors. Eventually the player did not seem to know what he wanted to do. One day he was for staying and the next he was leaving. Several special Board meetings were held to discuss his case because the directors did not want to lose him.

Among great efforts to retain him the Board offered him the captaincy of the club following Billy McNeill's retirement which everyone knew would come within a couple of years. Then, just when Hay seemed to have made up his mind to stay, Chelsea came on the market with over £200000 and the player, just back from a successful World Cup in West Germany and no doubt influenced by Anglo players, found the offer too tempting.

With that unhappy background one would have expected a poor start to the new season (1974–5) yet it was the exact opposite. Celtic won the brewery-sponsored Drybrough Cup in a penalties decider against Rangers at Hampden and then went on to win the League Cup in spectacular fashion against Hibs. The 6–3 victory was doubly welcome in that it ended a run of four consecutive defeats in the Final at the hands of Rangers, Partick Thistle, Hibs and Dundee.

The offside experiment which saw the 18-yard line extended to the touchlines was in operation and contributed to the goal feast. Inevitably Dixie Deans scored a hat-trick against the club which had come to regard him as a jinx. The unhappiest man on the field was Joe Harper, the Hibs centre-forward. He scored a great Cup Final hat-trick yet ended up on the losing side. As in the 1972 Scottish

Cup Final, Deans scored the goal of the match when he intercepted a Johnstone shot-cum-cross with his head and crashed the ball into the net with the power of a full-blooded shot. Other Celtic scorers to give the club their eighth League Cup were Johnstone, Wilson and Murray. Celts had accounted for Motherwell, Dundee United and Ayr United in the qualifying section, beaten Hamilton Accies 6–2 in the quarter-finals and Airdrie 1–0 in the semi-finals at Hampden.

In the Championship they began by hammering Kilmarnock 5–0 at Parkhead and Clyde 4–2 at Shawfield. A 2–1 defeat by Rangers at Celtic Park was quickly overcome with five goals against Ayr and Hibs and six against Airdrie and Dundee at Dens Park. The unbeaten run went on for sixteen games in which only two points were dropped but in the New Year game against Rangers at Ibrox disaster struck. After running Rangers ragged in the opening half-hour, mainly due to the magic of Paul Wilson, Celtic paid the penalty for missing four great chances. Rangers broke away and scored and in the end easily won by 3–0.

The following week saw Celtic lose at home to Motherwell by 3–2 and further points were dropped to Arbroath and Dumbarton before a 2–1 defeat at Easter Road ended any hopes of the Championship. It was sad that the terracing chant of 'It's magic you know, we'll make it ten in a row' never came to fruition. But as Jock Stein said afterwards: 'It was a great disappointment but it would have been sad whether the run finished at ten, eleven or twelve. It had to end sometime.'

The season finished on a high note, however, with the club's twenty-fourth Scottish Cup win against Airdrie at Hampden on 3 May. Paul Wilson, whose mother had died just a couple of days before the match, bravely turned out and scored two fine goals. Pat McCluskey scored a third from the penalty spot and the match ended 3–1. The Celtic legions thundered their acclaim as the players hoisted skipper Billy McNeill onto their shoulders and carried him across the field and they cheered themselves hoarse as he lifted the Cup high. What they were all quite unaware of was that it was the great Billy's last match. He had told his team-mates before the kick-off that he was retiring and they gave him the best possible send-off.

Billy McNeill was the most successful club player ever in British football. Into retirement he took a European Cup medal, nine League Championship, seven Scottish Cup and six League Cup medals. He also won international honours with Scotland. Caesar, as he was known to his team-mates, was a proud leader. It was because of the pride he had in his appearances for Celtic that he quit while still at the top. After eighteen years with the club he knew his latter performances were not among his best. During 1974–5 Billy was having trouble with his knees and back and the decision was gradually taken over a few months in consultation with manager Stein. Billy also asked the advice of former English internationalist Bobby Charlton before taking the final decision. Bobby told him he might just be a tired player and need a rest. But at that stage of his career Billy knew there was no resting place and he quit.

Among the many tributes to him came this one from former England team manager Sir Alf Ramsey: 'Billy will be remembered as one of football's great captains. He did nothing but good for the game. He was a gentleman on and off the field.' Bill Shankly, the former Liverpool manager, said: 'Billy was the kind of centre-half I didn't like to see in the opposition – good in the air, strong in the tackle, determined to win.' Don Revie, the former Leeds United manager, said: 'He was one of the men who killed my dreams of winning the European Cup. In our semi-final games in 1970 he inspired Celtic to victory.'

The season of 1974–5 had brought Celtic the Drybrough Cup, the League Cup and the Scottish Cup, yet because of their own high standards it was not looked upon as one of great success. That greatest test of consistency – the Championship – was gone and somehow Celtic Park did not seem the same without it after so many years. And there had been the first-round knock-out in the European Cup at the hands of the little-fancied Greek team of Olympiakos who had gained a 1–1 draw at Celtic Park and won 2–0 on their own ground. There was one outstanding fixture held over to the end of the season, the Glasgow Cup Final, which ended in a 2–2 draw against Rangers and it was decided to carry the replay forward to the following season.

After the match it was announced that Jim Brogan, who had skippered the side, was leaving for Coventry City as he could no longer be guaranteed a first-team place. But a further announcement a few days later brought great sadness to Celtic fans. It was announced from Celtic Park that Jimmy Johnstone was being released. It was felt that Jimmy had climbed all the mountains he could with Celtic and since he had reached the age of thirty-one the directors and manager felt the time had come for this all-time Celtic great to leave.

No transfer fee was involved and he was allowed to fix his own terms with the club of his choice. There is so much that could be said about Jimmy Johnstone. He was certainly one of the most courageous players football has known. He threw his slight frame into every battle which came Celtic's way and never flinched in a tackle. Although there was not much of him every ounce was 22 carat. In his time he caused Celtic many problems both on and off the field with his temperament and had he looked after himself better at training he could have gone on a few years more. But he was always worth any bother he caused. He was gutsy, immensely skilful and a real entertainer. The departure of Jimmy and Billy McNeill meant that of the Lisbon Lions only Bobby Lennox remained.

It was also in the final months of that season that speculation began once more that Jock Stein would be leaving Celtic. He had been given permission by the Celtic directors in February to run the Scottish Under-23 Team and not surprisingly made a success of it with several good results abroad. Stein, of course, had been manager of the full Scotland team in 1965 on a temporary basis while also with Celtic. Ever since then, when he bossed Scotland against Poland and Italy, there had been a faction at the SFA who wanted him to take the job permanently.

In 1975 there were people in the same SFA who wanted to get rid of manager Willie Ormond despite the fact that his record was a good one. By March speculation had begun that Stein was about to take over and the SFA's attitude towards Ormond was difficult to comprehend. There were those at the time who felt Jock Stein should immediately have made his position clear. He had remained silent for some considerable time. The Celtic Board were obviously very perturbed at the amount of Press coverage and the unsettling effect on players, supporters and everyone else connected with Celtic. In the month of June, and following a Press campaign which had backed Ormond, the dust seemed to have settled again and finally Stein came out with the firm statement: 'I stay with Celtic. I'll be here next season.'

That last sentence was to become a false prophecy because one morning in the close season Scotland awoke to banner headlines that Jock Stein was in a Dumfries hospital fighting for his life after a terrible car accident on his way back from a holiday. One writer got quite lyrical and suggested that Stein being Stein he would already have turned the ceiling above him into a football tactics board for the new season. But there was to be no new season for Stein in 1975–6 and there was the distinct possibility that there might never be another one. Everyone connected with Celtic was shattered by the event.

Billy McNeill was quite prepared to come out of retirement only because he knew the club faced a crisis situation and he was very disappointed that no one from Celtic Park contacted him. Celtic had decided to persevere with young Highlander Roddy McDonald at centre-half and during the course of the season he shared the centre-half spot with the rugged Icelander Johannes Edvaldsson who had joined the club towards the end of the previous season. Other signings around then had included Ronnie Glavin of Partick Thistle and goalkeeper Peter Latchford from West Bromwich Albion.

Assistant manager Sean Fallon was given the daunting task of taking the team into the new highly competitive ten-club Premier League in which sides would play each other four times.

Celtic reached the League Cup Final but lost 1–0 to Rangers. They had also lost the opening League match against Rangers at Ibrox by 2–1. In the second Premier game at Celtic Park in the November Celts could manage only a 1–1 draw and their fate was sealed in the New Year game at Ibrox when they lost again by 1–0. The fourth meeting at Parkhead towards the end of the season ended 0–0 which meant that in five meetings Celtic had not won a victory. Disaster had come in the first round of the Scottish Cup at Motherwell, with a 3–2 defeat after leading 2–0.

The European Cup Winners' Cup had also ended in disappointment at the quarter-final stage after Celtic beat Valur of Iceland 9–0 on aggregate in the first round and Boavista of Portugal 3–1 in the second. Celts went crashing out to the moderate East German team Sachsenring Zwicau. They had overrun Sachsenring in the first leg at Celtic Park, taken a one-goal lead, missed a barrowload of chances and in the final minute the East Germans had equalized. A 1–0 defeat in East Germany finished interest in that competition. It had been a dreadful season for Celtic and their followers as they had watched a hard-working but certainly not highly talented Rangers side win the Treble.

There was further disappointment too in the Home International matches. Kenny Dalglish had thirty-three successive Scottish caps and was all set to equal the record of thirty-four held by ex-Ranger

George Young when he was unaccountably dropped for the match against Wales. It had Celtic fans thinking back to the 1971 match at Wembley when regular right-back David Hay was also dropped to make way for John Greig of Rangers who was the only Ibrox player in the Scottish pool. It was stated by the SFA that Greig had been included because it was felt Hay might not be experienced enough. Yet the same player had played in a European Cup Final the previous year and was deemed good enough for all the other international matches around that period. Greig's inclusion was for one reason and one reason only, especially as he was well past his peak by then. He was there to appease the huge Scottish support which traditionally is 90 per cent Rangers. In the Twenties and Thirties Celtic players often complained because they were being overlooked for international matches. In the Seventies it would appear that there are certain occasions where talent has to make way for other considerations.

But there was a memorable night to whet the appetites of the fans for the following season. More than 60000 fans packed Parkhead to salute Jimmy Johnstone and Bobby Lennox in their joint benefit match. On show was the newly signed Johnny Doyle from Ayr United, Celtic's most expensive-ever buy at £90000. The occasion was also marked by the official return of Jock Stein in charge of the team. It was around that time that the Board, because of the manager's health problems following the accident, began their moves for McParland, who was appointed assistant in charge of training, and it was hoped that the new appointment would take much of the strain off Stein. Jock Stein, despite lingering pain, obviously relished being back in the dug-out and as the match progressed his tactic of playing new boy Doyle through the middle with Dalglish looked highly promising. David Hay, back for the night, also played well.

In a night of great emotion Jimmy Johnstone summoned reserves of energy to show much of his old jinking magic and Bobby Lennox opened the scoring in a 4–1 win over Manchester United. People wept unashamedly at the end in scenes which rivalled any European Cup atmosphere. Green and white scarves were raised in never-ending chains around the stadium as the fans sang 'And You'll Never Walk Alone'. The two great little men came back out for a lap of honour. Jimmy knew it was his farewell whereas Bobby had the comfort of knowing he still had some Celtic days ahead of him. Both wiped tears as they ran, arms around each other's shoulders, two men who had been inseparable for so many years. In a final gesture to his fans Johnstone removed his boots and threw them into the 'Jungle' before leaving the Parkhead field for the last time.

The season of 1976–7 opened at Celtic Park with a 3–1 defeat by Rangers in the Glasgow Cup Final and although Celtic had played well and been unlucky to lose, manager Stein acted quickly in the transfer market. Pat Stanton, a player of silky touches and vast experience, was brought from Hibs in an exchange deal which saw young Jackie McNamara go to Easter Road. Hibs fans, like Celtic fans, were stunned by the move. Even though Stanton had been at odds with Hibs for some time everyone thought that after more than a decade there he would have finished his career with Hibs. His arrival had an immediate steadying effect on Roddy McDonald and the partnership grew in strength as the season progressed.

Joe Craig, a promising centre-forward with Partick Thistle, was bought for £40000. Just before Craig's arrival Celtic had drawn 2–2 with Rangers in the Premier League at Celtic Park after being 2–0 down. It had been two full seasons since Celtic's last win against them so it seemed the tide was at last turning. In the November match at Ibrox Joe Craig got off to the best possible start by scoring a spectacular winning goal in a 1–0 victory and Celts never looked back. They won the next Old Firm match at New Year – again by 1–0 – and were in unstoppable form. Early in the year they were odds-on favourites to take the Championship and on 16 April at Easter Road, scene of their 1973 win, the club's first Premier League was clinched – by a Joe Craig goal. The scenes were fabulous as skipper Kenny Dalglish was carried shoulder-high by his team-mates. He held aloft a Celtic scarf just like the majority of the 40000 crowd all around him on the terraces.

Those scenes or the goal which gave Celtic their 1–0 victory were never recorded by television because in the days leading up to the match Hibs chairman Tom Hart decided to ban the cameras, saying that television was killing the game. Strange that he should wait until the end of the season to take such action. Strange that he should choose a game in which Celtic were likely to win the League. Or was it? He had even gone to the extreme of instructing the Hibs secretary to ban the Celtic Ciné Club although they had already been issued with special passes by Hibs. Celtic chairman Desmond White, while realizing that Hart was in charge of his own football ground, had said to him in disbelief regarding the Ciné Club: 'I think there has been a mistake.' But Hart's reply was: 'There's no mistake. All cameras are banned.'

There can be little doubt that it had all stemmed from a row between the clubs the previous month over the playing of a postponed League fixture at Easter Road. The Hibs chairman had shown a lack of basic manners in having the match fixed up with the Scottish League and then advertising it in the newspapers without even letting Celtic know it was on. The background to the playing of the match was incredible. It had brought the following comment from manager Stein in the *Celtic View*: 'Where Celtic are concerned natural justice doesn't seem to apply. This incident merely adds to the evidence that has accumulated over the years to support this contention.'

Just before Hibs had advertised the match the SFA had told Celtic that they would not be required to play a Scottish Cup semi-final tie on the night of 30 March as two of their young players would be on international duty in Switzerland. Both players, Aitken and Burns, had been figuring in the first team as Celtic went for the League and Cup. Then came a decision by the Scottish League Management Committee, of which Mr Hart is a member, which decreed that Celtic would have to travel to Easter Road on the night of the 30th to fulfil the fixture with Hibs. Celtic were livid, especially as Hibs had gone ahead and advertised the match. They certainly seemed to have a hidden confidence in their action. Celtic travelled under protest and gained a 1–1 draw. But the story was far from finished.

In one of his last acts as secretary of the SFA the retiring Willie Allan launched a broadside at the League for their handling of the situation. In his report to the AGM of the SFA on 9 May 1977 he stated: 'Although a reasonable and convincing explanation may yet emerge, an apparently absurd and somewhat illogical decision was taken by the Scottish Football League Management Committee almost on the eve of the party's departure for Switzerland causing not a few ripples on the surface.' Mr Allan went on to point out that after studied deliberation and with commendable foresight the SFA ensured that Celtic would not have to play on 30 March to avoid the old club–country clash. He added: 'The League Management Committee provoked such a clash by decreeing that the Celtic club should fulfil a fixture on that date and by refusing a request by the club for postponement on the grounds that two players were in the international pool. The Association [SFA] agreed to release one of the players, the choice to be made by the club. Whether or not this had any bearing on the match in Switzerland will never be known.' On Celtic's behalf, director Tom Devlin put forward a motion to the League that in the event of two players being called for international duty, their club's match be postponed. It was carried.

Those at the Scottish League who had been unhappy about Stein's outburst were left in a bit of a quandary as the SFA obviously shared some of the manager's views. The latter part of Mr Stein's statement concerning 'an accumulation of evidence' could refer to several actions by the League over the years to Celtic's disadvantage. These included the order to Celtic and Hibs to play their League Cup semi-final replay at Ibrox in 1965 although both clubs had protested after the first game on the Rangers ground. They had stated that as their fans were paying top prices they had the right to Hampden's better facilities and their players had the right to sample the occasion there before the Final as the other two semi-finalists had done. There had also been a protest by both clubs about the standard of the Ibrox flood-lights. Despite backing from both Supporters' Associations the League insisted that the game should go on at Ibrox although there was no rule to state that a venue could not be changed.

The following year, as discussed in Chapter 4, Celtic got little sympathy from the League following their arduous flight home from the Soviet Union and had to play a vital League match with Hearts at Tynecastle less than twenty hours after arriving home. Then came the censuring of chairman Desmond White in 1971 when, in the interests of safety, he insisted that an Old Firm match could not go on at Parkhead because of reconstruction work (see Chapter 14).

In November 1972 a serious breach of confidence followed a League Management Committee meeting which caused great concern at Celtic Park. Someone from that committee room leaked a story to the Press that Celtic director Tom Devlin, a member of the com-mittee, had officially protested against referee Bobby Davidson of Airdrie being retained for a League Cup quarter-final decider against Dundee. Mr Devlin had in fact asked the committee in the course of discussion to consider the interests of the game and the referee if he were to control a third game between the clubs. This was based on the feeling that, following controversy surrounding the previous game, an intolerable burden could be placed on Davidson. The committee, however, decided that Davidson would also take charge of the third game. Celtic, and Mr Devlin, were naturally furious that his comments had been twisted and that any information should have been leaked from what was a private meeting. Had Celtic wished to protest about the referee no one would have been left in any doubt that they were registering a complaint.

Celtic's position as regards the Scottish League is quite clear. They hope that in future the management committee will exercise more sympathy and discretion in such matters as have been mentioned. These, as far as Celtic are concerned, are now in the past and the club, as they always have done, wish to live in harmony with the ruling bodies of Scottish Football. Men like Tom Hart should not ban a body such as the Celtic Ciné Club which does a fine job, without pay, in providing fans all over Scotland with evenings of football entertainment. Actions such as Mr Hart's can only lead to a deterioration in club relations.

If supporters on the terracing see these things going on among men who should know better then they can hardly be criticized for stepping out of line.

In the event, a Pressman had a ciné camera with him that day behind the goals and managed to capture Joe Craig's winner, and afterwards about half an hour of film was shot in the Celtic dressing-room. So Celtic's first Premier League win is very much recorded for posterity.

The Championship win more than made up for the earlier season disappointment when Celtic had fallen to Aberdeen in the League Cup Final. After winning a section which included Dundee United, Dumbarton and Arbroath, Celtic had reached the Final at the expense of Albion Rovers and Hearts before lining up against Aberdeen on 6 October at Hampden. Again it was the old story of missed chances after Dalglish had scored from the penalty spot. Aberdeen equalized and won 2–1 after extra time. If ever Celtic threw away a cup it was that day. The UEFA Cup had also been a disappointment with a first-round knock-out at the hands of Wisla Krakow of Poland who won 2–0 on their own ground after a 2–2 draw at Celtic Park. Had Celtic survived that first round during what was for them a sticky spell their form in the latter part of the season was such that they might have done well in the competition.

They reached the Scottish Cup Final again and had a trick or two up their sleeves when they lined up against Rangers on 7 May at Hampden. For a start they had ex-Ranger Alfie Conn in their line-up and they ran out onto the pitch wearing tracksuit tops emblazoned with the words 'League Champions 1976–77'. A real piece of one-upmanship.

Conn's signing had come as a great surprise to everyone and the man behind it had been Jock Stein. It was his suggestion to the Board that the club should bid for the Tottenham player. He was signed at the beginning of March, just in time to play in the Championship-clinching games and the Cup Final. The signing was a master-stroke and done not without some devilment. It had come at a bad time for Rangers who were struggling on and off the field. Once more their fans had disgraced them – this time at Birmingham – and in the aftermath of the riot the Rangers Board said that if by signing a Catholic player they could stop the trouble then they would sign one. That statement caused them further problems because thousands stayed away in protest. For the rest of the season Rangers played to very poor gates.

The Conn signing was proof once again that Celtic will sign players of any creed or colour provided they are good enough and want to play for the club. It was a signing which caused great embarrassment to Rangers and induced anger among their fans who felt that the Ibrox Board should have taken Conn back as he had been a great favourite with the Ibrox support and had played in the Rangers team which won the European Cup Winners' Cup in 1972. There is no doubt that he could have given a struggling Rangers team a much needed lift.

His signing had the historians delving back into their files to see how many players had played for both Celtic and Rangers. The most popular list is as follows.

Dr Willie Kivlichan, a Catholic, played for Rangers in the early 1900s but he was given a free transfer after only a short spell at Ibrox. Celtic signed him just after Alec Bennett had shocked everyone at Celtic Park by going to Rangers after winning four Championship medals in the famous team which won the League six years running between 1904 and 1910. He had formed a great partnership with Jimmy McMenemy. George T. Livingstone left Parkhead at the turn of the century for Manchester City and was later transferred to Rangers. He was at Ibrox from 1902 until 1907 and was capped while playing for all three clubs. Then there was Tom 'Tully' Craig who was freed by Celtic after three years and moved on to Alloa. Rangers, in a piece of shrewd business, signed him for £750 in 1923 and he went on to win five caps. Tom Sinclair, a reserve goalkeeper, was loaned to Celtic by Rangers in August 1906 after regular keeper Davie Adams had torn his hand on a nail protruding from one of the Ibrox goalposts. The great Davie had been taking part in a benefit match for a Rangers player. Tom Sinclair played a total of eight matches without losing a goal and won himself a Glasgow Cup medal in the process. He went back to Rangers where he won a Reserve Scottish Cup medal, then moved to Newcastle where he won an English League medal – all in one season! Other players, like Patsy Gallagher, signed on a temporary basis to play in benefit matches but this list gives the main personalities involved.

So Alfie Conn was part of a very select band when he lined up for the Scottish Cup Final of 1977. The last time he had played at Hampden had been in the 1973 Final when he had scored one of Rangers' goals in their 3–2 win over Celtic. Now he was facing most of his team-mates from that day. Some of the tension had been taken out of his particular situation, however, by playing him in the final Old Firm Premier League match of the season at Ibrox the previous month which had ended in a 2–2 draw.

Celtic's team was: Latchford, McGrain, Lynch, Stanton, McDonald, Edvaldsson, Aitken, Wilson, Craig, Dalglish, Conn. The substitutes were Doyle and Burns. Rangers sent out: Kennedy, Jardine, Greig, Forsyth, Jackson, Watson, McLean, McDonald, Parlane, Hamilton, Johnstone, with substitutes Miller and Robertson. The referee was Mr Bob Valentine of Dundee who had created a bit of a sensation the previous week at Pittodrie by ordering off Rangers skipper Greig. Before the end of the afternoon he had angered Rangers again with a penalty decision.

Ronnie Glavin had been injured during his international début the previous week so Stein had to rethink his successful line-up which had won the Championship. He brought in Edvaldsson to play alongside Roddy McDonald at the back and they snuffed out Rangers' only real threat – the high ball to Parlane and Johnstone. Paul Wilson was preferred to Doyle because of his scoring successes against Rangers in the past. Celtic were awarded a penalty in the twentieth minute after Derek Johnstone handled on the line. It was an award which was hotly disputed by the Rangers players. Full-back Andy Lynch took the kick and it was enough to give Celtic their twenty-fifth Scottish Cup. Rangers failed simply because they had no alternative route to goal.

It was a superb win for Celtic and gave them their sixth League and Cup double under Jock Stein.

As though it was becoming an annual event, the season ended with more rumours about Stein taking the Scotland job. Willie Ormond had moved on to Hearts but after a few days Stein again said: 'I stay with Celtic.'

With the tenth anniversary of Lisbon just a couple of weeks away the club tried to fix up a glamour match with their opponents from that famous occasion – Inter Milan. But playing commitments kept the Italians at home. There was, however, a night of great nostalgia to commemorate Lisbon. The Celtic Ciné Club put on a show to remember at a Glasgow cinema including the Lisbon game and other Celtic films. The League Championship trophy was presented by League President Mr Tom Laughlan as the entire team appeared on stage. But the greatest roars of the night came when all the Lisbon Lions walked on individually and spoke a few words to the fans.

And so the club prepared to set off on its longest-ever tour, to Singapore and Australia, in the hope of rebuilding the spirit of 1966. But on the eve of departure came the shock that Kenny Dalglish, just back from Scotland's tour of South America, did not want to travel. At first it was stated he was tired. But there was considerably more to it than that. Although he had signed a new contract with Celtic to play in the Cup Final in May against Rangers as a registered Celtic player, his heart was no longer at Parkhead. He wanted away and had been attracted to other pastures for some time.

Liverpool had originally expressed considerable interest in Dalglish and had asked if there ever was any chance of the player being sold, that they would be informed. Celtic did not in any circumstances want to lose Dalglish but had to face the reality of the position. It was now made known to Liverpool that Dalglish might just possibly become available. Would they still be interested? Celtic left for Singapore without him. Liverpool indeed were so interested that they contacted Celtic in Australia with a view to being allowed to approach the player. This was turned down out of hand. The Celtic Board were determined to make one final effort to retain Dalglish.

The Chairman had a meeting with the player on his return home and offered him the red carpet treatment to stay. But Dalglish said it was not just a question of money. He wanted to move to England or the Continent. A meeting was arranged with Liverpool's chairman and manager. Before entering the meeting Jock Stein once more approached Dalglish: 'Is there anything we can do to make you change your mind?' he asked. The answer was no. Liverpool paid a British record of £400000 for one of the game's great players.

The season of 1977–8 saw Celtic kick off in the unusual position of having a team of players bought mainly from other clubs. There had been so much promise shown in the close-season tour which saw Celtic beat Red Star Belgrade, Arsenal and the Australian national side to win a prestigious competition. But hard on the heels of the Dalglish transfer came a series of blows for the club. Stanton and Conn were seriously injured in the opening match of the season. They in turn were followed by new captain Danny McGrain, Tommy Burns and Johnny Doyle – all of whom were out for months. It left the club with no alternative but further moves in the transfer market as the team struggled badly in the Premier League. Tom McAdam was bought from Dundee United and Joe Filippi from Ayr United, which involved Celts' Brian McLaughlin moving to Ayr. Then Frank Munro signed from Wolves after a trial period.

Despite the set-backs the club has much to look forward to in the years which will take them to their centenary. The burning ambition is to bring another European Cup to Parkhead. It will be no mean task but this must be the yardstick for Celtic now. They can settle for no less. They have a proud history behind them as the most successful club side Britain has ever known. They are part of a European élite, only seven countries having won the coveted European Cup. No club has a story to equal the story of Celtic. It is unique and for reasons more than football. Jock Stein perhaps summed it up in a recent chat with your writer when he said: 'This club is all about three things. The reason behind its foundation, its fight against those who tried to put it out of existence and being the first British team to win the European Cup. No one can ever take that away from Celtic.'

The reason behind Celtic's foundation was to provide money for the poor children's dinner tables and other charities in the poverty-stricken East End of Glasgow in the late Eighties of the last century. The club today does not forget. In recent years they have sent £25000 to the United Nations Save the Children Fund, proceeds from a special match against Benfica at Parkhead. Large sums of money have gone to Biafra and Bangladesh to help relieve suffering there and other sums have gone to non-denominational charities.

Celtic now see poverty in a world context as opposed to the once local situation. Although poverty still remains in their midst in the city's East End there is a Welfare State now. The people of the Third World have no such help and Celtic's charitable horizons now stretch to those far-off lands.

It was St Paul who said: 'Though I speak with the tongues of men and of angels and have not charity, I am become as sounding brass or a tinkling cymbal.

'And though I have all faith, so that I could remove mountains, and have not charity, I am nothing.'

Long may their successes on the field of play – and their good deeds off it – continue.

Appendix

Belgian War Relief Funds Game

The full list of men in the photograph, between pages 70 and 71, of
Celtic (League Champions) *v.* Rest of League, Hampden Park,
20 May 1916.

Back row: Director Dansken (Rangers), A. Stewart (Falkirk),
A. McNair (Celtic), J. Gordon (Rangers), C. Shaw (Celtic),
W. Reid (Rangers), J. McMenemy (Celtic), J. M. Dickson
(linesman), A. Allan (referee).

Middle row: T. Robertson (Queen's Park), Director Furst (Hearts),
T. Cairns (Rangers), J. McMaster (Celtic), A. L. Morton (Rangers),
P. Johnstone (Celtic), R. Mercer (Hearts), P. Gallagher (Celtic),
Director Hart (St Mirren), J. Binnie (linesman), W. Maley (Celtic),
J. Nutt (trainer).

Front row: W. McAndrew (League Secretary), Director Bowman
(Motherwell), J. Simpson (Falkirk), J. Cassidy (Celtic), J. Wilson
(Hearts), A. McAtee (Celtic), J. McTavish (Partick), J. Young
(Celtic), P. Nellies (Hearts), J. Dodds (Celtic), R. Manderson
(Rangers), J. Browning (Celtic), W. Quinn (Celtic trainer).

Index